Choice
Yacht
Designs

Choice Yacht Designs

RICHARD HENDERSON

International Marine Publishing Company

CAMDEN, MAINE

Copyright © 1979
by International Marine Publishing Company
Library of Congress Catalog Card Number 78-75112
International Standard Book Number 0-87742-112-9
Typeset by A & B Typesetters, Inc., Concord, New Hampshire
Printed in U.S.A.

Published by International Marine Publishing Company
21 Elm Street, Camden, Maine 04843

In memory of two early mentors:

"Cap" Kenney and "Salty" Marks

Contents

Preface

When I was a small boy, at the ripe old age of five, I'd row our dinghy over to investigate any new yacht that would venture into our harbor at Gibson Island, Maryland. Propped up in the stern sheets of the dink would be my sailor doll, which was almost as big as I was. After the yacht had anchored or picked up a mooring, I'd circle around her close aboard and say to myself in a loud clear voice, "I wonder what she looks like below." In most cases, the owner of the visiting yacht would ask me aboard to have a look. I could almost count on the invitation if there was a lady aboard, because she'd inevitably be taken with that sailor doll. That was the real reason I carried it.

Almost half a century later, I'm still investigating new boats that come into our harbor (or boatyard), and my boarding tactics are only slightly more subtle. At any rate, I've been curious about boats, especially sailing cruisers, for a long time, and I've investigated more than just a few.

This book is about some of the craft I've become familiar with, and they are among my favorites. There is no common denominator for these boats except that they are smart-sailing, versatile cruisers, and many are considered classics. Of course, compromises are a necessary fact of yacht design as well as of life, and certain qualities of these boats are accentuated at the expense of others. I don't think that the yachts in this book are seriously deficient in any respect, but minor weaknesses in one aspect are compensated by strengths in other areas. At any rate, all the boats in this book are good or great, in my humble opinion, and I hope my overall admiration will be apparent to the reader.

Some of the qualities I think are important are: seaworthiness, sailing ability, ease of handling, comfort, and looks. Seaworthiness should be a prime consideration, because a lack of it could endanger the lives of the crew. Now, I don't claim that all the boats on these pages are rugged offshore passagemakers, but they are basically safe for their intended design purpose when well handled. When and if there is a lack of safety features I consider important, the deficiency will be pointed out.

Sailing ability is obviously an important requirement in a sailboat, and most of the boats in this book are competent performers upwind. As the noted expert on tank testing, Pierre DeSaix, once remarked, "yacht hulls are designed primarily by the requirements of windward work." Nevertheless, an offshore cruiser does not always need the upwind capability of a racer or an on-soundings cruiser. Thus, I have included a few boats that excel on a reach, but still they can perform reasonably well on a beat. I insist that each "choice yacht" can make at least some progress to windward in difficult conditions. Without this ability, she would be less fun to sail, and she might not be able to reach an upwind destination or escape if caught on a lee shore.

Most of the yachts on these pages can be handled with reasonable ease. This is a desirable requirement for anyone who likes to sail with a small crew, but even the skipper who normally sails with a large crew will find himself short-handed once in a while. There may be times when he will want to daysail or weekend cruise with his wife alone or with his wife and small children, or there may be greenhorn guests aboard. Therefore, I think it is fair to insist that cruisers be reasonably forgiving and that they can be managed in a fairly relaxed manner without the need of a large, skillful crew. This quality requires a wholesome hull as well as a sensible rig.

The macho-ascetic or gung-ho racer may not care about comfort, but his wife probably does, and I think many cruising sailors want as much comfort as they can get. My own feeling is that this quality is tremendously desirable when there is no great sacrifice to seaworthiness, performance, or looks. The larger the yacht, of course, the greater her capacity for comfort, but even small cruisers, such as the smallest ones shown on these pages, can have pleasingly snug cabins when the accommodation details are carefully worked out.

As for looks, this is an important quality for me, and most of the "choice yachts" are handsome, in my opinion. Aesthetics involves personal taste and not everyone agrees on what is beautiful, but there is no doubt that many modern boats are somewhat less than good-looking, to put it kindly. Many of their owners and even some designers will admit this. There may be some excuse for an ugly racer if her aesthetic defects produce speed, but there is no good reason why a cruiser cannot be handsome or at least show character in her looks.

Most of the yachts in this book are racing-cruising types, because I prefer their versatility, but an old cliché tells us that "variety is the spice of life"; so the attempt has been made to present different kinds of racing-cruisers. There are long-keel boats, fin-keelers, centerboarders, a twin-keeler, and even a boat with double trim tabs. The majority of these yachts have counter sterns, but there are some double-enders, and boats with round and transom sterns. Sloop and cutter rigs predominate, but there are also some yawls, ketches, and schooners. The merits and disadvantages of the various rigs and hull types are discussed. The "choice yachts" vary in size between 25½ feet and 54 feet overall, but the vast majority are small- to medium-sized. They span a period of almost half a century, but most are still available (on the used boat market at least), and many are affordable for the sailor of modest means.

One interesting but at times frustrating aspect of putting together this book has been the acquisition of lines drawings. The publisher and I were most anxious to show the shape of each hull. In the old days, it was the normal practice for designers to publish their lines drawings, but today many designers are reluctant to do so for fear of plagiarism. Fortunately, many of the designers of boats in this book were tremendously cooperative, and the lines of some famous racing-cruisers, such as the Owens cutter, Cal 40, L-27, and C&C 35, are shown for the first time. One designer, Carl Alberg, was more than willing to allow that the lines of his popular Triton be published, but the boat's producer would not give permission; so Mr. Alberg drafted, especially for this book, new lines with very minor changes, which I have noted and labeled as the Mark II version of the boat. When designers were unwilling to release their lines, they were often willing to allow me to commission perspective drawings, which could then be published. Al Mason, a noted draftsman and naval architect, did nearly all the perspectives in this book.

The designers whose work I've featured have been so kind that I am reluctant to criticize their boats in any way, but I'm determined that this book will not read like an advertising brochure. So when I see something I don't particularly like, there will be an appropriate comment. If I say anything that offends a designer, I apologize, but it is only fair to the reader that I be completely candid. Actually, I've found little to criticize, and the few faults that caught my eye might not be objectionable to another sailor.

Choice Yacht Designs has been a fascinating and educational project for me, and I only hope the reader has half as much fun as I have had in studying these boats. Gotta go now—I think I see a new boat coming into our harbor.

Richard Henderson
Gibson Island, Maryland

Acknowledgments

I want to express my thanks to the following sailors for supplying me with plans, photographs, or information about the boats in this book: Dr. Gifford B. Pinchot, E. Newbold Smith, Francis C. Stokes, Thomas H. Closs, Charles F. Stein III, H. Parker Matthai, John F. Quinn, Harry C. Primrose III, William O. Fordiani, Thomas and Barbara Moore, Steven D. Batchelor, A. Homer Skinner, Paul M. Rosenfield, William G. Homewood, John R. Sherwood III, William T. Stone, Harold R. White, Victor Jorgensen, John A. Aufhammer, Stuart S. Orrick, James Cancil, Marcia Wiley, William H. Shaw, William A. Swartz, William Breitbach, Ian Smith, Mitchell C. Gibbons-Neff, Richard F. Sheehan, B.J. Lavins, and especially Roger C. Taylor.

Also, my extra special thanks go to the following designers and boat producers: Roderick Stephens Jr.—for answering many questions and releasing the lines of the Sparkman & Stephens boats as well as arranging for perspective drawings; William C. Lapworth—for releasing the lines of the Cal 40; Gary W. Mull (and Mr. Mull's associate Shelley Hayse)—not only for supplying lines and plans of the Rangers 26 and 28, but also for helping persuade Bill Lapworth to release his lines; the C & C Design Group (J.R. Forsey, Mrs. S.L. Milne, and Rob Ball)—for lines of the Redwing 30 and the C & C 35; A.E. (Bill) Luders Jr.—for his interesting correspondence and for redrawing the lines of *Storm* especially for this book; Charles J. Owens (the senior partner of Owens Yacht Co.) for much information and permission to reproduce the lines of the Owens cutter (kindly supplied by Rolfe L. Pottberg); Peter Van Dine—for much information and the lines and plans of the Tancook schooner; Henry R. Hinckley III—for plans of the Hinckley boats in this book and lines of the Bermuda 40; John S. Letcher, Jr.—not only for supplying me with lines of his *Aleutka* but also for making a number of comments on the designs of other boats; Einar Ohlson (and P.F. Wood of Tyler Boat Co.)—for drawings of the Ohlson 38; Edward S. Brewer and Robert E. Wallstrom—for photographs, lines, and other plans of the Brewer and Brewer-Wallstrom-designed boats; Alvin Mason—not only for supplying me with lines and plans of his own Mason 31, but also for drawing most of the perspectives in this book; and Carl A. Alberg—for his great interest in this project and especially for modifying the lines of his famous Triton for use in *Choice Yacht Designs*.

Finally, I'd like to thank all the designers mentioned on these pages for creating the "choice yachts" in the first place. These fine boats have given and will continue to give a lot of pleasure to a great many sailors.

1/ Kelpie

A Reaching Fool

Length overall: 34 feet 3½ inches
Length on waterline: 25 feet 4½ inches
Beam: 9 feet 8½ inches
Draft: 5 feet 1½ inches
Sail area: 712 square feet
Designer: John G. Alden
Year designed: 1928

One sunny afternoon in early September many long years ago, a 34-foot yawl and a similar-size cutter squared off to have a go at each other. This was not a true race but merely a "brush," a kind of informal comparison of sailing performance (with the crew of each vessel deadly serious but with an outward show of casualness if not apathy). The yawl, named *Kelpie*, was owned by my father, William L. Henderson, and the cutter was the famous *Hotspur* belonging to yachting author Alfred F. Loomis. *Hotspur* had come down for a visit to the Chesapeake Bay and to compete in the 100-mile Cedar Point Race, which would start the next day. Mr. Loomis had suggested the brush for tune-up purposes, but we suspected that he also had a bit of psychological warfare in mind. He had an old score to settle with *Kelpie*, because she and two sister boats had beaten *Hotspur* in the New London-Gibson Island ocean race a number of years before.

Although only a young boy at that time, I was being allowed to crew on the Cedar Point Race, and I was aboard *Kelpie* during the brush with *Hotspur*. After having spent every summer since I was four years old living aboard my father's yawl, I knew *Kelpie* quite well, and I had no illusions about her ability to go to windward. However, I was somewhat taken aback by what *Hotspur* did to us when we went against her hard on the wind. Repeatedly, the cutter would start to leeward of us and soon work across our bow and leave us wallowing in her wake. She carried three headsails (staysail, jib, and jib topsail) that seemed, in those days at least, to be the epitome of multi-slot, aerodynamic efficiency.

If Alf Loomis wanted to psych us out, he right well succeeded, for we soon began to feel that we would have no chance at all against *Hotspur* in the Cedar Point Race. As it turned out, however, the race was a reaching affair, with little opportunity for the cutter to show her upwind prowess. Not long after the start, *Kelpie* pulled ahead under started sheets while carrying her large reaching jib. *Hotspur* slowly sank below the horizon astern, and we never saw her again. That race was a clear demonstration

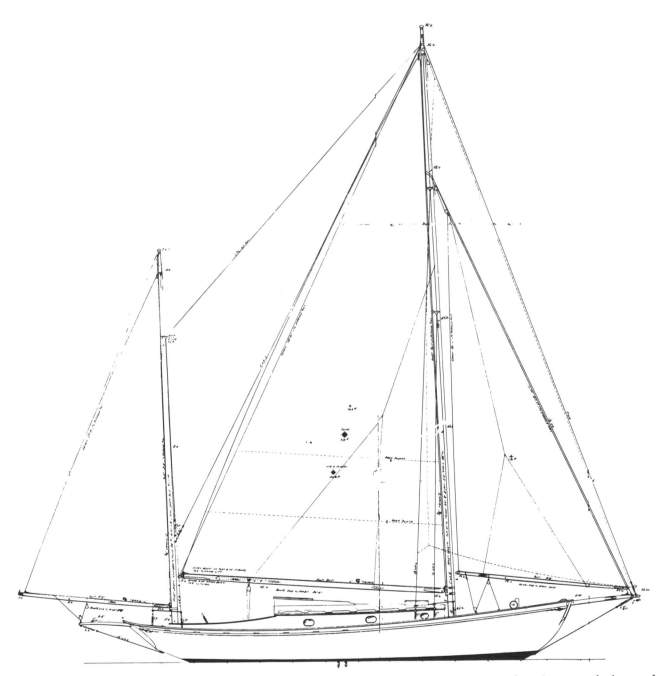

Kelpie's original sail plan. Note the low main boom, which prohibited carrying a dinghy on the cabin top. The boomed jib was surprisingly efficient, but the lower sheet block made an awful clatter on the iron bar traveler when Kelpie *came about.*

that windward ability is not everything. Reaches are the points of sailing very often encountered on point-to-point races and on offshore passages.

Kelpie was not much to windward, but she was a reaching fool. On another occasion, in more recent times, I remember reaching past a fast Owens 40-foot cutter that had been cleaning up in the local races. Later I happened to overhear a conversation between a member of the cutter's crew and her owner: "That old

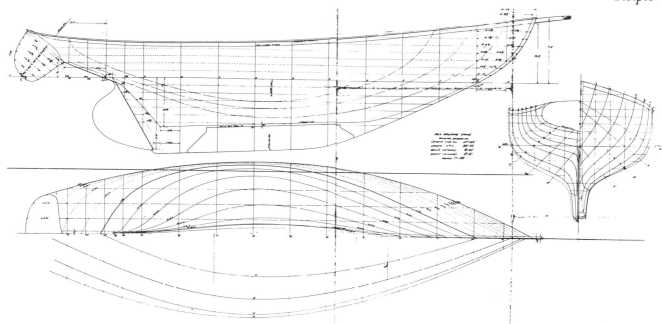

The lines of Kelpie *show her fine entrance and rather full afterbody. With her moderately long keel she would track well yet was fairly quick in stays.*

Accommodation plan of the Alden 34. *Since* Kelpie *was used almost entirely on the Chesapeake Bay during the summer, she didn't have the vented stove, but instead had a hatch in the foredeck for extra ventilation.*

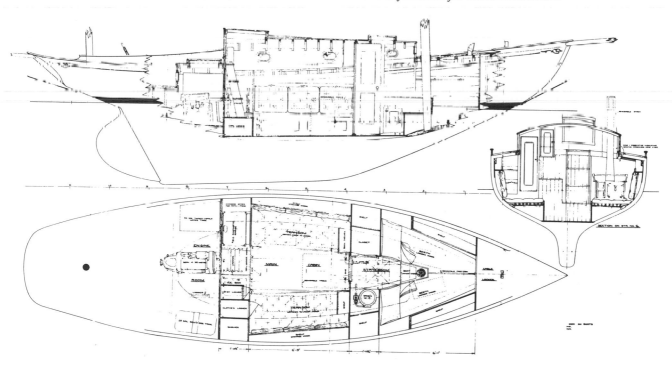

The Alden 34 Cynara *being finished at Blaisdell's in Woolwich, Maine.*

Kelpie certainly does fly on a reach," said the crew. "I don't know about that," the owner replied, "she must have had her motor on." Somehow, I resisted the urge to tell him that we never ran the engine.

It is not surprising that *Kelpie* was a good reacher, for she was designed by John G. Alden, who was famous for his ocean-racing schooners that could pick up their skirts and fly when their sheets were well eased. Of course *Kelpie* was yawl rigged, but her lines bore some resemblance to the fast Alden schooners, which in turn had been influenced by the commercial fishing schooners. Those fishermen had to be reasonably fast, because they often had to race each other to port in order to get the best price for their catch. Probably the main reason for *Kelpie*'s speed off the wind, however, was her large sail area of 712 square feet for working sails. This did not count the masthead reaching jib that added approximately another 300 square feet. That is a lot of sail for a boat only a little more than 25 feet on the waterline.

With a mainsail luff length of over 40 feet, *Kelpie* had a tall rig even by today's standards, and originally she had solid spars, which meant there was a lot of weight aloft. Her beam of nine feet eight inches was only moderate, so she needed plenty of ballast to carry such a large, heavy rig. The original plans called for 6,560 pounds of iron on her keel, but I think that before *Kelpie* was built, the keel's weight was increased to well over 7,000 pounds. In addition, she carried 300 pounds of lead pigs in her bilge for trimming ballast. The yawl was never tender, but later in her life, when the original sticks were replaced with hollow spars, she became fairly stiff.

My father complained to John Alden about the original spars, which soon became cracked and twisted, and the designer replied: "The question of Marconi spars is quite a problem, and if Oregon pine sticks are used, they would be so heavy that the boats would be tender and quite unsatisfactory. It is necessary to use the spruce unless hollow spars are used, which, of course, are a great deal more expensive. Spruce is bound to crack and this, of course, is not desirable, but I do not see just what other solution there is." Finally, Dad decided that hollow spars would be worth their cost, and not surprisingly, they were very helpful to stability.

Kelpie was built by N. Blaisdell and Sons at Woolwich, Maine, in 1929 for a cost of $5,700, which seems dirt-cheap now, but during the depression years, equivalent boats could be bought for even less. She was planked with 1⅛-inch cedar over oak frames and fastened with galvanized iron nails. During the 30 years my family owned her, we never had much trouble with the fastenings, but like many boats of that vintage that were tightly ceiled, we had our share of problems with dry rot.

Insofar as sailing characteristics are concerned, *Kelpie* was a well-mannered lady, unlike many of the temperamental racers of today that must be pampered and coaxed. She was a wonderful ghoster in light air and would reach her hull speed with ease, although her considerable displacement would not permit rapid acceleration, and she was prone to some rhythmic rolling when driven beyond her hull speed in a hard blow running before the wind. Despite her somewhat asymmetrical waterlines, with a fine

Kelpie crossing the finish line during her victorious Oxford race when William Henderson sneaked her through the Poplar Island narrows.

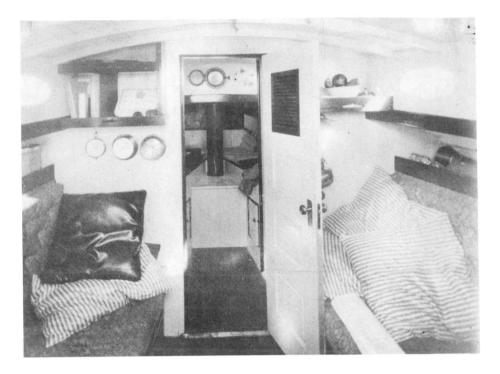

Below decks in an Alden 34. The main bulkhead door in Kelpie *was hinged so that it swung forward, thereby allowing more room in the main cabin and permitting a sizable dining table.*

bow and full afterbody, she was well balanced, directionally stable (except in difficult quartering seas), and the full waterlines aft gave her some bearing when heeled. The slightly hollow entrance helped her drive through choppy seas, yet she had sufficient sheer and flare at the bow to keep spray off the deck. The keel was moderately long, which was helpful to directional stability, but the forefoot was sufficiently cut away and the rudder large enough to give her good maneuverability. *Kelpie*'s freeboard amidships was a bit low by today's standards, but I don't remember putting her rail under very often.

In 1956 her rig was modernized slightly with the hope of making her more competitive on the race course. The jibstay was moved farther aft to facilitate tacking a large genoa, the mizzen was shortened, and its boom and the main boom were raised somewhat. The latter modifications lowered her handicap rating a little and enabled her to collect some silver in certain reaching events, but she was not really competitive in closed-course racing that included a lot of windward work. I always felt the old yawl did

reasonably well when you consider that she was not designed to any rating rule.

Racing aside, there were many advantages to *Kelpie*'s original rig. She had a very powerful working rig, unlike contemporary boats, and this meant that she could be handled by one person with ease. Her large working jib had a boom and traveler, which made the sail completely self-tending, and it wasn't necessary to touch a line when coming about. With this arrangement we were able to sail and even race the boat for years without the need of winches, although two watch tackles were used when the large reaching jib was set.

Of course, the working jib was not as powerful as a large genoa, but it was ever so handy for cruising and daysailing when shorthanded. I can even remember how the self-tending jib helped to win a race, because it enabled such fast tacking up a narrow channel.

During an early race from Annapolis to Oxford, Maryland, *Kelpie* and her competitors were beating down the Chesapeake Bay against a fresh southerly wind and a foul current. The old yawl was taking a bad licking from the more

Kelpie *showing her handsome oval stern. The author as a young boy is sitting in the cockpit; incidentally, his present home is on the shore directly behind the mainmast.*

Kelpie *(number 86) after the start of the Cedar Point Race in 1939. As the author's wife said when she first saw the picture, "Another lousy start."* Kelpie *is carrying a borrowed six-meter genoa jib.*

weatherly single-masted boats, much to the delight of my first cousin, who was crewing on one of the leading sloops. My father decided to duck in out of the current and short tack up the Poplar Island narrows, a channel with not much more width than a superhighway, running between Poplar Island and the Eastern Shore. It was a desperate gamble, but there wasn't a lot to lose, since *Kelpie* had no hope if she followed her weatherly competition outside in the bay. The working jib allowed the dozens of tacks to be made with ease, and when *Kelpie* came out of the channel and once again into the Chesapeake, she was far ahead of her competition, much to the amazement of everyone, including her crew. She managed to hold her lead and went on to win the race. Obviously, the weaker current and smooth waters of the narrows made the difference. Dad never had the opportunity to pull that trick again, because race instructions thereafter required the passing of a buoy near the middle of the bay opposite Poplar Island, which made it impossible to use the narrows.

The accommodations below decks were simple and functional. In the days when *Kelpie* was built, it was not the fashion to see how many bunks could be crowded into a small cabin. Our boat had four sizable berths, two in a forward stateroom and two in the main saloon. There was plenty of space for lockers and shelves. Of course, the accommodations were not perfect. There was no sink in the galley, the head could have been more private, and the dining table had to be removed completely after each meal. Nevertheless, my mother, father, and I (and even my sister for a while) lived aboard *Kelpie* in reasonable comfort for many summers.

The old yawl was an important part of my youth, and I loved every plank in her hull. But she did have that one weakness of being slow to windward, and she made me resolve that the dream boat I would acquire when I grew up would be a lively performer against the wind. In many other ways, however, I wanted my boat of the future to be like *Kelpie*.

2/ Stormy Weather

A Certain Character

```
Length overall: 53 feet 11 inches
Length on waterline: 39 feet 8 inches
Beam: 12 feet 6 inches
Draft: 7 feet 11 inches
Sail area: 1,300 square feet
Designer: Sparkman & Stephens
Year designed: 1933
```

As recently as 1969, when I asked the noted marine architect and design critic Robert G. Henry for his opinion of the best kind of boat to take to sea, he replied: "I'm still in favor of a modern able boat for offshore work. A hull like, say, *Stormy Weather*." Other designers and yacht seamen of the highest caliber have been equally impressed with this early design by Sparkman and Stephens. For example, there is the story told by the late William H. Taylor of *Yachting* magazine that designer John Alden was once strolling through the Nevins Yacht Yard in New York and was stopped in his tracks by a beautiful hull unidentifiable under the winter cover. Alden studied the underbody and then remarked: "In my opinion a better design would be impossible to achieve." The boat was *Stormy Weather*.

The creators of this much-admired boat are, of course, the world-famous Stephens brothers, Olin the designer and his younger brother Rod, who is the expert on rigging and seamanship. The brothers achieved great fame in the early 1930s with their somewhat radical ocean-racing yawl *Dorade*. In fact, they received a Broadway ticker tape parade à la Charles Lindbergh after *Dorade* won the transatlantic and Fastnet races in 1931. The yawl actually beat her larger rivals across the Atlantic boat-for-boat, finishing nearly two days ahead of the elapsed-time runner-up. Of course, the margin of victory was due mainly to the Stephens' strategy of sailing the northern great circle route, but there was no doubt that *Dorade* was fast and weatherly. She was also easy to handle and an able boat in heavy weather.

Stormy Weather, designed near the end of 1933, was intended to be a somewhat improved version of *Dorade*. The latter was narrow and slack-bilged, almost like a meter boat, and if she had any faults, they were some initial tenderness and a tendency to roll under certain downwind conditions. Olin Stephens gave *Stormy* considerably more beam, and this was quite helpful to her handicap rating under the newly devised CCA (Cruising Club of America) Measurement Rule. One might suspect that Olin had some second thoughts about *Stormy*'s beam soon

11

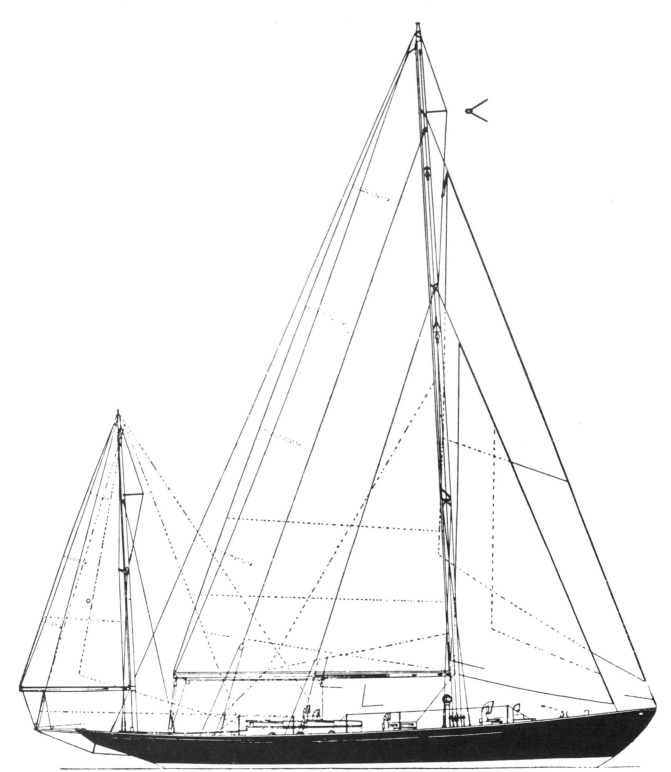

Stormy Weather's sail plan. The running backstays are not really needed except in heavy weather, but they prevent a large catenary in the headsail stays for efficiency when beating to windward. (Courtesy Uffa Fox Ltd.)

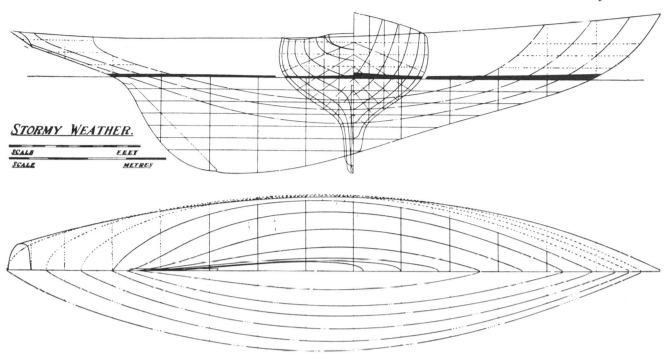

STORMY WEATHER.

| SCALE | | FEET |
| SCALE | | METRES |

The lines of Stormy Weather *show a quite symmetrical hull with easy curves that cause minimal confusion to the water flow. She appears fairly narrow by today's standards but was considered beamy when she made her debut. (Courtesy Uffa Fox Ltd.)*

The accommodation plans *of Stormy Weather show a fine arrangement for a live-aboard paid hand. (Courtesy Uffa Fox Ltd.)*

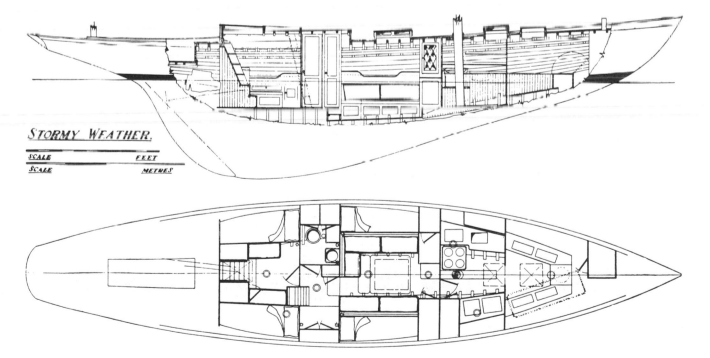

STORMY WEATHER.

| SCALE | | FEET |
| SCALE | | METRES |

Stormy Weather *under sail in 1948. Those old-fashioned genoa jibs let plenty of air under the foot, but they allowed* *good visibility forward. (Freddie Maura)*

after she was built, for he said: "Personally, I should like her better with less beam, although she should be faster under the rule as she is." As it turned out, she not only rated well, but she proved unusually stiff, for it was written that she was the only boat not forced to shorten sail in the 1934 Bermuda Race. Furthermore, Rod Stephens told me that *Stormy* had much less of a problem with rolling.

Narrow cruising boats will often develop a severe roll when running before the wind with quartering seas. Eric Hiscock has said that he considers his *Wanderer III*, in which he made two circumnavigations, to be one of the finest sea boats, but he would have preferred that she have a little more beam to help counteract her tendency to roll. Of course too much beam can create problems in resistance, steering, and even quickness of motion. *Stormy*'s beam, which would be considered quite moderate compared to offshore racers of today, proved to be a very happy medium. The CCA rule was based on a number of "ideal" measurements that designers and experienced seamen felt would produce a fast but seaworthy hull; and it is interesting to note that *Stormy Weather*'s load waterline beam is almost exactly (about three inches less than) the ideal beam for a boat of her waterline length under the last revision of the CCA rule.

The well-known British designer Uffa Fox was so enthusiastic about *Stormy* that he suggested the formation of a one-design class of ocean racers built to her lines. In *Uffa Fox's Second Book*, published in 1935, he gave the following, almost lyrical, description of her: "*Stormy Weather* is one of Olin Stephens' favorite designs, and her lines show her to be beamy and powerful, yet very easily driven, and therefore fast. She has moderate overhangs, and is exactly the type of vessel favored by the new American rule for ocean racing, a type that should gladden the hearts of those who go down to the sea in such small ships. Her diagonals are very fair and sweet, and her buttocks have the easy sweep that speaks of speed easily attained and main-

tained. *Stormy Weather* should glide along with the effortless grace of a bird soaring through the air, totally different to the clumsy, brutal way in which the 'wholesome, sturdy cruiser' smashes her way along at half of *Stormy Weather*'s speed. The sections show her high, easy, yet powerful bilge, which tells of easiness in a seaway, for though *Stormy Weather* will sail fairly upright she will not be stiff and jerky in her movement. The water-lines, it will be noticed, are sharp at their fore ends above and at the load waterline, gradually getting fuller as they get lower, until the lowest, through the keel, is virtually a true streamline."

In 1935, Rod Stephens skippered *Stormy* on the transatlantic race from Brenton Reef off Newport to Bergen, Norway. He won this race partly by repeating the strategy used with *Dorade* of sailing a northern great circle route. This course involved some risk, since it led through foggy waters and a rather large region of icebergs east of Newfoundland. However, the dangerous waters were safely negotiated, and the strategy proved so successful that *Stormy* came abreast of the much larger *Vamarie* off the Shetland Islands after about 3,000 miles of racing. The larger boat finished first, but only five hours ahead of *Stormy*, which easily saved her time. Later that year *Stormy* entered and won the Fastnet Race, and then she sailed back to America across the north Atlantic against the prevailing winds in the remarkable time of 24½ days, arriving home during the peak of the hurricane season.

During the time between the transatlantic and Fastnet races, Rod and his crew cruised the waters of northern Europe. The engine and fuel tanks had been taken out of *Stormy* because her skipper thought them unnecessary weight, so a great deal of ditch-crawling was done under sail alone, or by hitching tows from barges or canal boats. Rod told me how they once had to beat to windward along the North Sea Canal in Holland making about 150 short tacks and, incidentally, with a large jib that was not self-

3/ Aweigh

Bally's Boat

Length overall: 47 feet 2 inches
Length on waterline: 35 feet 8 inches
Beam: 11 feet 9 inches
Draft: 6 feet
Sail area: 929 square feet
Displacement: 32,000 pounds
Designer: Sparkman & Stephens
Year designed: 1933

A much-admired blue-green cutter that was moored for many years in our harbor at Gibson Island, Maryland, was the Sparkman & Stephens-designed *Aweigh*. Her plans were drawn the same year as *Stormy Weather*'s, and the two boats have similarities, but there are important differences. Aside from the obvious difference in rig, and the fact that *Aweigh* is seven feet shorter overall than *Stormy*, the cutter is relatively heavier, huskier in appearance, and has less draft, less overhang aft, and a somewhat longer keel.

To my way of thinking, *Aweigh* is the slightly better design for cruising, even though she gives up a little in being competitive on the race course. Actually, she was designed to be a comfortable live-aboard boat and to excel as a shorthanded cruiser for both shallow and deep water. It was some surprise, perhaps, that she also proved exceptional when she gave the southern ocean racing circuit a try.

Aweigh was built for a famous character, Lawrence M. Bailliere. A book could be written about the prankish antics of Bailliere, known far

and wide as "Bally," and his friend, "Monk" Foster. The pair were sometimes called the Katzenjammer Kids, and indeed they rivaled those comic-strip characters in creative mischief. Bally had a reputation as a great sailor (and as a great imbiber), so I would feel very flattered as a young boy when he would ask me aboard his beloved *Aweigh*. Incidentally, I had Bally to thank for almost losing me my girl friend, now my wife, because he told her I had webbed feet. Of course, he meant this as a compliment; it was his way of saying that I was a good sailor, but Sally took the remark literally, and the thought of my duck-like extremities slightly repulsed her.

Bally's cutter was built at the yard of M.M. Davis and Sons of Solomons, Maryland. Her specifications called for mahogany planking, bronze fastenings, and teak decks and trim. She was expertly built, and Davis and Sons by this time had a fine reputation for yacht construction, although not many years before, the yard built only broad-beamed centerboard working craft.

Donald H. Sherwood, who gave the Davises their first yacht commission, tells the story of how Philip L. Rhodes, a struggling young designer, was horribly distressed and even pictured his ruination upon receiving a phone call from Clarence Davis after the launching of a newly built Rhodes-designed sloop. It seems that Mr. Davis had been used to the tremendous initial stability of the work boats, and when he stepped on the rail of the dainty yacht, which really had greater ultimate stability than the working craft, he thought her excessively tender. In fact, he told Phil Rhodes that he would be afraid to step the mast for fear the sloop would capsize. Mr. Rhodes was shocked and despondent, but it later turned out that his sloop was as stiff as a church and almost never had to reef. Of course, Rhodes went on to become one of America's greatest designers, and the Davises later produced many yachts of the highest quality, including *Aweigh*.

Not long after her building, *Aweigh* was taken south to try her hand at wintertime ocean racing. In early 1935 she won the fleet prize for the 186-mile Miami-to-Nassau Race, followed that with a third in her class on the Nassau Governor's Trophy Race, then took a class second in the St. Petersburg-to-Havana Race, and later won the Havana-to-Key West race. Not

The rakish rig of Aweigh. *Note the belt and suspenders arrangement of both a headstay and jumper stays. (Yachting)*

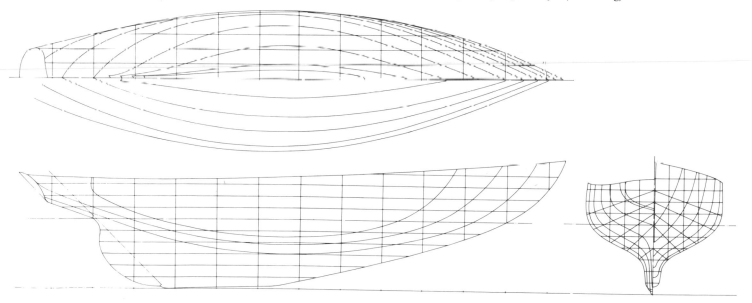

Aweigh's hull has ample freeboard, moderately shallow draft, and well-balanced ends.

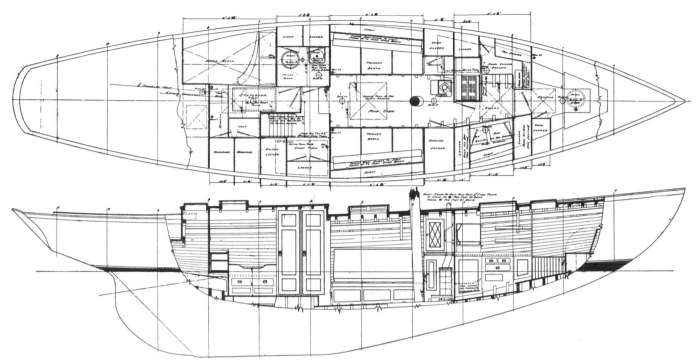

Aweigh's accommodation plans show the luxurious after cabin with double berth and the famous bathtub beneath the sole. (Yachting)

bad for a heavy, rather shoal draft cruiser. She did not have much success racing after returning to the Chesapeake Bay, because the airs were too light for her liking, and Bally acquired an increasing fondness for gunkhole cruising at the expense of racing. Nevertheless, *Aweigh* had proven she was fast and weatherly, given any kind of decent breeze, despite her weight and lack of draft.

Even by today's standards, or perhaps especially by today's standards, *Aweigh* is a near-perfect hull for cruising. Not only is she a smart sailer, unlike some modern boats intended purely for cruising, but she is handsome, able, and comfortable. Her freeboard is a bit high as compared to most boats of her day, but it is quite moderate by present standards. This feature gives her a lot of reserve stability and helps keep the lee rail out in a fresh wind. The moderate overhang aft nicely balances the handsome spoon bow and provides what seems to me just the right amount of reserve buoyancy with a minimum of counter that can slam in a seaway.

The lines show the stern sections to be somewhat V'd, which also mitigates slamming. *Aweigh*'s long keel gives her good directional stability without excessive wetted surface or undue sacrifice to maneuverability. Of course, the modest draft allows access to many shallow harbors without detracting too much from windward performance. Her considerable displacement of 32,000 pounds does not allow excellence in ghosting conditions, but there is plenty of working sail to drive her in a light wind, and her heavy weight gives an easy, comfortable motion in a seaway.

I have always thought highly of the cutter rig and in previous writings have extolled its many virtues. *Aweigh* gave me my first real introduction to the rig. Some advantages enjoyed by a cutter are: a three-sail divided rig with only one mast to garb, stay, and maintain; aerodynamic efficiency on most points of sailing (unlike many two-masted rigs); ease of shortening down to a really reliable and effective heavy-weather rig (with staysail and reefed

Photographed against a sparkling sea, Aweigh *shows her power in shouldering aside an ocean wave.*

main); great size of foretriangle and loftiness of mast for ability in light airs; mast location near the point of maximum beam for effective staying and the greatest width of deck for crew safety; and the mast weight concentrated nearly amidships for a favorable effect on the moment of inertia to alleviate pitching.

The small boomed staysail carried by *Aweigh* is especially handy when sailing shorthanded. Since it is tacked down well abaft the stem, jibs can be brought around quite easily when coming about, and ground tackle can be handled with the staysail hoisted without the interference of flapping canvas or fear of getting mud on the

*Aweigh under working sails flying the Gibson Island burgee. Note the two hatches in the foredeck for good ventilation below. (*Yachting)

Under power, Aweigh *shows off her shapely transom. (John Sherwood)*

sail. Of course, the staysail is self-tending, and it can be backed easily for maneuvering when a crew member is at the mast. Although I don't think Bally used it for this purpose, the staysail might be used for self-steering by backing it slightly with a windward sheet and leading the sheet back to the helm.

Aweigh's sail plan would be more powerful with a masthead jib, and obviously this would have helped her in ghosting conditions on the Chesapeake.

Below decks *Aweigh* is not unlike *Stormy Weather*, with the forecastle, forward galley, and main saloon amidships. Farther aft is a luxurious private stateroom with a double berth, bureau, two wardrobes, and, believe it or not, a bathtub housed under the cabin sole. A large enclosed head is accessible either from the main saloon or the stateroom. A chart table and oilskin locker are near the companionway.

My recollection of *Aweigh*'s cabin interior is that it was very posh, and the saloon was homey, with its large table and heating stove. However, it was somewhat gloomy, because the principal light source was only a small skylight. There are no side windows or portholes. Of course, the cutter is almost a flush-decker, and this gives the hull great strength. Nevertheless, there is a small cabin trunk that could have moderate-size windows, and I might prefer a few small, heavy deadlights in the upper topsides. Of course, nowadays translucent hatch covers of rugged fiberglass or Lexan add considerable brightness to the cabin on rainy days or when the spray is flying.

Although Bally had more than a few talents and a great deal of charm, he was a restless man who seldom stuck to anything for very long. But one constant element in his life was his beloved *Aweigh*. He kept her for about 30 years, until his death, I believe, and that is certainly the best testimonial for any boat.

4/ New York 32

An All-Time Classic

> Length overall: 45 feet 4 inches
> Length on waterline: 32 feet
> Beam: 10 feet 7 inches
> Draft: 6 feet 6 inches
> Sail area: 950 square feet
> Designer: Sparkman & Stephens
> Year designed: 1936

Over a long and distinguished sailing career, Tom Closs has been the proud owner of two New York 32s (*Fun* and *Raider*). He has won 176 racing prizes with these boats, and 22 of them, collected in one summer, were won as late as 1967. Tom calls the New York 32 the classic of all classics, and although he no longer owns one of these boats, he says he'd like another if it were made of fiberglass.

That's high praise indeed for a boat that was designed in 1936, but Tom is not the only experienced sailor, still actively racing, who admires the NY 32. The master seaman/designer/rigging expert Rod Stephens told me that this boat, designed by his brother Olin, is one of his all-time favorites. Rod owned the famous NY 32 *Mustang* (formerly *Revonoc*) for more than two decades and won numerous racing awards with her, including class prizes in four Bermuda Races. He also cruised the boat extensively, often with only his wife and daughter for crew, and on certain occasions he even sailed and raced *Mustang* singlehanded.

In 1905, the New York Yacht Club sponsored a one-design class of boats, created by Nathanael Herreshoff, which rated 30 feet under the Universal Rule and were referred to as the New York 30s. These boats replaced the few enormous New York 70s, and their main purpose was for use in an active program of non-handicap, boat-for-boat racing. This class was followed by larger one-designs, the New York 50s and 40s, but these boats were more expensive and harder to handle. So in the mid 1930s, there was a move by prominent members of the club to replace the old 30-footers with a similar-sized but slightly larger and more comfortable boat incorporating the latest thinking on hull and rig design for offshore racing. The result was the S&S-designed New York 32 (32 feet on the waterline), which not only turned out to be a superb racer, but also a seakindly and able cruiser.

Twenty New York 32s were produced by one of the best wood boatbuilders, Henry B. Nevins of City Island, New York. Specifications called for white oak frames and keel, Philippine mahogany planking, Everdur fastenings, and exten-

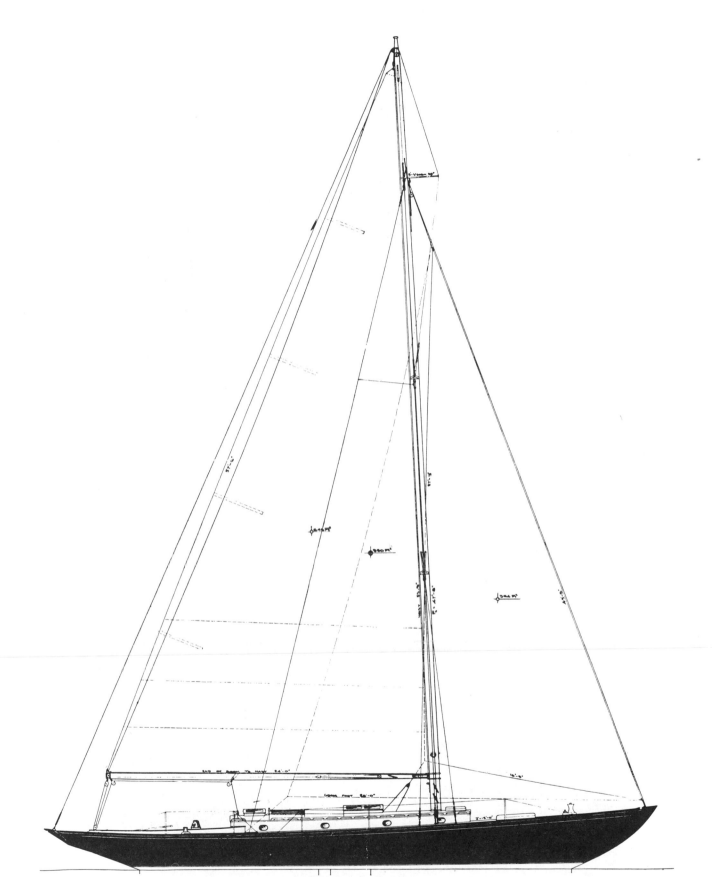

Original sail plan of the New York 32. A later plan shows much less mast rake and the jib tack at the stemhead, which would indicate an attempt to lessen weather helm.

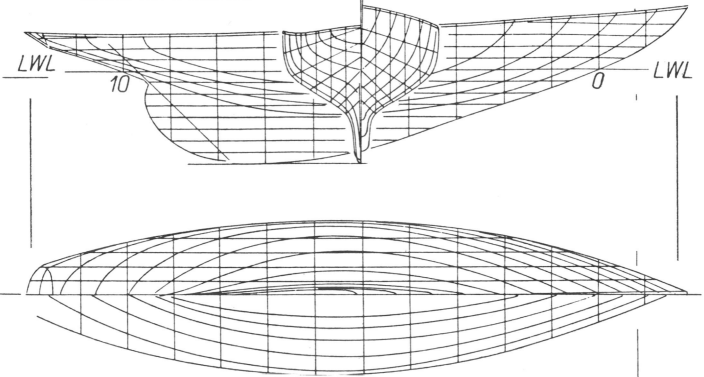

Lines of the New York 32 show a sleek, fairly symmetrical hull. The moderately long overhangs are not only aesthetically pleasing, but they are often helpful in damping pitching on heavy boats with symmetrical underbodies and spread-out keel ballast. (From Sailing Theory and Practice *by C.A. Marchaj, © 1964. Dodd, Mead & Company)*

Arrangement plans of the New York 32. The profile plan also shows many of the fine construction details. (Yachting)

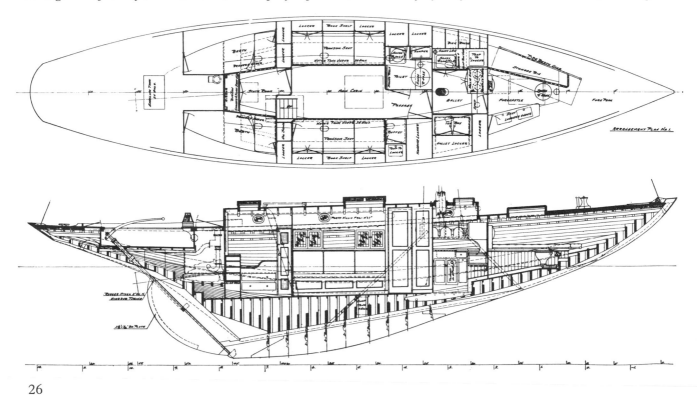

sive hull strapping. In the initial stages of construction, they were built upside-down. Construction details included such refinements as a bronze trailing edge to the rudder and large limber holes with a clearing chain. The cabin trunk was through-bolted to the deck, and a heavy tie rod held the deck steady at the mast partners.

The New York 32 and a forerunner design named *Starlight* seem to be developments of the *Stormy Weather* hull in smaller sizes. Obviously there are variations, with the 32 having slightly more beam proportionally, less tumblehome, and not quite as much deadrise as *Stormy*. The NY 32 has more overhang forward, and this is aesthetically pleasing, because the bow more closely matches the stern. The keel profiles of the two boats arc fairly similar, except that *Stormy*'s drag is more pronounced, and of course the rudder stock angle is considerably greater (almost 45 degrees) on the 32.

This view of the New York 32 Valencia *shows her many hatches and skylights, which provide a lot of light and air below decks. Note the jib sheet tackle arrangement used on the early boats. (Morris Rosenfeld)*

In the book *Nowhere is Too Far*, The Annals of the Cruising Club of America, author John Parkinson Jr. wrote that "in their first year the 32s carried considerable weather helm," but he reported that "this was subsequently eliminated by ballast changes." I notice that the original specifications called for 9,400 pounds of keel ballast, but Francis S. Kinney, a designer long associated with Sparkman & Stephens, recently wrote in his book *You Are First* that "the NY 32 ballast is 10,200 pounds of lead." Perhaps additional ballast was added to increase the boat's stiffness and thus alleviate any undue weather helm resulting from too great an angle of heel. The original sail plan shows much more rake in the mast than a later plan, and this change probably made the boat less ardent. But whether or not there was any significant helm fault originally, the 32 was tuned to balance well early in her life.

I did hear one owner of a New York 32 report that his boat would sometimes tend to knock down and broach to when carrying the spinnaker in a fresh breeze. However, this certainly doesn't correspond with a statement made to Mr. Kinney by Rod Stephens when he said, "We never hesitated about setting a spinnaker under running conditions in some pretty fresh breezes, and never was there any idea of broaching—the boat (*Mustang*) never broached, never in any condition." Undoubtedly, suitable spinnaker shape together with proper handling technique and careful attention to the helm are the keys to avoiding broaches. Nevertheless, I would be willing to bet a bottle of beer, perhaps even a bottle of rum, that if the New York 32 were fitted with a more modern type of keel-attached rudder, she could be controlled even better in difficult downwind conditions. Steering was noticeably improved on the Luders-designed Navy yawls when they were recently fitted with modern rudders. Originally, the yawls had rudders that were not unlike those on the NY 32s, but the new rudders are more like the one Olin

Stephens designed for the 12-meter *Constellation*—this type has greater area at the bottom, a hollow curve in the trailing edge, and a sharp corner at the bottom.

According to Francis Kinney, Olin Stephens has a theory that "sloops designed with a foretriangle and mainsail each of equal size do not seem to perform as well as sloops with these two sails of unequal size." This is a very interesting theory, and there's no denying that there have been some very fast boats with little jibs and big mains, and also fast boats with little mains and big jibs. Of course, the NY 32 is the former type, with her long main boom and seven-eighths foretriangle, and there are many advantages to this rig. The boat has enough area in the mainsail to sail quite well under main alone, which is a great asset in certain situations, such as when sailing into a harbor to pick up a mooring, or continuing to sail with reasonable balance (due to the forward location of the mast) after dousing a light headsail during a sudden squall. Also, with the small foretriangle there is not as much need to change jibs (provided they are heavy enough), because sail can be reduced quite easily by reefing the main. Long ago, Rod Stephens was able to reduce the mainsail on *Mustang* with a fast method that in some respects anticipated the modern jiffy-reefing system.

If the NY 32 had a modern aluminum mast of proper section and wall thickness, the jumper stays would probably not be needed, and then she could carry a slightly larger jib, and the mast could be flexed to some extent in order to help flatten the main in a breeze. I take a very conservative view of mast flexing on offshore boats, but it does help control the mainsail's draft, and moderate bend seems safe enough if the boat is properly masted and has a forestay that does not go to the masthead.

As with *Stormy Weather* and *Aweigh*, the below-deck arrangement of the NY 32 is designed to accommodate a paid hand. His quar-

Left: The famous New York 32 Mustang *with her skipper Rod Stephens handling the spinnaker sheet from the foredeck where he can easily see the luff of the sail. (Morris Rosenfeld)*

ters are in the forecastle, which contains a pipe berth and head. The galley is just abaft the fo'c's'le, so that the hand can stay forward when preparing meals. Of course, we have a different lifestyle today, and most people can't afford or don't want a live-aboard hand on a boat of this size. Thus the location of the galley on the NY 32 seems a little inconvenient for modern cruising. Nevertheless, Rod Stephens found *Mustang* to be very comfortable below during long cruises, and a few sailors I know actually prefer the forward galley location, because it keeps congestion away from the companionway/chart table area. My own preference, though, is for an after galley, because of its accessibility from the cockpit and also because there is less motion aft.

Although the accommodation plan here shows a different arrangement, *Mustang* has a transom and pilot berth on each side of the main cabin. There is a clever plan whereby the cushioned backrests of the transom seats can be swung upward to make bunkboards for the pilot berths. The dining table is a swing type that remains level when the boat heels. There is a stateroom abaft the companionway with two quarter berths, lockers, and a small hatch for ventilation. The arrangement precludes a chart table, but there is an oilskin locker near the companionway so that water need not be tracked into the cabin in wet weather.

The 32 has low freeboard by modern standards, but still she is a good sea boat, with ample reserve stability and the ability to claw off a lee shore in heavy weather. Several seagoing features are the low cabin trunk with small ports, small cockpit well, bridge deck, and high companionway (even if it is somewhat off-center). These boats have made some outstanding offshore passages, including a notable transatlantic crossing by Frederick Lyman in *Voyageur* (later named *Raider*). This boat got quite a dusting north of Scotland and later in the North Sea, but she was able to handle the heavy weather very well.

Sparkman & Stephens has recently designed another one-design class boat for the New York Yacht Club, a fiberglass centerboarder that measures 34½ feet on the waterline and 48 feet overall. This boat is magnificent and luxuriously comfortable, but it is not cheap, and it is a relatively complicated boat. In many respects, I still prefer the New York 32, which is far simpler, easier to handle with a small crew, and has an ageless kind of beauty.

Left: A dramatic aerial view of the New York 32 Tigress *hard on the wind. This view clearly shows the narrow cabin trunk and wide decks that provide safety during knockdowns and for the crew going forward or coming aft. (Bill Kuenzel)*

5/ The Concordia Yawl

No Stamped-Out Rubber Ducky

Length overall: 39 feet 10 inches
Length on waterline: 28 feet 6 inches
Beam: 10 feet 3 inches
Draft: 5 feet 8 inches
Sail area: 650 square feet
Displacement: 18,000 pounds
Designer: C. Raymond Hunt
Year designed: 1938

Owners of Concordia yawls tend to be connoisseurs, who deservedly have a great deal of pride in their classic wooden craft. Not so long ago, when I asked a New England woman who owned one if she might not be considering the replacement of her Concordia with a modern fiberglass boat, she drew herself up indignantly and replied, "What? Exchange my beautiful boat for one of those stamped-out rubber duckies?"

The design for the boat she was so proud of was drawn up after the hurricane in 1938 when three yachtsmen got together to create a replacement boat for one that was lost in the storm. The three sailors were the late Llewellyn Howland, his son Waldo, and C. Raymond Hunt, Waldo's partner at the Concordia Boat Company in Padanaram, Massachusetts, who later was to achieve considerable fame as a designer. Llewellyn, whose boat was lost in the hurricane, was descended from a line of prominent New Bedford whalers, and he had not only a family seafaring tradition but also a practical background of extensive small boat cruising. This new craft would be his "dream ship," and he

had some strong opinions on the characteristics she should have.

Some important considerations were the ability to cope with choppy seas, easy handling characteristics, windward ability, and speed under a wide range of conditions. The foremost requirement, however, was that the boat should be able to stay on her feet in the frequently windy conditions of Buzzards Bay where she would be sailed.

It has been said that Llewellyn had a strong aversion to boats that sailed with their lee rails awash, so Raymond Hunt, who drew the lines for the new boat, gave her hard bilges and considerable tumblehome. In addition, she was given a ballast-to-displacement ratio of 43 percent, which was substantial for a cruising boat of those days.

Roger Taylor, who knew Llewellyn Howland quite well, wrote an interesting article about the Concordia yawls in the *National Fisherman* (April 1976). In discussing the origins of the design, Roger said that it was inspired by a model of a French lugger, "probably of the

The standard sail plan of the Concordia, which is somewhat small for light air regions. Note the bridle for the mainsheet that relieves the bending moment on the boom. (Yachting)

Chasse Marée type," designed by Pierre Reynard; but Roger said the Concordia's actual lines were influenced by *Cinderella*, a boat Raymond Hunt had designed in 1936.

The result of these widely varied influences, in conjunction with some quite original thinking, was an eminently successful design. As one can plainly see from the accompanying plans and photographs, it is a strikingly handsome

boat with a spoon bow, narrow overhanging stern, moderately low freeboard, and a saucy sheer.

The lines show a rather symmetrical hull with well-balanced ends, and this characteristic tends to produce an easy helm. Although there is one theory that symmetrical hulls may have a tendency to hobbyhorse, the Concordias do not seem to pitch excessively in a seaway, despite

33

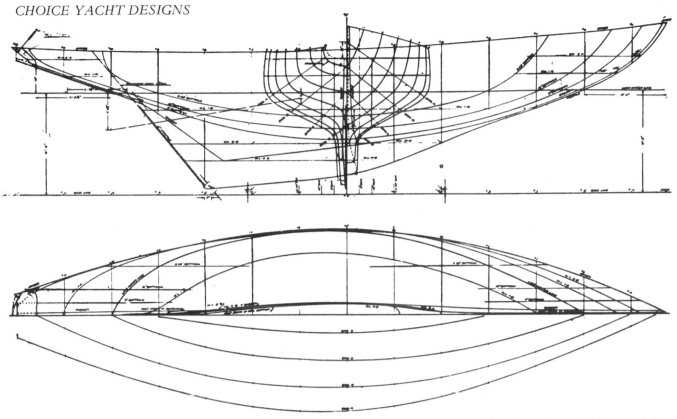

Lines of the Concordia show a symmetrical hull with balanced ends and sharp turn of the bilge. The tumblehome of the midsections helps keep the rail dry once the heeled boat has settled on her shoulder. (Yachting)

the fact that their sections and waterlines forward are rather full. Perhaps the long overhang aft and U-shaped sections above the waterline supply a damping effect to slow the motion. There is very little forefoot, and the after end of the keel has considerable rake. This keeps the lateral plane small for low wetted surface drag, and the raked rudder stock is helpful to steering when the boat is heeled. It is easy to see why the

Concordia is stiff, with her sharp turn of the bilge and maximum beam, as seen in the body plan, very close to the load waterline. As the boat heels, her center of buoyancy moves outboard rapidly to produce a considerable righting arm.

Greater emphasis was put on the boat's looks and sailing ability than on her accommodations; nevertheless, she is adequately comfortable for

Although the accommodations of the Concordia may seem a bit small for a boat of her size, there is a tremendous amount of stowage space. (Yachting)

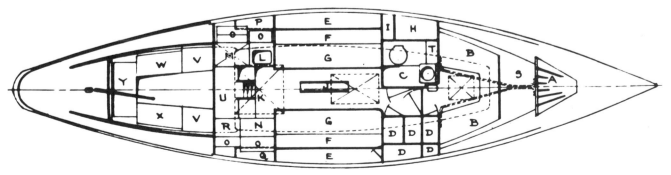

The venturesome Concordia Winnie of Bourne, *which cruised the sometimes treacherous waters described in Erskine Childers'* The Riddle of the Sands. *(Morris Rosenfeld)*

cruising and has a number of innovations, such as the famous Concordia berths. These are folding bunks somewhat similar to pipe berths but with wood slats on their undersides so that they make backrests when the bunks are folded up. Of course, the main value of these berths is that they can be adjusted to the boat's angle of heel so that a windward-side sleeper will not be rolled out. There is plenty of stowage space, including a platform forward for sails. The boat has an ample enclosed head and large galley; but personally, I would rather compromise part of the galley space for a small chart table near the companionway. With a cabintop skylight to admit light and air below, there is no need for large, ugly windows or ports in the cabin house sides. A nice feature for protected water cruising is the extra-wide companionway hatch; however, I would prefer that it be more narrow for offshore work. Then, too, I would want to modify the cockpit for ocean passages, because the standard boat has locker doors in the side of the well that are not entirely watertight.

The first Concordia yawl, *Java*, named after a lucky whaling vessel owned by Llewellyn's great grandfather, was built in 10 months by the old Casey yard in New Bedford and launched in 1939. She attracted great interest and was later followed by sisters with such exotic names as *Malay*, *Sumatra*, and *Suva*. The latter was the first of many Concordias to be built by Abeking and Rasmussen, the German yard with such a splendid reputation for excellence in wood construction. The original yawls were 39 feet 10 inches long, but a newer, slightly modified model was given an extra foot of overall length. This model is known as the Concordia 41.

Although the Concordias were not designed to any handicap rating rule, they fared well under the Cruising Club of America rule, and many had excellent racing records. Some consistent winners in New England waters were *Actaea, Sagola,* and *Gamecock,* while *Malay* attracted much attention in 1954 by becoming the smallest boat up to that time to win the prestigious Bermuda Race. Perhaps the most successful racer of them all, though, was Ray-

mond Hunt's own Concordia 41 named *Harrier.* She won a number of important races, but her performance at Cowes Race Week in 1955 earned her international recognition. At that time *Harrier* was newly built, had a modest sail inventory, and was sailed by an all-family crew consisting of skipper Ray Hunt, his wife, two daughters (age 21 and 14), and two sons (age 18 and 16). The Hunt family absolutely devastated their class by winning six out of six races against the cream of British racers. *Harrier*'s margins of victory were so considerable that her rating was questioned, and she was remeasured. To the astonishment of her competitors, the new rating was even lower, by three quarters of a foot!

Aside from their ability as racers, Concordias have excelled as distance cruisers. One of the most interesting cruises, to my way of thinking, is the one made by John Parkinson Jr. in *Winnie of Bourne* when he cruised the Frisian Sands along the coast of Holland in an attempt to visit the scene of *The Riddle of the Sands*, the famous nautical mystery book by Erskine Childers. Perhaps the most adventurous cruise was made by the Steve Loutrels in their Concordia yawl, *Lacerta.* The Loutrels cruised the coast of Labrador as far north as the sixtieth parallel. In poorly charted waters they experienced fog, gales, fierce currents, and pack ice. On one occasion they had to short tack through a labyrinth of channels in the ice to reach an anchorage, and later, while at anchor, they were rammed by a large ice pan measuring 50 by 100 feet.

The standard Concordia is rigged as a yawl with a seven-eighths foretriangle as shown in the accompanying sail plan. But many of the most competitive boats were masthead rigged, and some of these were rigged as sloops. A few that sailed in areas of predominantly light winds had bowsprits added. Raymond Hunt experimented with several rig variations—even a catboat rig with a large single sail—but it seems that *Harrier* proved more successful as a seven-eighths or masthead sloop with a bowsprit. With the seven-eighths rig she sacrificed some area aloft, but the rating was kept reasonably low and the

The famous Concordia Harrier. Her larger-than-standard foretriangle gives her a respectable sail-area-to-displacement ratio of 17.5. (Morris Rosenfeld)

extension of the foretriangle's base produced a well-shaped spinnaker. Of course, the bowsprit demands extra caution when changing jibs off-shore, and I would prefer an inboard rig for extensive ocean cruising on this type of boat.

The standard yawl rig is a good one for cruising in regions where there is a high percentage of fresh winds. The boat balances quite well under main and jib, mizzen and jib, or mainsail alone; and the jib has a boom to enable tacking without the need to touch a sheet. About the only detail of the rig plan I might question is the length of the main boom. During a Chinese jibe, or even a reasonably well executed jibe when the sheet is not shortened quite enough, the boom could lift and foul the permanent backstay. This has happened to me a couple of times, so I'm a bit sensitive on the subject. Rather than shorten the main boom, however, which would reduce sail area, it might be better to have a slightly taller mizzenmast so its boom could be raised to allow moving the backstay farther aft.

In an article that William W. Robinson wrote for *Yachting* magazine (December 1972) about Raymond Hunt, he pointed out that in the 1968 Bermuda Race the Concordia *Westray*, a 30-year-old design, topped her class. The article went on to say, ". . . it really wasn't until the IOR Mark III became established that this very traditional-looking design could really be called out-of-date." I'm sure Bill Robinson is aware that in the highly competitive Annapolis Fall Series in 1977, a Concordia racing under IOR with an old-age allowance ended up second in her class. This same yawl, *Babe,* won fleet first in the MHS (Measurement Handicap System) division of the 1978 Bermuda Race, while the Concordia *Malay* (not the original *Malay*) finished second!

It seems a shame that Concordia hulls have not been produced in fiberglass, simply because wooden boats are so expensive and troublesome to maintain in this day and age. Of course, I realize that such an idea must be repugnant to many wood boat buffs, but regardless of the material from which it is made, I don't think a Concordia could ever be considered a stamped-out rubber ducky.

6/ The Owens Cutter

Ahead of Her Time

> Length overall: 40 feet 6 inches
> Length on waterline: 28 feet
> Beam: 10 feet 6 inches
> Draft: 5 feet 10 inches
> Sail area: 651 square feet
> Designer: Norman G. Owens
> Year designed: 1944-45

How could a leading powerboat company with no prior experience in producing sailboats create a sailing cutter that would be years ahead of its time? That is the question many sailors have asked themselves after the creation of the 40-foot Owens cutter in the mid-1940s. The powerboat company, of course, was the Owens Yacht Company of Baltimore, Maryland, and it turned out a one-and-only sailboat design that all but dominated her racing class for about two decades or more. I can't answer the question about the precocity of the boat's conception except to say that the three Owens brothers, who ran the company, had been avid sailors from way back; and one of them, Norman, was a naval architect and a keen student of the most up-to-date sailboat design. Also, the brothers were able to use some of their powerboat technology in the construction of the cutters to produce rigid hulls that were quite light for their day.

Many people have been credited with having had a hand in the design of the Owens cutter. In this connection some well-known names

have been mentioned: Olin Stephens, Phil Rhodes, Sherman Hoyt, and Ernest Tucker. But Charles (Chuck) Owens, the senior partner, gives full credit to his brother Norman. It is true that Ernest Tucker (later the designer of the Dickerson ketches) was working for the Owens company when the cutter was designed, and I understand he drafted some of her plans. Also, I have heard that the company had previously considered building a Rhodes design measuring 27 feet on the waterline, and it has been said that this had some influence on the Owens cutter. But whether this is true or not, Norman certainly came through with a racing-cruising design that was unique for its time.

The cutter was designed during World War II, and M. M. Davis of Solomons, Maryland, made the first five hulls. In 1946 the first boat, named *Den-E-Von*, went south and won the St. Petersburg-to-Havana race, thereby serving notice that this was a design to be reckoned with. The Owens company soon took over construction and built 41 boats, using modern, almost assembly-line techniques. Decks were

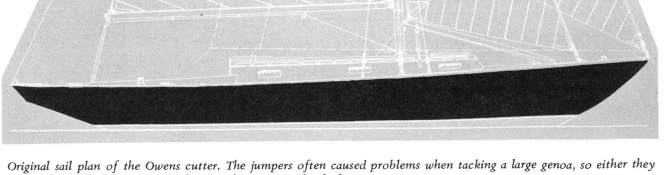

Original sail plan of the Owens cutter. The jumpers often caused problems when tacking a large genoa, so either they were removed or the struts were fitted with a semicircular fouling preventer.

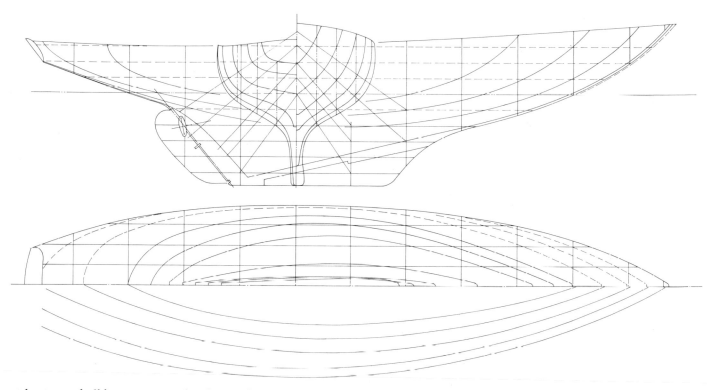

The Owens hull has a cutaway forefoot with a prominent keel toe. Her sections aft are quite flat, but the radius is large at the turn of bilge amidships.

built separately using a specially designed jig, and the hulls were made by what the company called "Duraform" construction. Fabrication consisted of outer mahogany planking bonded with phenolic resins and bronze fastenings to an inner skin of marine plywood laid diagonally from sheer to keel. The result was a moderately light, nearly monolithic hull that was rigid enough to satisfy the racing skipper, who likes to carry his rigging taut. The first boats cost a mere $7,850. The Owens-built cutters have held up very well, except that some were fitted with aluminum chainplates that in time severely corroded. In the early 1950s the Henry R. Hinckley Co. of Southwest Harbor, Maine, took over building the cutters. These were more

One disadvantage to the layout of the original Owens cutter is the rather small galley with stove facing the wrong way for gimbaling.

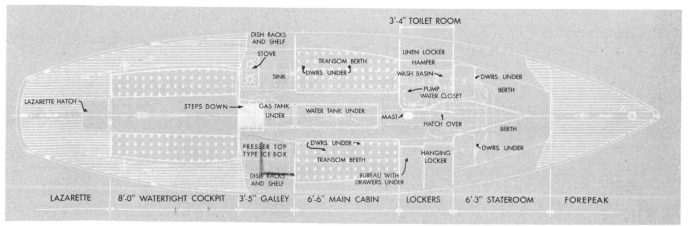

heavily built, lead ballast was increased from 6,000 to almost 7,000 pounds, and the sail area was also increased somewhat. The Hinckley boats were exceedingly strong, but they didn't seem to be quite as fast as those made by the Owens company.

Some prominent Owens cutters in the Chesapeake area were *Fandango* (the Owens brothers' boat), *Sashay, Prim, Trig, Rubicon, Bay Wolf,* and *Snallygaster.* Morton (Sunny) Gibbons-Neff, the owner of *Prim,* certainly has to be considered the most tenacious owner, because he refuses to give up his cutter. He has altered the boat to an unbelievable extent, but underneath the disguise she is still the same old *Prim,* formerly *Whirlaway,* which was built in 1948. When the International Offshore Rule first came into being, Sunny took a brief "fling" at racing with an IOR boat, but he soon came back to his beloved Owens cutter. As late as 1972, he raced *Prim* across the Atlantic to Spain, and actually won his class. On the way home, *Prim* sailed from the Canary Islands to Grenada in the remarkable time of 18 days 9 hours. She averaged over 171 miles per day, which must have been close to a record for a displacement (nonplaning) monohull with a designed waterline length of only 28 feet. This was before *Prim* was extensively modified. I saw her on the ways in Grenada in late 1972, and from a long distance off I could instantly recognize her as an Owens cutter.

Perhaps the two most famous boats of this class have been Ash Bown's *Carousel* sailing out of San Diego, California, and *Finn MacCumhaill*, a top performer in New England waters. A friend of mine, who occasionally crewed on *Finn,* said that the skipper, Robert Coulson, had a strong aversion to carrying extra weight. Lightening holes were cut in the bulkheads, and heavy cooking utensils were so scarce that canned foods were sometimes heated in their own cans. Accommodations were Spartan, but the boat won more than her share of silver. *Carousel* did even better in West Coast racing. For nearly 20 years she was able to beat with great regularity the toughest competition not only in local races but

also in distance events, including a member of Acapulco races of more than 1,400 miles.

I had the good fortune to sail a number of times on Charlie Stein's Owens cutter, *Snallygaster,* one of the most winning boats on the Chesapeake Bay. It was a thrill being able to best all but one of our class in the widely attended Block Island Race Week of 1967. I was amazed to see how well *Snally* moved against the famed Cal 40s. One of them beat us, but we beat seven others, if I remember correctly.

Charlie had a nonstandard aluminum mast, and he carried the rigging taut as bowstrings. Before the series, I remember sighting up the mast and seeing that it was slightly bent to one side. I suggested that we slack the shrouds on one side to straighten the mast, but Charlie insisted on tightening the shrouds on the boat's opposite side. Carrying out his orders, another crew member and I tried in vain to tighten the turnbuckle with two large screwdrivers. Charlie disappeared below, then came back with a huge wrecking bar, and instructed us to use that on the recalcitrant fittings. Why we didn't drive the mast through the bottom of the boat I don't know, but I became convinced that the boat had to be strongly made. Incidentally, for those who might try to emulate this form of tuning, I should warn that overly taut rigging not only is hard on the hull, but too much leverage applied to an open-barrel turnbuckle can weaken the fitting.

Since the Owens cutter was such a success, one might ask why it has never been produced in fiberglass. The answer is that it has been, but in slightly modified forms by three different companies. The Allen Boat Company of Buffalo, New York, built one version called the Borsaw 40, and then sold the mold to the Allied Boat Company. Designer Robert Harris was commissioned by Allied to redesign the after section of the underbody to incorporate a skeg with attached rudder and to modify the transom. The result was the well-known Allied 39.

The other fiberglass version is the Hinckley 41. *Finn MacCumhaill* was used as a plug for the mold after considerable work was done to her

The famous Owens cutter Finn MacCumhaill *strapped in and hard on the wind. (Morris Rosenfeld)*

Perhaps the winningest of all Owens cutters, Ash Bown's Carousel *of the San Diego Yacht Club. (Beckner Photo)*

The author at the helm of Charlie Stein's fast Owens cutter Snallygaster *during Block Island Race Week.*

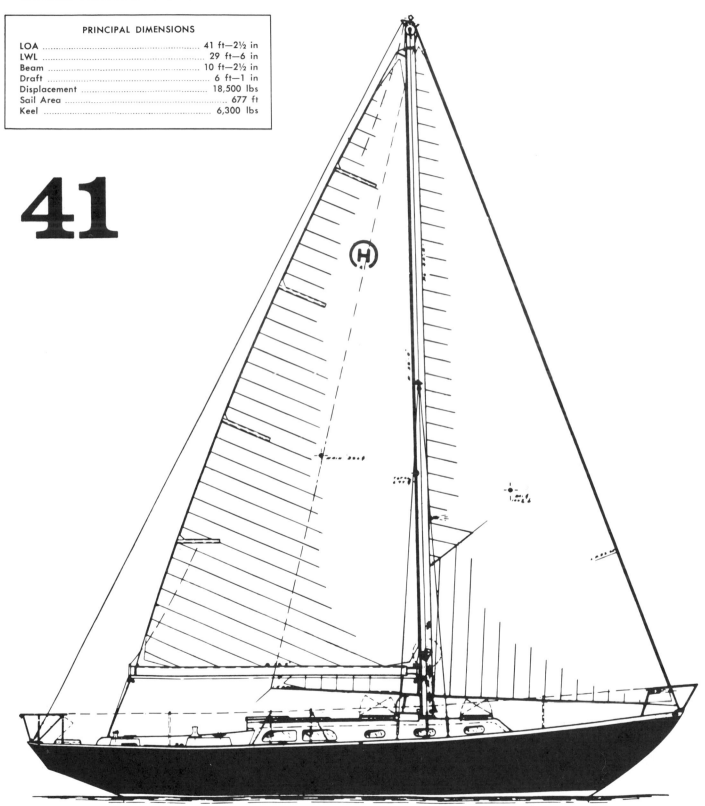

PRINCIPAL DIMENSIONS

LOA	41 ft—2½ in
LWL	29 ft—6 in
Beam	10 ft—2½ in
Draft	6 ft—1 in
Displacement	18,500 lbs
Sail Area	677 ft
Keel	6,300 lbs

41

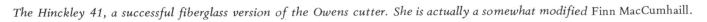

The Hinckley 41, a successful fiberglass version of the Owens cutter. She is actually a somewhat modified Finn MacCumhaill.

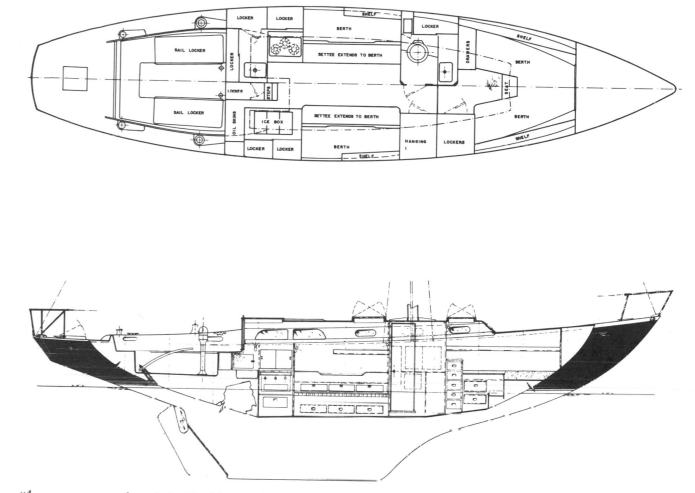

7/ The S & S Pilot

Leaving Well Enough Alone

> **PILOT 35** (fiberglass model)
> Length overall: 35 feet 9 inches
> Length on waterline: 25 feet
> Beam: 9 feet 6 inches
> Draft: 5 feet
> Sail area: 554 square feet (sloop)
> Displacement: 13,500 pounds
> Designer: Sparkman & Stephens
> Year designed: 1945 (original underbody)

The arrangement plan of the Hinckley 41 shows a number of improvements over the original Owens cutter, especially the rearranged galley and the addition of a sizable oilskin locker.

measure of the worth of a yacht the length of time it remains in The Sparkman & Stephens-designed een around for a long time, and new is class are still being requested. The ot 33 was designed right after World was built of wood by the Thomas pbuilding Corporation, and also the Works, I understand. In 1956 the was lengthened to 35 feet overall ion by Henry R. Hinckley and A write-up in *Yachting* (January that the new Pilot "retains the from her 24-foot waterline down, have been drawn out to a 35-foot length. . . ." Six years later Hinck- ducing the boats in fiberglass, but ey are not in production at the

tive lines drawing shows a lesome hull that is moderate in is an unspecialized boat with no duly compromised for another. f thinking, it is a splendid

combination of speed, seaworthiness, looks, and easy handling characteristics. The bilges are fairly slack, and the turn at the garboards has a large radius. These features not only reduce wetted surface and inhibit pounding in a seaway, but they allow an integral keel of great strength with room for a proper bilge water sump. With her easy bilges and a fairly modest ballast-to-displacement ratio of 31 percent, one might expect the Pilot 35 to be a trifle tender, but the ballast is external lead to achieve about the lowest possible center of gravity, and there is ample waterline beam for adequate initial stability. If the ballast were more spread out fore and aft, the center of gravity would be slightly lower, but the weight is concentrated amidships at the forward end of the keel, which is helpful in reducing the moment of inertia to inhibit hobbyhorsing.

There are two schools of thought concerning the merits of external ballast on fiberglass hulls. Ballast encased in a keel avoids the use of keel bolts, which can cause leaks and will eventually corrode, but the fiberglass exterior is subject to

hull. Henry R. Hinckley III, the former president of the Hinckley Company, wrote me: "In addition to re-shaping we also changed the keel, rudder, and sheer on the boat." Nevertheless, the original Hinckley 41s bear a marked resemblance to the Owens cutter. Later the company turned out a "souped up" version of the boat with a shorter keel and spade rudder called the Hinckley Competition 41. Some of these boats, especially the Hinckleys' own *Night Train*, did very well racing.

I am very pleased to be able to show the lines of the Owens cutter, because to my knowledge they have never before been published. The body plan shows an almost wineglass shape with a moderately thin keel that gives high lateral but

low head resistance, despite the bluntness at the toe. With the slackish bilge amidships, moderate beam, and an approximate one-third ballast-to-displacement ratio, it is a wonder the boat is so stiff, but the wide, flat stern sections give her a lot of bearing aft. The waterlines forward are fairly full especially above the LWL to balance the stern's buoyancy. The profile is quite cut away forward and aft for a cruising boat of her day, and of course this reduces wetted surface. I don't think the rudder could be moved much farther forward without creating steering problems in a hard chance downwind. With her long overhangs she is an exceedingly handsome boat in the traditional sense, although she had a lot of freeboard for her time. When the Owens cutters

This view of a Hinckley 41 shows her handsome lines to good advantage.

first appeared, I remember thinking that they were a mite too high-sided, but their freeboard now seems normal compared with the boats of today.

The fiberglass versions of the cutters do not seem to show a great deal of improvement in speed, but they afford definite advantages in maintenance and provide more room below. The original cutters have only four bunks and a smaller cabin, due in part to their wood construction. Also, the accommodations are quite far forward even on some of the fiberglass boats, because there is a considerable after deck and stern lazarette. This is a good feature on boats having a lot of overhang aft, because it helps keep the crew forward where their weight will not adversely affect the boat's motion and trim. The drawback is that the after deck pushes the cockpit and thus the cabin farther forward, at some sacrifice to cabin space. A disadvantage of

the origina
that they l
feature, tc
barred so
races, al
modifiec

The r
not just
boats l
skippe
remer
Stein
have
exhi
cut'
bla
ful
to
g'
t

One good
design is
demand.
Pilot has b
boats of th
original Pilo
War II and
Knutson Sh
Fisher Boat
basic design
for product
Company.
1957) claim
original lines
but the ends
2-inch overall
ley began pro
regrettably th
present time.
The perspe
thoroughly wh
every respect. I
one attribute u
To my way

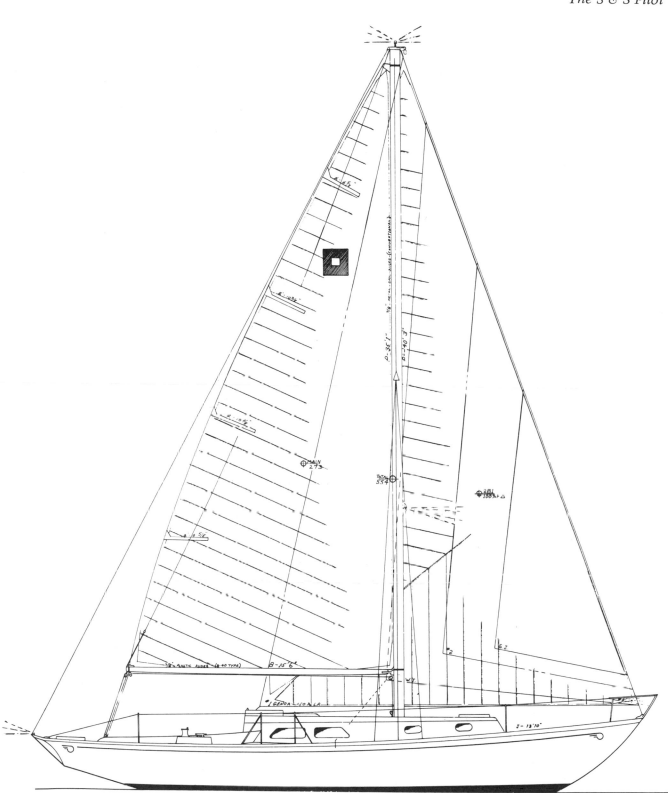

The aspect ratio of the Pilot's rig seems a bit low by today's standards, but it is helpful to stability and minimizes difficulties in sail handling.

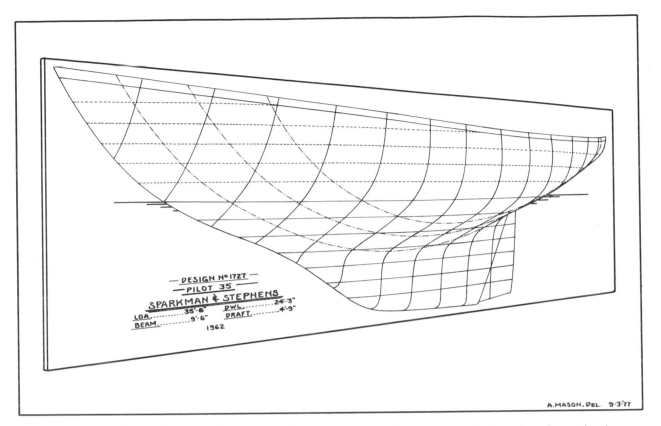

This perspective of the Pilot shows her moderately sharp entrance that cuts so well through a chop. The sheer appears slightly powder-horned from this point of view. The rudder has been modernized in this drawing, which is based on 1962 plans.

The two accommodation plans are almost identical, except that one arrangement provides four berths while the other has six.

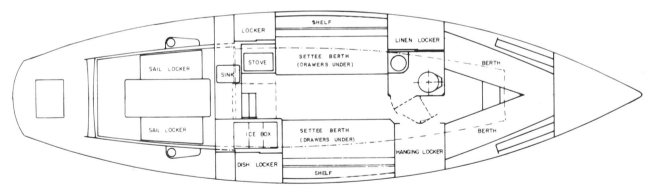

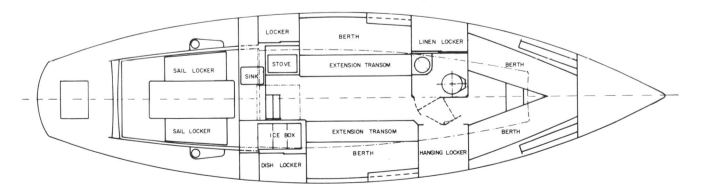

52

The Pilot seems to be one of those rare boats that appears more sightly in actuality than she does in the designer's drawings. (Courtesy Henry R. Hinckley & Company)

damage during a hard grounding. External ballast not only provides a slightly lower center of gravity, but it protects the fiberglass during a grounding. My own preference is for internal keel ballast in areas where the bottom is soft, such as in the Chesapeake Bay, but for external ballast where the bottom is rocky, such as in the waters of Maine where the Hinckley firm is located. Of course, the after end of a Pilot's keel is not protected, but the lead toe will take the brunt of the impact during a grounding.

Incidentally, the bottom of the Pilot's rudder is well raised so that it cannot be damaged by running aground. The rudder shown on the perspective drawing is a modern kind with most of its area at the bottom. Regarding this type, Pierre DeSaix, the acknowledged authority on tank-testing model yachts, has written that the use of a straight trailing edge rather than the traditional curved edge on the rudder can increase the efficiency of the lateral plane. Also, he has said there is evidence that a sharp corner to the heel of the rudder may be highly beneficial.

The Pilot has a moderately sharp entrance, and this allows her to knife through choppy head seas. For several years I raced a very fast Ohlson 35-foot yawl against a wooden Hinckley Pilot 35. We usually had a slight edge on the Pilot in light airs, but she was a bit better to windward in a seaway. The blunter bow of the Ohlson would tend to squash the seas, whereas the Pilot would seem to cut through very cleanly without throwing much spray.

Pilots have been a threat on the race course from the time they first appeared until the advent of the International Offshore Rule. As late as 1969, the fiberglass Pilot 35 *Ergo*, racing under the Storm Trysail Club Rule, won the coveted Everett Morris trophy for the out-

53

standing boat in Block Island Race Week. She won three out of four races in her class. It wouldn't surprise me if Pilots continue to give a good account of themselves under the new Measurement Handicap System.

The Hinckley yard has a reputation for building quality boats. They are expensive but solidly put together and carefully finished. I am impressed with a number of details on the Pilot 35, including the specially made stemhead fitting; the recessed deck scuppers, which help prevent puddles from lying against the toe rail; the joinerwork below; and the handsome teak and holly cabin sole for which Hinckley is famous.

One feature I don't especially like is the deck-stepped mast, which is not as strong as one that passes through the deck and is stepped on the keel. Deck-stepped masts can be perfectly acceptable on small boats that do not sail long distances in the ocean, but in my opinion, a seagoing boat of the Pilot's quality should have her mast stepped on the keel. At least the Pilot will not suffer from a sagging cabintop, because directly under the step is a sturdy pipe that transfers the mast thrust to the keel. This arrangement does nothing to strengthen the mast, but it does strengthen the cabintop, takes some strain off the main bulkhead, and assures that doors in way of the mast will not jam when the mast is loaded. About the only other criticism I have is that I'd prefer a slightly larger forward hatch so that sail bags could be hauled on deck more easily through the hatch.

There are several accommodation plans. One of the original drawings shows a small saloon with a dinette to port and the galley running fore and aft along the starboard side. This arrangement may be satisfactory for harbor living, but it is not very practical for offshore work. I would rather have the optional arrangement that puts the galley aft and bunks on each side of the saloon. With this arrangement, Hinckley provides the choice of a four-berth or six-berth layout. The four-berth layout is probably better for the boat that carries a small crew and seldom makes long passages, since the bunks

in the saloon are fairly wide and comfortable, and there is plenty of room for large lockers outboard of the bunks. But the six-berth layout, with a pilot berth and sliding transom on each side, is the arrangement I prefer for distance racing or passagemaking with a full crew, because there are always two bunks aft, near the pitching axis, that are on the low side when the boat is heeled.

Many years ago my father decided to try out a pilot berth on our Ohlson 35. When I asked him how he liked it, he replied with two lines from a limerick: "Caesar's bones lie on the shelf, and I don't feel so well myself." Thereafter, that berth was always known as Caesar's shelf. It was not the most comfortable or convenient bunk, but it was a blessing at times when the boat was heeled, and quite often it made a convenient stowage area for sails.

The galley, stretching across the after end of the cabin, provides a lot of counter space, but I might want the sink slightly farther away from the stove. The large gimbaled stove with oven may somewhat block access to the sink when the boat is well heeled on the port tack. It is not always convenient to have the chart table above a top-loading ice box, but this is perfectly excusable in a boat of the Pilot's size. At least the chart table is convenient to the companionway, and there is a fine chart locker above the table. Although there is no seat for the navigator, he can perch on the companionway steps.

The original Pilot 33 had a seven-eighths rig, which moved her very well in moderate winds and well enough in light airs. But Hinckley boats tend to be heavy, so it is just as well that the Pilot 35 was given a masthead rig. This not only allowed more powerful headsails and kept a respectable ratio of sail area to displacement, but it simplified the rig by eliminating the need for jumper stays and struts.

At one time the Hinckley yard considered producing a fin keel version of the Pilot to be called the Competition 35. The project never really got off the ground, although one of the boats was built. I had the opportunity to race against her some years ago, and she didn't

A yawl-rigged Pilot with her dodger up and carrying a handy lapper jib. It might be preferable for the mizzen to have a slightly shorter boom and taller mast for less effect on the helm, easier furling, and the ability to carry a larger mizzen staysail. (Courtesy Henry R. Hinckley & Company)

The handsome interior of a Hinckley Pilot. The six-berth arrangement limits sole space, but it is convenient for sleeping under sail. (Courtesy Henry R. Hinckley & Company)

impress me as being much if any faster than the conventional Pilot. I don't think the elder Henry Hinckley, who was running the yard, was happy putting fin keels on lightweight seagoing boats. In an interview with *Yachting* magazine (October 1975), he expressed a distrust of lightly constructed IOR boats for offshore use. He said that the Hinckley yard had built one such boat, but

he "wouldn't want to take it to sea." I must say that I'd rather go offshore in a boat with a conventional integral keel, although I would tend to be quite confident in any fin-keeler built by the Hinckley company. When it comes to a product as satisfactory and well proven as the S & S Pilot, however, I'd be tempted to leave well enough alone.

8/ Loki

"A Superb Sea Boat"

Length overall: 38 feet ¾ inch
Length on waterline: 26 feet
Beam: 9 feet 7 inches
Draft: 5 feet 8 inches
Sail area: 701 square feet
Displacement: 18,000 pounds
Designer: Sparkman & Stephens
Year designed: 1947

According to the dictionary, a Loki is a Norse god who created discord, especially among his fellow gods. To my knowledge, however, the celebrated 38-foot yawl named *Loki* never created any kind of discord, unless it was among her racing competitors. Certainly she's a harmonious creation in form and manner, and it seems most unlikely that she would ever cause any discord among her crew.

The yawl was designed in 1947 by Sparkman & Stephens for Dr. Gifford B. Pinchot of New Haven, Connecticut, and she attracted so much interest that the design was developed into a stock boat class known as the Loki class. The original *Loki* first came into the limelight when she won her class in the 1950 Bermuda Race. Then the boat received further notoriety in 1953 when Dr. Pinchot and a crew of three, which included his wife, sailed *Loki* across the Atlantic along a northern route to Norway.

Dr. Pinchot was kind enough to write me the following brief account of his passage: "We left Norwalk, Connecticut, on June 4th, stopped one night at Woods Hole and went into St. John's,

Newfoundland, for about 24 hours for some radio repairs. We got into Bergen, Norway, at about 2 o'clock in the morning on July 4th for a total passage time, if I remember correctly, of 27 days. We had one gale on the way over and hove to for a few hours and were almost totally becalmed north of the Shetland Islands. Our worst day's run was 12 miles. We did, however, have some whale sharks there and rowed around them in the dinghy."

After the passage, *Loki* cruised down the Norwegian coast to Christiansted, and then crossed the rugged North Sea to Cowes, England. Dr. Pinchot said that the only time the boat pounded extensively was during the North Sea crossing, when she experienced seas that were just the wrong size. It took about a week to reach England because of the rough seas and hard winds that were mostly dead on the nose.

Dr. Pinchot then entered his yawl in the Fastnet Race and did very well, although with a little better luck he might have won a fleet first. He wrote: "Rounding the rock we were well up with the bigger boats and almost all the way

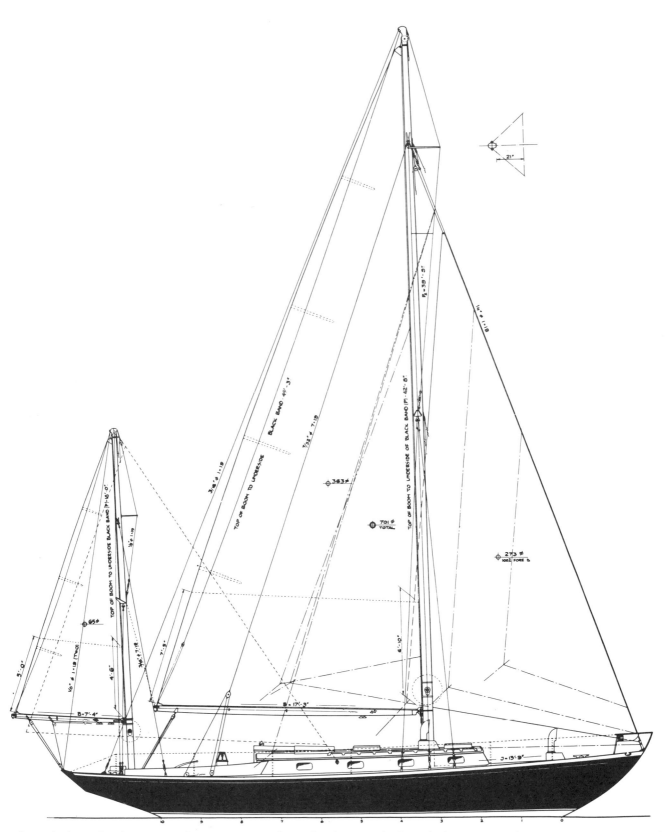

The sail plan of Loki. Despite her 701 square feet of sail area, which is fairly generous for a boat with a designed waterline length of only 26 feet, Dr. Pinchot feels she was slightly under-rigged for light airs.

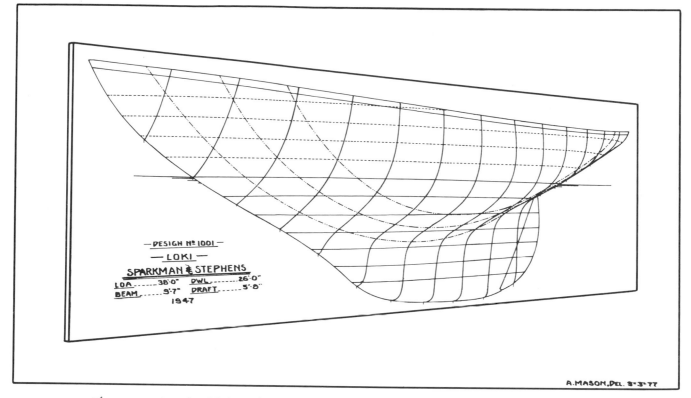

The perspective of Loki shows her moderate, seakindly hull with easy curves and slackish bilges.

Loki's accommodation plan. The pipe berths forward may not be particularly comfortable for harbor sleeping, but they are functional at sea, and they allow a lot of room for stowage forward.

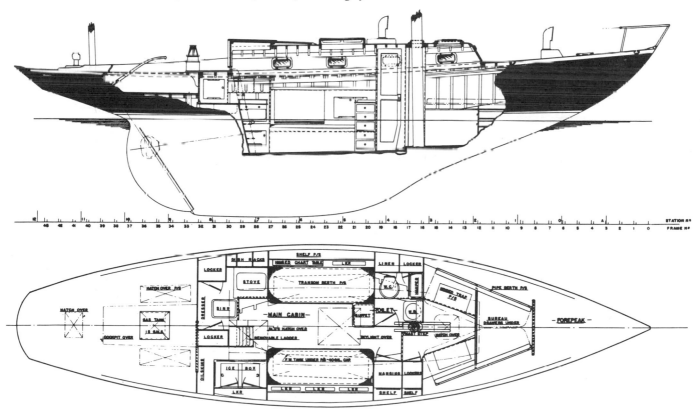

back to Plymouth in that position we were an easy winner of the race, but we got in very calm weather for the last day and dropped down to third in our class and fourth in the fleet."

Aside from her cruising and racing achievements, *Loki* attracted attention because she had no engine, and Dr. Pinchot and his wife, Sally, very often sailed the boat alone. When I wrote to Rod Stephens about the possibility of including *Loki* in this book, he was enthusiastic and said he thought the boat was particularly interesting because of the Pinchots' skillful handling without power. Rod recalled an incident when *Loki* and some other boats anchored in a channel at night after a Stamford Race. He said that the next morning a tug came through the channel blowing, and the anchored boats felt obliged to make a hasty departure. *Loki* sailed her anchor out under jib and mizzen and made her departure more quickly than many other boats that had engines. It takes a bit of doing to impress Rod Stephens with a feat of seamanship, and there is no doubt that Dr. Pinchot is a very talented sailor, but it is also true that *Loki* is a superb handling boat, one that is rarely dependent on auxiliary power to get out of difficult situations.

The profile plan of *Loki* shows her ample lateral plane, which inhibits leeway at low speeds, and the moderately long keel helps make her steady on the helm. Dr. Pinchot wrote, " . . . particularly noteworthy was that she held her course well and had no tendency to broach when pushed hard downwind." How many owners of modern racers could make that statement?

Her lines shown in perspective reveal her fairly slack bilges, a generally acknowledged characteristic of a seakindly hull. The hull is moderate and wholesome in every way, and it is not surprising that Dr. Pinchot called her "a superb sea boat."

By modern standards her overhangs might be a bit long, but these provide reserve buoyancy, which is desirable in a boat of considerable displacement so she can lift her ends in a seaway. The overhangs also tend to lengthen her

waterline as the boat heels; this is apparent in the photograph of *Loki* under sail in Hamilton harbor, Bermuda. Another advantage of the long overhang aft with the raked transom is that it provides a good sheeting base for the mizzen. With a cut-off stern, sheeting would be more difficult, and the crew would have a hard time reaching the after end of the mizzen boom.

One of the few weaknesses of *Loki* perhaps is her light air sailing ability. Dr. Pinchot feels that she was "slightly under-rigged for light weather work." Actually, the sail plan shows an area of 701 square feet (100 percent foretriangle), and this seems ample, but *Loki* is a fairly heavy boat, displacing 18,000 pounds, and her longish keel gives her a fair amount of wetted surface. These features, which tend to produce seakindliness, also inhibit speed in light airs. Her mainsail seems ample, but the foretriangle is small, and the stays passing over the jumper struts restrict the length of the jib luff.

A masthead rig with the mast stepped a bit farther aft would supply more light-weather power, of course, but at some sacrifice to ease of handling when sailing shorthanded. With the seven-eighths rig, more power is consigned to the mainsail, and this sail is relatively easy to shorten down in heavy weather with modern reefing systems. I did hear that at least one *Loki* yawl, *Bikini*, racing on the Great Lakes, had great success after she was converted to a masthead rig.

In changing the rig, of course, one has to be careful not to disturb the boat's fine balance. Too much sail forward might give her a lee helm in light airs. Dr. Pinchot praised his boat's balance, and it is interesting to note the apparent ease with which his wife (I presume) is handling the tiller in the photo of *Loki* in Hamilton harbor. Many boats with that much heel would develop a fair amount of weather helm, which would require some strength to counteract with a tiller, considering the size of the boat and the fact that her mizzen is trimmed in flat.

Dr. Pinchot wrote me that the boat was fairly closewinded, but I used to race against a

Loki under sail in Hamilton Harbor after winning Class C in the 1950 Bermuda Race. The numerous small wrinkles in her main and mizzen didn't seem to slow her in the least. *(Bermuda News Bureau)*

Loki *with all sails set while racing at Cowes, England, in 1953. (Courtesy Gifford Pinchot)*

sloop-rigged *Loki,* and I would describe her upwind ability as a little better than fair. Of course, yawls normally are not quite as close-winded as sloops. At any rate, with a modern rig and sails made of the latest cloth, her speed made good to windward should be excellent.

Since *Loki* was intended for handling by a small crew, except on ocean races when the crew would be standing alternating watches, she was only provided with four bunks. Of course, this allows more room for lockers and stowage, and when there are no sliding berths, the passageway can be kept open. The forward bunks are pipe berths, which makes good sense, because they can be adjusted to the boat's angle of heel and folded back to provide more room for sail stowage and the like. Although forward bunks are often bouncy in a seaway, pipe berths with firm mattresses tend to dampen the bounce, and on *Loki* the berths are a little farther aft than normal because of her extra large forepeak.

The galley is large, and there is a good oilskin locker near the companionway so that wet foul-weather gear will not have to be taken into the main cabin. Ventilation is ample, with three Dorade vents, opening ports, a forward hatch, and a skylight. About the only criticism I have of the accommodations is that there is no fixed chart table, although there is a hinged one over the port transom. On a boat the size of *Loki,* however, I think a proper chart table could be worked in, especially since she has only four berths. The head is large and well laid out, with the wash basin near the boat's centerline to avoid possible flooding and enable drainage when heeled, but I prefer a WC that is aligned fore and aft rather than athwartships. A friend of mine with an athwartships WC got so many

complaints from his crew that he was "always on the wrong tack," he finally mounted the device on gimbals.

Loki class boats were constructed of wood, of course, and they were built to last. As an indication of their strength, the *Loki* yawl *Katrina*, which made two transatlantic passages, was undamaged by a violent collision with a large sperm whale. Specifications called for mahogany planking on steam-bent white oak frames. The keel and deadwood were also white oak, and fastenings were Everdur bronze. The standard deck construction was canvas over waterproof plywood, but I would prefer teak decks or fiberglass covering the plywood. The original *Loki* was built before the heyday of fiberglass, but there is little doubt that glass construction would offer a big advantage in low maintenance and watertightness. Francis S. Kinney, a designer at Sparkman & Stephens, has written that *Loki* developed a leak at the garboards from violent rolling in a calm during her Atlantic crossing. This problem, as well as seams in the topsides opening up in hot weather, is not at all unusual for wood boats. Obviously fiberglass construction would avoid these troubles.

Aside from her sailing and cruising abilities, *Loki* is a joy to behold. Granted, she has a traditional look, but I think there are few modernists who could honestly deny that she is handsome. It seems unlikely that a *Loki* will ever become anachronistic, even if she doesn't conform to the latest rating rule, because she is just too good a boat. Surely there will always be some demand for a lovely boat that can take her owner anywhere with grace and in haste.

9/ The Nevins 40
The Record Speaks

> Length overall: 40 feet
> Length on waterline: 27 feet 6 inches
> Beam: 11 feet 3 inches
> Draft: 3 feet 11 inches (board up)
> Sail area: 739 square feet
> Designer: Sparkman & Stephens
> Year designed: 1954

I don't suppose any readers of this book need to be told about *Finisterre,* the 39-foot yawl built by Seth Persson for Carleton Mitchell from designs by Sparkman & Stephens. But for that rare sailor who has never heard tell—some castaway, perhaps, who spent most of his life marooned on a desert island—I need only say that this boat has the unique distinction of having won the Bermuda Race three times in a row. The odds against this feat are so great that it seems unlikely it will ever happen again. Of course, the boat has received an unusual amount of publicity, and Mitchell and others have extolled her virtues in numerous magazines and books as well.

The Nevins 40, otherwise known as the Series A yawl, might be considered the production model of *Finisterre.* The Nevins-built boats are essentially *Finisterre* with her bow drawn out a bit, as I was told by Rod Stephens of Sparkman & Stephens. The 40-footers, like their slightly shorter prototype, were beautifully built of wood, and the construction plan gives some indication of how solidly they were put together.

The highly regarded Nevins yard of City Island, New York, not only built the hulls but also made a lot of the rigging, fittings, and hardware.

I had the opportunity to become really familiar with the boat when William T. Stone, the noted columnist for *Yachting* magazine and author of cruising guides, was kind enough to lend us his Nevins 40, *Brer Fox,* for a week's cruise in the Abaco Cays some years ago. The boat proved ideal for our cruise, because she was comfortable, sailed well, and was able to negotiate the shallow waters of the area quite easily with her centerboard retracted.

Needless to say, variable draft is advantageous in shoal waters, but centerboards have disadvantages too. There are sometimes problems with worn pins and jammed or corroded pendants; servicing can be difficult in some regions; thumping of the board in its trunk is sometimes an annoyance; and there can be highly concentrated stresses on the hull, trunk, or board in rough weather or when grounding. Perhaps the greatest drawback of a shoal-draft seagoing boat, however, is that for a given weight of ballast

Sail plan of the Nevins 40. A larger mizzen might have improved balance and speed in light airs, but it is important to keep the spar light when it is stepped abaft the waterline ending.

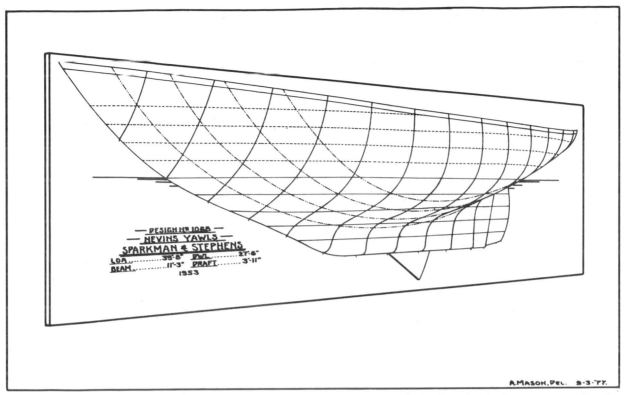

Although this perspective drawing shows the Nevins 40's centerboard fairly far aft, the location is said to be slightly forward of the board location on Finisterre.

These plans show many details of the Nevins 40's accommodations and construction. Note such features as the large forepeak, chart drawers forward, large hanging space for oilskins, adequate ventilation below, and well-planned galley that utilizes the top of the centerboard trunk as a dresser.

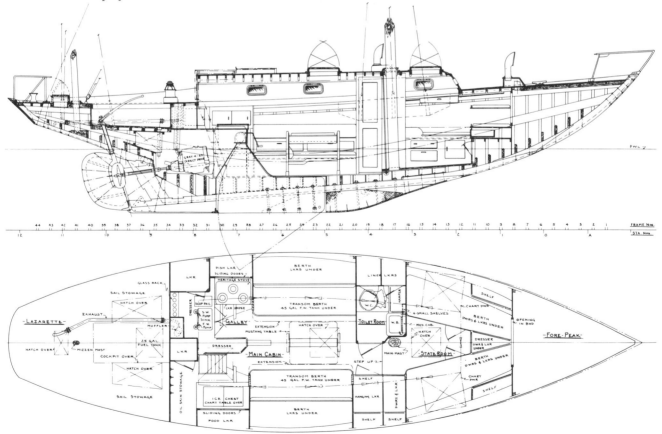

Colin E. Ratsey's Golliwogg, *one of the most successful of the Nevins 40s that raced under the CCA rule. Not surprisingly, her sails set well, and they resemble racing sails of today except that the jib is not a deck sweeper. (*Yachting)

there is some sacrifice to the range of stability.

Carleton Mitchell has praised the seakeeping qualities of his *Finisterre,* but I tend to agree with Rod Stephens, who wrote me, "In spite of a certain amount of propaganda from centerboard enthusiasts, I certainly feel a reasonable keel with the stability range provided would be my choice for bad weather offshore." In dis-

cussing the pros and cons of the keel-centerboard yacht, the late naval architect and design critic Robert G. Henry expressed this opinion: "For offshore cruising, I prefer the normal draft, full keel type. Basically the center of gravity of the lead ballast is considerably lower, and the rudder, being deeper, is not in danger of rolling out when the going gets rough." Specifically in regard to *Finisterre,* Bob Henry wrote me: "I've crewed a few times on *Finisterre* with lots of beam and shoal draft. She was an exception and always got along well due partly to good handling. But I had the feeling that when we buried the rail the hull was really rolled out, and there would be not too much rudder in the water."

Naturally, yacht design involves compromises, and with the shoal-draft keel-centerboarder it is probably true that a slight amount of seaworthiness is sacrificed for the ability to cruise in shallow water. Nevertheless, strongly built and well-handled boats of this type are certainly capable of long-distance passagemaking. *Finisterre* made a number of outstanding ocean passages, and Wright Britton's *Delight,* a similar type of yawl, has successfully weathered numerous heavy gales at sea. There is, however, a lesson to be learned from the heavy weather experience of the 39-foot keel-centerboarder *Doubloon.* This yawl rolled over twice as a result of lying ahull in a Gulf Stream gale with her board down. It seems likely that she would not have been so susceptible to tripping and rolling over if her board had been retracted. For a boat having a limited range of stability in seas with spilling breakers, the preferable tactic might be to keep her as much as possible end-on to the seas, with perhaps a riding sail aft (a tactic used by *Delight*), or by running off while towing drags astern.

Even if lacking the ultimate stability of a deep keel boat, the Nevins 40 has numerous seagoing features. She has plenty of beam for high *initial* stability, and thus the ability to carry sail in a breeze. This characteristic, together with her modest freeboard of low windage and her moderately sharp entrance, gives her the ability to drive to windward in a blow and claw away from a lee shore. She has very wide side decks for the crew's security, and there are no large "picture" windows that are vulnerable to breakage in heavy weather. The cockpit well is small, and there is a proper bridge deck and high sill, although I would prefer that the companionway be closer to the boat's centerline. The mast is stepped through the deck, as it should be for

greatest strength, and there is a tie rod running from the partners to the step to ensure that the cabintop will not move. I know of a boat that nearly sank because of a broken hose that housed the centerboard pendant, but on the Nevins 40, the after part of the centerboard trunk is raised, and the pendant exits well above the waterline.

The broad beam of 11 feet 3 inches not only adds to initial stability and allows ample width for the side decks, but also it provides plenty of room below decks. There are no quarter berths, but the beam permits a pilot berth and sliding transom to fit easily on each side of the boat. The dining table is a drop leaf gimbaled type, or actually a swinging kind called a mustang—which I presume was named after the table used on Rod Stephens' New York 32, *Mustang.* These tables have a heavy weight underneath to keep the top level and to damp the swinging movement.

In the planning stages before *Finisterre* was built, Carleton Mitchell made a full-scale mock-up of the galley to be sure it would be exactly right, and the same general arrangement plan was used for the Nevins 40s. My only quibble is that in a boat of this size, it should not be necessary to have the chart table over the ice box. It's most annoying having to clear the table when a crew member wants a cold beer. The arrangement plan shows a seawater pump as well as a freshwater pump for the galley sink. This is a very handy feature for a boat that will sail far offshore, but the pumps should be clearly marked. I remember one night at a large raft-up in a crowded harbor when I took a huge gulp of sea water, because the person who fixed my drink was confused by the two pumps. I survived, but it is a wonder that I didn't come down with typhoid fever or something about as bad. No doubt the rum in my drink killed the germs, so I learned two valuable lessons: (1) plainly mark the galley pumps, and (2) always be sure to add plenty of rum to the drinking water.

Some of the other features I like about the cabin of the Nevins 40 are the abundant lockers,

The famous Finisterre, *forerunner of the Nevins 40. It looks as though the jib lead block should be moved farther forward to improve the genoa's trim, but if that were done, the clew would be pulled into the block. (Courtesy Mrs. Fred Thomas)*

Wright Britton's seagoing Delight, *which is quite similar to a Nevins 40. (Bermuda News Bureau)*

large forepeak, oilskin stowage convenient to the companionway, large drawers for chart stowage (even if they are not close to the chart table), and ample ventilation. The hatches are double-hinged so that they can be opened at either the forward or the after end, and this allows changing the direction of the air circulation below when desired. The ability to open a hatch at its after end also allows it to be cracked in wet weather at anchor when the rain is being blown aft.

In sailing performance the Nevins 40s closely match *Finisterre*. During the 1958 Bermuda Race, for instance, Colin E. Ratsey's Series A yawl *Golliwogg* finished less than an hour behind the fleet winner, *Finisterre*, after a tooth-and-nail battle the whole way. The Nevins 40s have *Finisterre*'s ability to drive to weather in a blow, but with less weight and slightly more sail area, they are a bit faster in light airs.

It is plain to see from the sail plan that nearly all the sail area is supported by the mainmast. The tiny mizzen of only 65 square feet is little more than a balancing sail, although its mast can support a fairly large mizzen staysail, which gives some extra drive on a broad reach. Several details on the sail plan are somewhat puzzling to me. I should think the mainsheet would have a better lead angle from the very end of the main boom, and this would also allow the use of roller reefing, which was so popular at the time the plan was drawn. Also, I notice several turnbuckles aloft, which makes their inspection and adjustment very difficult at sea. I would especially want the turnbuckle on the headstay (if I felt a turnbuckle necessary) to be at the deck.

In an article written for *Yachting* in July 1976, Carleton Mitchell speculated on how *Finisterre* would sail against a modern one-tonner. He reckoned that his former boat would be "murdered" downwind but not upwind in head seas. My own feeling, after having seen *Finisterre* in action a number of times, is that she would be quite respectable against almost any boat her size in a good breeze, but a great many boats can beat her in drifting conditions. Very much the same could be said about a Nevins 40, except that she would probably be a little better in light airs. Rod Stephens told me that *Finisterre* had a slight lee helm in light airs, but this was corrected on the Nevins 40s by moving the board farther forward.

At any rate, I would far rather be aboard *Finisterre* or a Nevins yawl than a current one-tonner for anything much longer than a day's sail, because the former boats are real cruisers. Aside from the fact that they can poke into shallow gunkholes and are relatively placid at anchor, they are far more comfortable; their motion is more pleasant; they are much easier to handle with a small crew; steering is normally less demanding at moderate angles of heel; and I, for one, have more confidence in their construction and strength of rig.

Carleton Mitchell said in his article that *Finisterre* wrote him a letter dictated to the boat's present owner, but the Nevins 40 *Brer Fox*, in the tradition of Uncle Remus, "lay low" and like the tar baby, "she ain't sayin' nothin'." As a matter of fact, these boats don't have to say very much, because the record speaks for itself, loud and clear.

10/ The L-27

Taking the Competition by Storm

Length overall: 40 feet
Length on waterline: 27 feet
Beam: 9 feet 10 inches
Draft: 5 feet 5 inches
Sail area: 800 square feet
Designer: A. E. Luders Jr.
Year designed: 1955

The L-27 *Storm,* designed, built, and skippered by A.E. (Bill) Luders Jr., was certainly well named, because she took her competition completely by storm, and at one time or another she stirred up a storm of controversy. For over a decade she all but dominated the racing scene in the vicinity of Long Island Sound, and repeatedly won or did exceedingly well in such events as the Vineyard Race, New York Yacht Club cruise, Block Island Week, and the Whitmore Trophy series. The latter, a hotly contested series spread throughout the summer, was won seven times in a row by *Storm.*

The occasional controversies had to do mostly with Bill Luders' propensity to experiment with unusual rigs. One year *Storm* was raced as a ketch with a pocket handkerchief-sized main, and another year she was rigged as a normal sloop but carried no mainsail at all. When Luders won with these rigs, he was often accused of rule beating. Actually, though, he was pointing out, in a decisive way, glaring loopholes in the Cruising Club of America rule. Of course, he demonstrated that headsails were not being suf-

ficiently penalized, and this led to major rule changes. I understand he offered suggestions that were incorporated into the changes. *Storm's* great success, however, had nothing to do with beating the rule or freakish rigs. She was such a fast boat and was so well sailed that she usually won no matter what the rig. In fact, she did best as a conventional sloop.

Storm was built in 1955 by the Luders Marine Construction Co. in Stamford, Connecticut. The company had pioneered in building boats of molded plywood during World War II, so that method of construction was used for the L-27s. Although these boats are a class, only six of them were built by the Luders yard, and each one is slightly different from its sister. Perhaps *Storm* is the most different, because she has less freeboard and no cabin trunk. As can be seen from her plans and photographs, she is a sleek, graceful craft with the look of a pure racer. However, she is really a highly refined racing-cruiser with a rather seakindly hull.

I seem to have strong leanings toward cruising boats that come from the boards of meter boat

One important reason for Storm's phenomenal success on the race course under her standard rig was her generous sail plan.

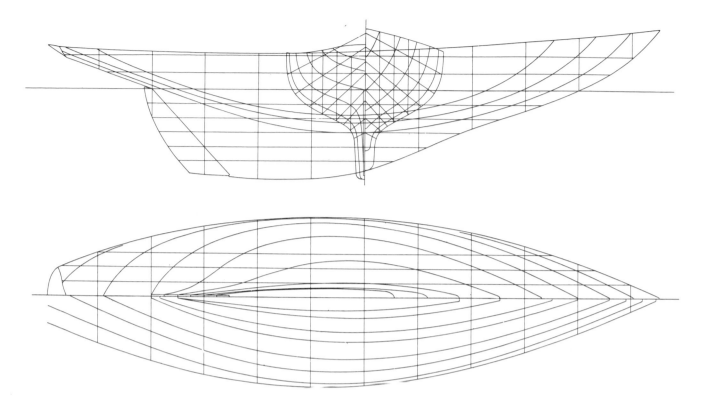

The lines of Storm *show well-rounded sections amidships and almost straight buttocks aft. The reason for the extraordinary flare in the after sections is that* Storm *is an L-27 with less than standard freeboard.*

designers. At least I greatly admire the work of such meter boat designers as Olin Stephens and Einar Ohlson. They have splendid records for producing cruising boats that are untemperamental, smart sailers with unusually good balance and an easy motion. These are the kinds of cruisers that Bill Luders also turns out with great consistency, and he, too, is famous for his meter boat designs: champion sixes, five-point-fives, and the well-known twelve meter *American Eagle.*

With her low freeboard and long overhangs, *Storm* has something of the meter boat look, although she has more beam and less deadrise than most twelves and sixes. The original lines plans of the L-27 were badly damaged in a fire at the Luders yard, but Bill Luders was kind enough to redraw the lines for use in this book. When I first saw them, I was struck with their similarity to the lines of the U.S. Naval Academy yawls, which were drawn by Luders back in 1939. When I mentioned this to Bill, he wrote back: "In regard to the lines themselves, you have a good eye. The L-27 is a scaled down Navy yawl in the proportion of 9 to 10, and the

only original difference was that we moved the rudderpost a little further aft for more lateral plane." This similarity may surprise some readers, because the Navy yawls have never been thought of as red hot racers. However, they are exceptional all-around boats, being seakindly and fast, with recent racing records that are remarkably good when you consider the age of the design. The after location of *Storm*'s rudderpost adds somewhat to her wetted surface area, but it provides a bit more lateral resistance and better steering control. Despite her moderately long keel, *Storm*'s wetted surface is not excessive, because her sections are quite rounded.

I was interested to learn that a year or two after she was built *Storm* had 580 pounds of lead added to the bottom of her keel. Some people think that the Navy yawls are a trifle tender, so I was anxious to know what Bill Luders thought about *Storm*'s stability. He wrote: "Due to the fact that the *Storm* was lighter than the standard L-27 we put in some inside ballast. I never thought she was tender, but I did think she was making more leeway than we wanted so that's why we put some or all

74

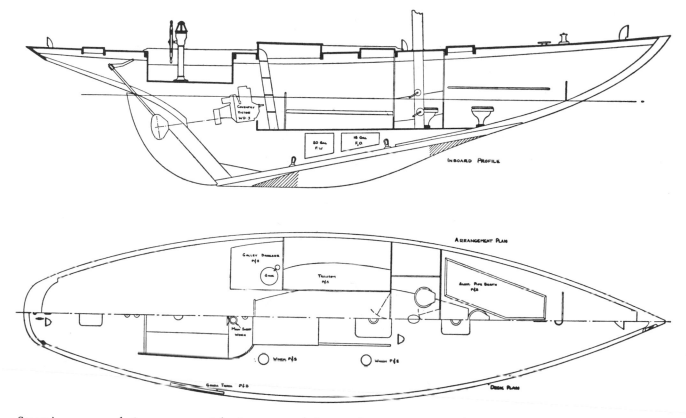

*Storm's accommodations are certainly Spartan, and there is less than standing headroom, but notice the two heads.
(One-Design and Offshore Yachtsman)*

of the inside ballast on the outside of the keel at a later date. I suppose this cut down the leeway a little but it wasn't noticeable. I don't think *Storm* made more leeway than the average cruising boat, but I was just looking for an improvement if possible. I am not sure whether we did this after one season's use or two seasons', but she performed well both ways."

Some sailors have expressed the opinion that *Storm's* success was largely due to her light displacement, but this has probably been overrated. In the first place, she weighs 17,500 pounds, and that is not really light for a boat that measures only 27 feet on the waterline. It is true that *Storm* has rather Spartan accommodations (even though she has two heads), but Bill Luders could not have had any great hangup about weight, since he often raced with a crew of eight. The gifted designer Ted Brewer, who often crewed for Luders, told me about a race during which *Storm* sailed for a considerable time alongside a heavier, more standard L-27. He said that *Storm* took what seemed like forever to get past her sister and that he didn't think the

difference in weight had a tremendous effect on the relative speeds. Of course, weight has some effect in some conditions, but not as much as many sailors seem to think when the hulls are deep displacement types such as the L-27s.

Bill Luders has said that *Storm* is not intended for long-distance racing. Nevertheless, the standard L-27, having a bit more freeboard than *Storm*, is a fine sea boat. With her slackish bilges, moderate displacement, and rounded sections, the motion is easy; and the moderately deep keel with over 45 percent of the hull's weight assigned to outside ballast should assure an ample range of stability. About the only feature I might quarrel with for offshore work is the long counter, which might slam under certain rugged conditions; however, Navy yawls have been sailed across the Atlantic and driven hard in many offshore races, and to my knowledge they have had no problems with the stern overhang.

It can be seen from *Storm's* standard sail plan that she has ample area for speed in light airs. There is a fair amount of rake to the mast, and

There are two methods of beating your competition, by sailing fast with a high rating, or by sailing more slowly with a low rating. Here Storm *demonstrates the latter method using her unconventional ketch rig. (Morris Rosenfeld)*

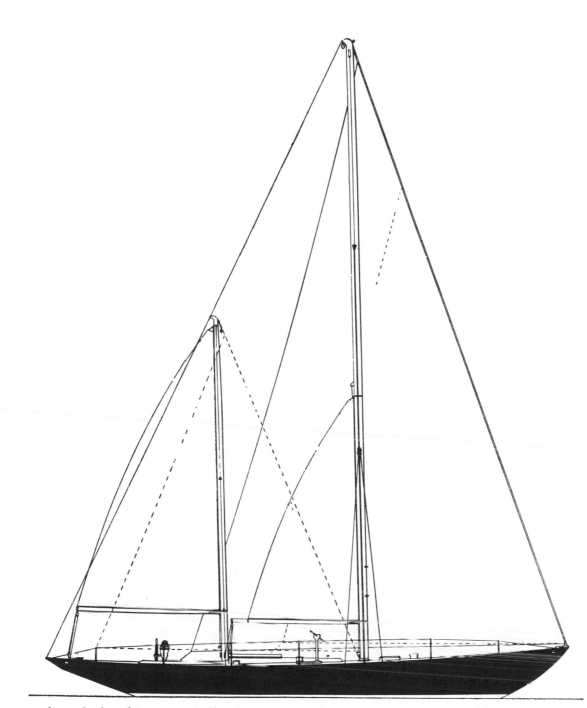

The sail plan for Storm's *offbeat ketch rig. The mizzenmast is partially supported by the permanent backstay, and it appears that the mizzen's generous roach might foul the stay. Note the coffee grinder abaft the mainmast. (*One-Design and Offshore Yachtsman*)*

this is not surprising, because it moves the center of effort aft to properly lead the center of lateral resistance, which must be rather far aft as compared to the CLR of a Navy yawl. Also, the rake facilitates keeping the headstay taut when beating in a breeze. It's a wonder that *Storm* did not have an intolerable lee helm during the sea-

son when she was raced with no mainsail. The fact that she did not shows that the hull is exceptionally well balanced. A hull with inherent good balance can seem to tolerate considerable shifting of the sails' center of effort, but a bad helm can seldom be relieved to any great extent on a really poorly balanced hull,

Storm *driving over a sea. Her mainsail should give encouragement to those with less than perfectly setting sails.* (*Morris Rosenfeld*)

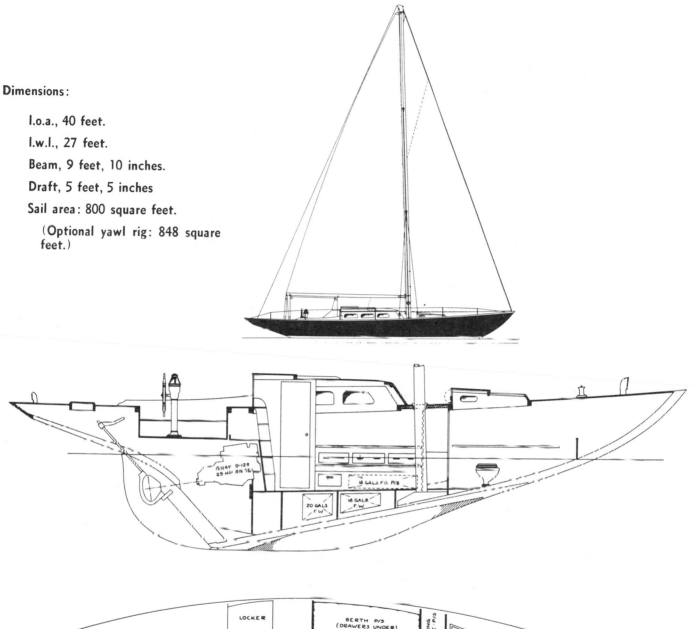

Dimensions:

   l.o.a., 40 feet.

   l.w.l., 27 feet.

   Beam, 9 feet, 10 inches.

   Draft, 5 feet, 5 inches

   Sail area: 800 square feet.

     (Optional yawl rig: 848 square feet.)

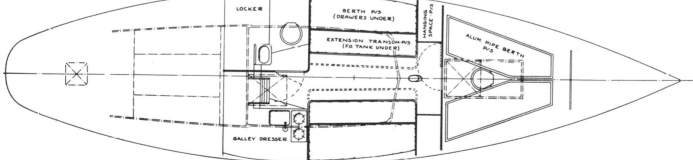

A cruising version of an L-27. Quite a bit of privacy is afforded by having two heads and a forward cabin that closes off and has its own companionway. (The Skipper)

even with considerable shifting of the center of effort. Every so often you hear of a bowsprit being added in a futile attempt to correct a weather helm. Sometimes the bowsprit helps, but it will not solve the problem completely if the hull itself is very poorly balanced.

Obviously *Storm* would not have been so successful if she had not been well sailed. Bill Luders and his crew were aggressive, skillful, and imaginative. I use the latter word because Bill constantly experimented with ways to improve the boat with new rigs, sails, deck layouts, ballast placement, rudder shape, rating adjustments, and methods of trimming sails. Judging from photographs of *Storm* in her heyday, it seems as though Luders and his crew anticipated some of the modern trends in sail trim, such as opening up the slots between sails in order to carry the genoa (or large staysail) along with the 'chute. Also, I understand that Bill Luders was very particular about getting the very best helmsmen to relieve him at the wheel. Ted Brewer is justifiably proud of the fact that he was often asked to steer.

Because of her lower sheerline and flush deck, *Storm* doesn't have full standing headroom below, and her accommodations are not really adequate for extended cruising; however, the other L-27s are relatively posh. One trunk cabin version of the L-27 is illustrated, and it can be seen that she has accommodations for six with adequate locker space and two heads. Unfortunately, the large enclosed head aft moves the companionway slightly off center and somewhat restricts the galley space on the starboard side. This arrangement also necessitates having a galley sink that might need closing with a valve or plug to keep it from overflowing when the boat is heeled on the port tack. The booby hatch forward is a nice touch, which augments headroom, provides good ventilation, and adds character to the boat.

Bill Luders believes in having two heads on a cruising boat. In a recent letter to me he said, "We raced it (*Storm*) with a crew of eight, including my wife and sometimes other girl crew, and for privacy we liked two heads, and also as insurance in case one of them broke down. I still think this is a good feature on any cruising boat." This reminds me of a remark my cousin made after he took a large crowd off for a weekend cruise on his new Morgan 34. After returning home he said, "I've decided to name my next boat *Janus,* because she's definitely going to have two heads."

11/ The Triton

A Little Gem

TRITON (MK I):
Length overall: 28 feet 4 inches
Length on waterline: 20 feet 6 inches
Beam: 8 feet 4 inches
Draft: 4 feet
Sail area: 371 square feet (sloop)
Displacement: 6,930 pounds
Designer: Carl A. Alberg
Year designed: 1958

When the Triton class was introduced at the New York Boat Show in 1959, it was an immediate sensation. The trim little 28-footer was one of the early cruising sailboats to be made of fiberglass, and it is now considered a classic. Many a sailor who had been undecided about what boat to buy must have made up his mind on the spot after a look at the boat show sample, because 16 orders were placed at the show.

My uncle, Charles E. Henderson, a stern critic of stock designs, had spent over 20 years looking for just the right boat. His sons, Ed and Charlie, had all but given up hope that he would ever do anything but window shop, but he finally did decide to buy a Triton. Of course, he didn't buy her immediately—the inevitable bugs in any new design had to be ironed out first—but he determined that this was the right boat, and eventually the cautious Scotsman plunked down his money. Neither he nor my cousins, who did most of the sailing, ever regretted the choice.

Occasionally, I sailed with my cousins on their Triton named *Ojigwan,* and I'll never forget competing in an early spring series held at Oxford, Maryland. The competition was rough, because we were up against two of the top racing sailors on the Chesapeake Bay: Bill Meyers, sailing a Morgan-designed Columbia 31, and Doug Hanks, sailing a red-hot Cal 28. *Ojigwan* was well prepared, with a beautiful new suit of sails including an oversized main that could be flattened and reduced a bit in fresh winds with Cunningham cringles and a foot lacing line. Charlie decided that standard bottom paints were not fast enough, so he mixed up and applied his own concoction, which turned out not to be very good as an antifoulant but made the boat slippery as a greased eel for several weeks.

The series was a tight one, but *Ojigwan* came out on top, and it showed me firsthand that a well-tuned Triton could sail with the best of her contemporaries, including fin-keelers and centerboarders. We were at a distinct disadvantage when sailing downwind because of the three-quarter rig and tiny spinnaker, but the Triton could usually recoup her losses on the upwind legs.

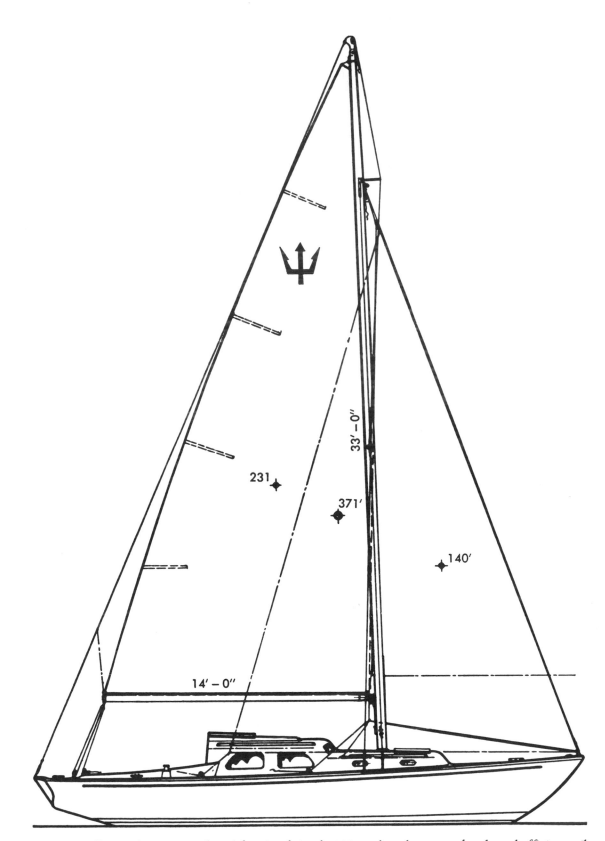

*With her tall mast, large mainsail, and fractional rig, the Triton sloop has a very handy and efficient sail plan. Such a rig will allow some flexing to flatten the main in a breeze, but it would be important to use great restraint, because the mast was not designed to bend very much. (*The Skipper*)*

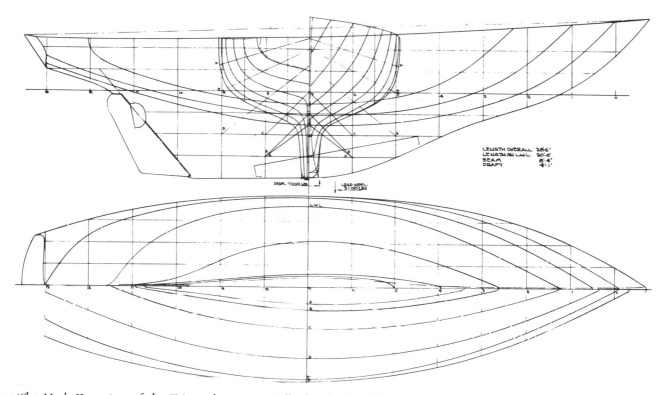

LENGTH OVERALL 28'6"
LENGTH ON L.W.L. 20'6"
BEAM 8'4"
DRAFT 4'1"

DISPL. 7000 LBS   LEAD KEEL 3100 LBS

The Mark II version of the Triton drawn especially for this book by Carl Alberg. Notice the firm bilges, which give her good stability. Her upper stem is a little more straight than the Mark I Triton, and the rudder has a more modern shape.

About the only thing lacking in the Triton's accommodations is a stove, but a portable one might be used on the drop leaf when at anchor and a bulkhead-mounted swing stove can be used underway. (The Skipper)

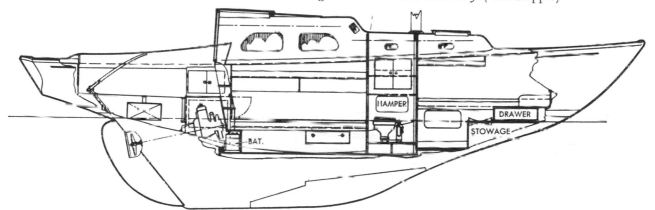

HAMPER
DRAWER
STOWAGE
BAT.

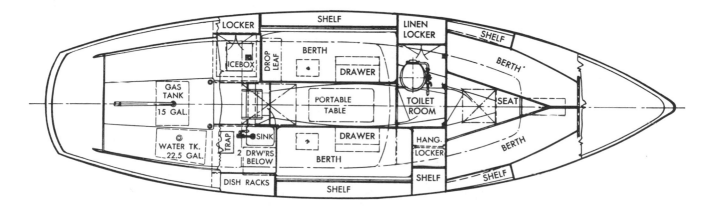

LOCKER   SHELF   LINEN LOCKER   SHELF
ICEBOX   DROP LEAF   BERTH   SHELF   BERTH
DRAWER
GAS TANK   PORTABLE TABLE   TOILET ROOM   SEAT
15 GAL.
TRAP   SINK   DRAWER   HANG. LOCKER   BERTH
WATER TK.   2 DRW'RS BELOW   BERTH
22.5 GAL.   SHELF   SHELF
DISH RACKS   SHELF

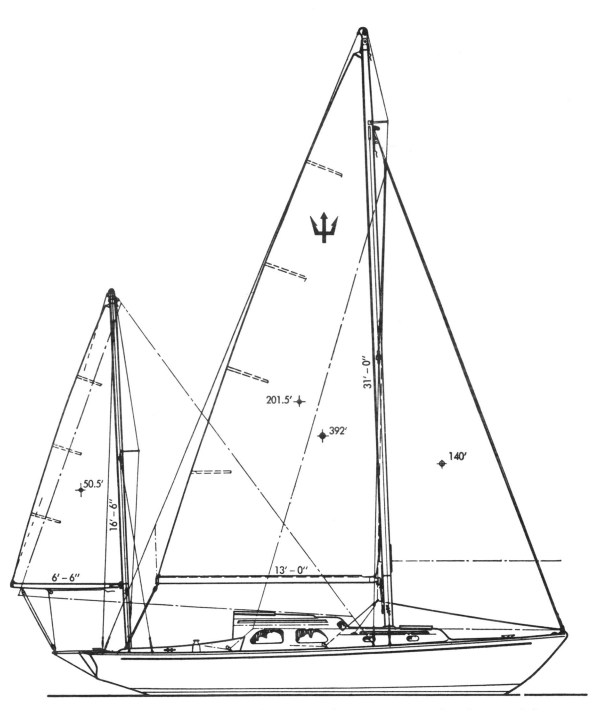

The yawl-rigged Triton. In comparison with the sloop rig, the mainmast is two feet shorter and the main boom one foot shorter. Despite the smaller main, the total center of effort of the yawl is about a foot and a half abaft the TCE of the sloop, which should produce a little more weather helm under certain conditions. (The Skipper)

Charlie was the usual skipper, but on one race when he was away, I filled in for him. We got off to a good start and led Hanks by a few boatlengths to the first mark, which was Bononi Point lighthouse. There was a riprap of rocks surrounding the lighthouse, and Hanks, a native of that area, yelled a warning that there were some underwater rocks we should keep clear of. In my naiveté of Eastern Shore gamesmanship, I gave the mark a wide rounding, and this gave Hanks a perfect opportunity to slip inside us and take the lead. Actually, there really were rocks under the water, and Hanks had done nothing at all unethical, but I was too cautious, and as a

Ojigwan II *in the fall of 1962 with the author at the helm and Ed Henderson manning the windward rail. The vang at the end of the main boom is a makeshift substitute for a traveler. (Fred Thomas)*

result, we were plainly outmaneuvered. We never could regain the lead, but *Ojigwan* finished close behind the Cal 28 and easily saved her time to win the race, despite my lack of finesse.

The Triton is not only a smart sailer, but she's a good looker. Her designer, Carl A. Alberg, to my knowledge never drafted an ugly boat. He had previously designed such well-known attractive craft as the Coastwise Cruiser, when he worked for the John Alden Company, and much later the saucy little Sea Sprite that resembles the Triton in some respects. It would seem impossible to get six-foot headroom in a boat only 21 feet on the waterline without ruining her appearance, but Carl Alberg pulled it off with the Triton. He did this by using a high but attractive doghouse, so there was no need to detract from the looks of the hull with excessive freeboard. Of course, the trouble with a tall doghouse is that it is hard to see over, but this difficulty can be alleviated, if the helmsman is not too short, by sitting on a seat, even one or two cushions.

Pearson Yachts of Rhode Island built the Triton, and it might be said that the Triton built Pearson Yachts, for the company was reportedly in bad financial shape before it began producing the popular Alberg design. Even though this particular class is no longer produced, many hundreds of Tritons were sold, and this gave the company a much-needed boost. In fact, the late Everett B. Morris, a highly respected yachting reporter, once wrote that the Triton allowed Pearson Yachts to narrowly "escape from the oblivion of bankruptcy."

To my regret, Grumman Allied Industries, Inc., of which Pearson Yachts is a division, refuses to release the lines of the original Triton, despite the fact that the boat has not been produced for many years and the designer is more than willing to have the lines published. However, Mr. Alberg was kind enough to draw up, especially for this book, a new set of lines that might be labeled the Triton-Mark II. This plan closely resembles the original boat, and in one respect the Mark II lines more accurately resemble the actual late-model Tritons, for Mr. Alberg wrote me the following: "Starting with boat #385, Pearson put the lead keel inside the hull, which of course made the keel almost two inches thicker and about one inch deeper. This change is incorporated in this plan." The Mark II plan also differs from the original lines in that Mr. Alberg "straightened the upper part of the stem line, increasing the overall length by two inches, from 28 feet 4 inches to 28 feet 6 inches; lengthened the aft end of the LWL two inches by making a slight change in the profile of the lower part of the stern overhang; and gave the rudder a more modern shape."

The hull is certainly beautifully shaped, to my eye at least. There seems to be just the right amount of overhangs with the bow and stern nicely matched but with sufficient waterline length for speed in a breeze and also to inhibit hobbyhorsing. The keel is long enough to give directional stability and to supply ample lateral plane for the sake of minimizing leeway. A shorter keel would reduce wetted surface, of course, but it might require more draft to supply the same lateral resistance, and this would not be helpful to gunkhole cruising. The Triton's hull is fairly symmetrical by modern standards, and her waterlines are rather straight amidships. These characteristics, together with her modest beam and generally moderate proportions, give her an easy, predictable behavior unlike so many of today's temperamental racing cruisers. Her sections show fairly firm bilges, and this feature, together with a 44 percent ballast-to-displacement ratio, enables her to carry her sail well in a breeze.

Although the Triton is rather small for offshore work, it is a good sea boat. Triton number 8, named *Olé*, made a rugged trip from New York to Bermuda in 1960 and came through a bad Gulf Stream storm unscathed. The early models, however, need certain modifications before going to sea. On those boats, for instance, the cockpit seat lockers open from the side rather than the top, and the standard unhinged locker doors could leak or possibly be washed out by a sea breaking into the cockpit. But if the lockers can be kept sealed, there is little danger from a filled cockpit, because the well is quite small. In fact, I read that Carl Alberg once

On a spinnaker run in light airs, the Triton is at a disadvantage, because her 'chute is so small. In real drifting conditions, however, the small 'chute can often be kept filled when larger ones collapse. (Fred Thomas)

calculated that a full cockpit would "only" lower the stern 5½ inches.

Another shortcoming of the early Tritons was that they came with single rather than double lower shrouds, and a number of masts were lost as a result. It is my understanding that after boat number 120, however, another set of lower shrouds was added, and shroud kits were supplied to the earlier boats.

Most Tritons are sloop rigged, but some were rigged as yawls. Personally, I can't see much advantage in having two masts on such a small boat. The mizzenmast can be used as a backrest, of course, and it is fun to hang up a mizzen staysail, but that sail has a very narrow range of effectiveness. The standard three-quarter sloop rig is very efficient on the wind, but as mentioned earlier, it is not advantageous for downwind handicap racing. Some Tritons were fitted with slightly shorter than standard masts and were masthead rigged, but for some reason these boats did not seem to do as well in closed-course racing. Two Tritons of my acquaintance were fitted with bowsprits to extend the base of the foretriangle, and one of these boats did extremely well despite the fact that she might have had some lee helm in light airs.

Back in 1959, when the Triton was first introduced, many sailors were amazed at the room below. They had been used to the cabin of a wood boat with ribs and ceilings that seemed to shrink the interior. Nowadays, in this age of fiberglass, the Triton doesn't seem so large; but nevertheless, she is roomy for a boat only 21 feet on the waterline and with a beam of 8 feet 4 inches. Also, she is well laid out with four full-sized bunks 6 feet 3 inches long, a head that can be closed off, and plenty of stowage space. Her wide beam forward allows sufficient foot room for the forward bunks. On many boats of this size, the forward bunks converge into a V, and this means that the sleepers compete for foot room. About the only drawback to the accommodations is that the galley is quite small, and there is not much of a place for a proper stove. Some owners have solved this problem satisfactorily by using a bulkhead-mounted Sea Swing that burns Sterno or kerosene. Another very minor problem is that the 22½-gallon water tank is located on one side of the boat, which could cause a slight list when it is topped up, but it is somewhat counterbalanced by the ice box on the opposite side.

A friend of mine used to own a Triton named *Gem*. I always thought the name was most appropriate, because that's exactly what the boat is, a little gem in the world of molded stock designs.

12/ The Mason 31

A Blend of Science and Art

Length overall: 31 feet
Length on waterline: 22 feet 11 inches
Beam: 9 feet 4 inches
Draft: 4 feet 8 inches
Sail area: 426 square feet
Displacement: 10,400 pounds
Designer: Alvin Mason
Year designed: 1959

Not long ago, a well-known ocean-racing skipper, who has wrung more salt water from his socks than most of us have sailed on, told me about a sensational broach he had witnessed when a new IOR racer was running down the English Channel in a fresh breeze. She carried a 'chute, and all her crew were crowded aft on the fantail. Something went wrong with the spinnaker, and several crew members went forward to attend to the problem. At the same time, a moderately large following sea lifted the stern, and the boat drove her bow under and began to pitchpole. She came through the accident in one piece after a spectacular broach, but it was plain to see that with her lack of freeboard forward, narrow bow, and not much overhang, she seriously lacked buoyancy forward.

Such an accident would seem very unlikely aboard a Mason 31. Not only has she a shorter mast to reduce the spinnaker's leverage, but she has lots of reserve buoyancy forward. There is ample freeboard at the bow, some overhang, and plenty of flare forward, all of which are helpful in resisting the tendency to bury. Although the

entrance is fairly sharp, there is not much forefoot that can dig in when running off. In contrast, many IOR boats are deep just under the cutwater to obtain a measurement advantage, and this can encourage a fine bow to root in hard-driving conditions.

The Mason 31 is a development of the earlier Mason 30 design, known as the Venture class on the American West Coast. About the only difference between the hulls is that the 30-footer has a transom stern, while the 31 has a counter. There is still another Mason design of similar size and hull shape called the Vastkust, which has a pointed stern. For those who are partial to double-enders, the Vastkust is a very attractive boat that can sail exceedingly well. In fact, all of these models are smart sailers. The Mason 30 had a good racing record in the late Fifties and early Sixties with particular success in Off-Soundings events. One year she won first place in her competitive class in the combined spring and fall series.

Both the Mason 30 and Vastkust have outboard rudders, and there are some arguments for

89

The sloop version of the Mason 31 keeps the rig inboard while providing simplicity and efficiency upwind.

The schooner-rigged Mason 31 is not only delightful to look at, but she has great versatility and carries plenty of sail.

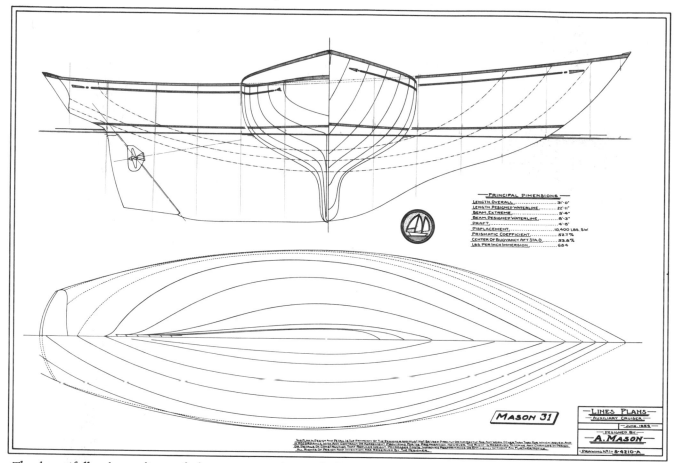

The *beautifully drawn lines of the Mason 31 show a hull that is quite symmetrical with well-balanced ends and a pronounced sheer.*

this arrangement. The outboard rudder is about as far aft as possible for the best steering control; the blade is more accessible, perhaps, and easier to remove; there are certain advantages if a trim tab is used for self-steering; there is no need to penetrate the hull with a rudder stock tube; and certain outboard rudders provide a rather salty look. On the other hand, there are very good reasons for an inboard rudder of the type seen on the Mason 31. The rudder can be relatively small and light, it is well protected, it is completely submerged to minimize ventilation (aeration of the water around the blade), it enables easy placement of the helm fairly far forward in the cockpit, and it allows a full keel of moderate length that need not extend far aft, thus permitting minimal wetted surface. Of course, it is sometimes impractical if not im-

possible to hang an outboard rudder on a boat with a counter stern.

To my way of thinking, the stern on the Mason 31 is a particularly attractive type. Although the overhang is modest, it allows a long waterline, which is important to a boat of this size for speed and to minimize pitching. I would never be concerned about this stern slamming in a seaway, since the counter is short and steep, while the sections aft are slightly V'd. The well-shaped transom has a pleasing rake, and it seems to harmonize with the bow.

Generally speaking, the Mason 31's hull is a moderate, seakindly type. The sections and buttocks show easy, smooth-flowing curves, and the submerged waterlines are quite symmetrical. At and above the LWL, the waterlines are much fuller aft, and this gives the boat some bearing

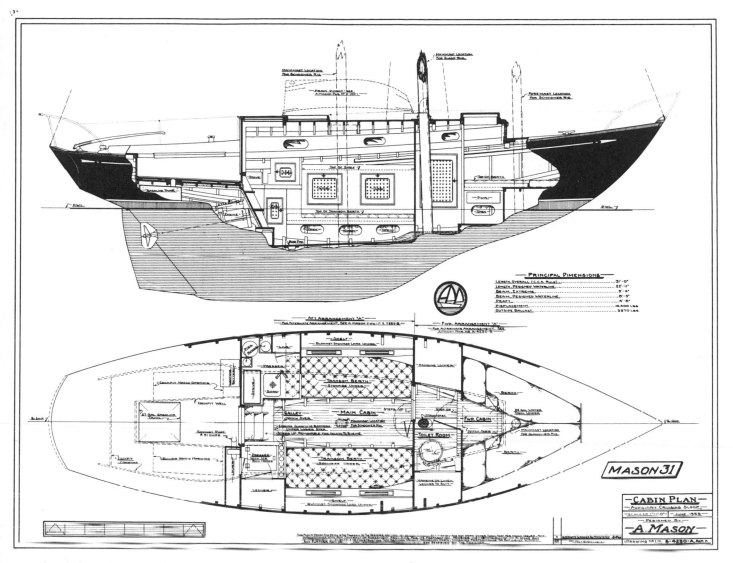

Details of the M-31's accommodations are well worth a study under the magnifying glass. Note such interesting touches as the double-hinged door, dust pan, transom berth foot well, and especially the glass rack next to the ice box, which is next to the companionway. Where would you set up your bar?

The deck plan of the M-31 shows such details as the dinghy, spinnaker pole, and anchor stowage as well as the bilge pump location, which is properly accessible from above the deck. Not all designers draw in the circles described by winch handles, and many sailors have experienced skinned knuckles to prove it.

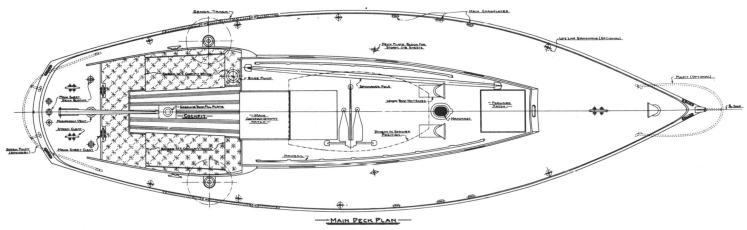

93

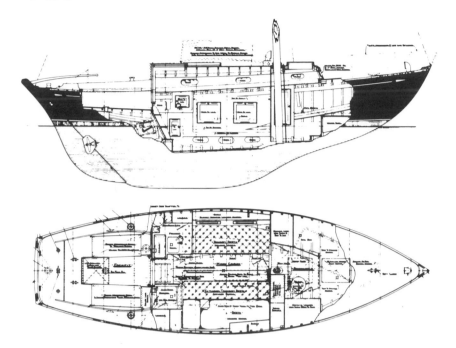

The Mason 30, which is essentially the Mason 31 with a transom stern and outboard rudder. (From 29 Designs from the Board of Al Mason © *1972, Seven Seas Press)*

when she heels. It is not surprising that she has proven to be a good sea boat. Her designer, Al Mason, wrote me that a yard fire destroyed most of the records of cruises and the like, but he has heard of some successful passages, including one across the East China Sea from Taiwan to Japan.

Al Mason is well known, especially among his confreres, as being one of the very finest draftsmen. His clean, sure lines and meticulous rendering of details are apparent in the plans of the Mason 31. Incidentally, one of Mr. Mason's specialties is perspective drawings, and most of those in *Choice Yacht Designs* were done by him especially for this book.

One of the distinctive features on the plans of the Mason 31 that typifies Al Mason's attention to details is the six-foot-nine-inch pram on top of the cabin trunk. Cruising boats need dinghies for a number of purposes, such as transporting the crew, hauling supplies, and carrying out a kedge anchor in the event of a grounding. But stowage is often impossible on many small boats, and the dinghy must be towed, which is far from satisfactory in heavy weather. One solution is an inflatable rubber boat, but pumping it

up is a nuisance, it won't last as long as a solid boat, and it doesn't row or sail well.

The cabin plan shows such details as dish and glass racks, perforated locker doors for adequate ventilation, and even a dust pan under the cabin sole. One feature I like very much is the privacy of the head. On many modern boats of this size, there is only a door between the head and the main cabin, but on the Mason 31 there is an additional door enclosing the head that can be swung athwartships to close off the forward cabin. One has the option, without sacrifice to privacy, of either closing off the head or closing off the forward and after cabins to utilize the entire width of the boat in way of the head.

There are alternate arrangement plans providing from three- to five-berth layouts, but I prefer the layout illustrated, which has four berths. With this arrangement there are always two bunks on the leeward side, and there is ample space for stowage. On boats of this size, especially those with quarter berths, sail stowage is often a problem, but this has been alleviated on the Mason 31 with large seat lockers on each side of the cockpit. The cabin trunk is attractive-

This Mason 30 is particularly handsome with her bright wood finish. Otherwise known as Ventures, Mason 30s are smart sailers with some important race wins under the Off Soundings Club rule. (Morris Rosenfeld)

ly small, but it is high enough for standing headroom aft, and its narrow width allows ample room for walking on the side decks.

A choice of two rigs is offered: a very sensible masthead sloop or a handsome schooner rig. The former is more efficient and easier to handle for normal sailing, but I must say that I'd be very tempted to opt for the schooner. It is a fun rig that gives the boat tremendous character. With the traditional hull, low cabin trunk having small old-fashioned ports, and bowsprit and boomkin extending the sweep of the graceful sheer, the tall schooner rig seems most appropriate. It should not even be overly difficult to handle with the boomed working jib, which is self-tending. There is plenty of sail area, and the boat should fly on a reach, especially if one takes the trouble to set the 126-square-foot fisherman staysail. Advantages and disadvantages of the schooner rig are fairly obvious, but there is at least one advantage that is seldom mentioned: most schooners will lie to an anchor without yawing excessively, because their windage is quite far aft.

Mason 31s have been built by several yards, but they are currently being produced in Taiwan. There are plans for two types of wood construction: conventional plank-on-frame or strip planking with slightly greater frame spacing. I believe that the strip-planked boat can be had with a covering of fiberglass.

It has been said that naval architecture in its best form is the blending of science and art. This is certainly true of Al Mason's work, for it is a combination of technical competence with an artistry that is at once apparent after a first glance at his excellent drawings.

13/ A Pair of Tripp 40s
Thoroughbred Boats

BI-40: Length overall: 40 feet 8 inches
Length on waterline: 27 feet 6 inches
Beam: 11 feet 9 inches
Draft: 3 feet 11 inches
Sail area: 743 square feet
Designer: William H. Tripp, Jr.
Year designed: 1957

B-40: Length overall: 40 feet 9 inches
Length on waterline: 27 feet 10 inches
Beam: 11 feet 9 inches
Draft: 4 feet 1 inch
Sail area: 741 square feet (MK II)
Designer: William H. Tripp, Jr.
Year designed: 1959

After the Sparkman & Stephens-designed *Finisterre* and her production model, the Nevins 40, showed the yachting world they could more than "cut the mustard" on the race course, many other designers turned out their own versions of a fat, comfortable, centerboard racing-cruiser. Perhaps the most successful versions were the fiberglass 40-footers drawn by the late William H. Tripp, Jr. In 1957 he designed the Vitesse class for Van Breems International, but shortly thereafter, American Boat Building Corporation, the molder, took over selling the boat, and its class name was changed to the Block Island 40. Two years later, a development of this hull called the Bermuda 40 was drafted by Tripp for production by the Henry R. Hinckley Company.

The Bermuda 40s and especially the Block Island 40s did extremely well racing under the CCA rule, and still today they perform well under true handicap racing and even the IOR when age allowances are used. In 1978 the BI-40 *Alaris* won her class in the Bermuda Race competing under the Measurement Handicap System.

Although the Block Island 40s are no longer being produced, a revised model will probably be made in the near future. Metalmast Marine, Inc., obtained the molds from the American Boat Building Corporation, and built or completed 14 boats, but Metalmast explained that production has stopped because "the molds became worn and are at a point where extensive retooling is needed." The company plans to resume production, but a schedule has not yet been set up. The Metalmast version as well as the original BI-40 is shown in the accompanying profile and arrangement plans. The newer version has her keel shortened and the rudder attached to a skeg well aft. Also, she has been given a reverse transom, although there is still plenty of overhang at the stern. The accommodations are quite different too.

As for the Bermuda 40, this boat is still being produced by Hinckley, and it has achieved the status of a classic shoal-draft fiberglass cruiser. It

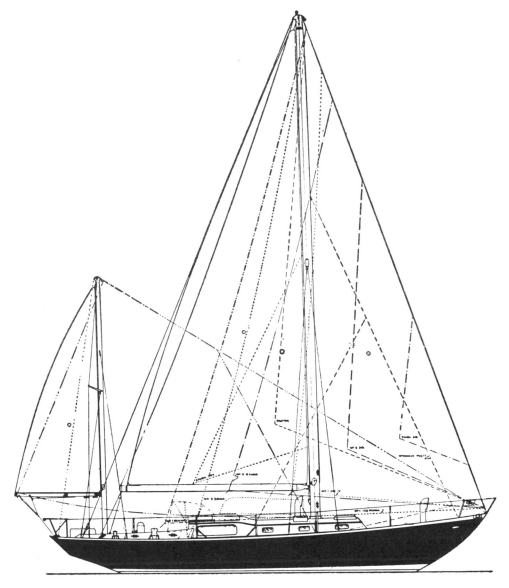

The sail plan of the Block Island 40 shows a great variety of sails, including storm sails and the unusual mizzen staysail that is held aloft by a line leading to the stemhead. (Yachting)

is constantly being refined and improved, but the hull is essentially the same as the 1959 design. Like most Hinckley boats, the Bermuda 40s are solidly built with great care and craftsmanship.

The fundamental difference between the original BI-40 and Bermuda 40 hulls lies in the shape of the sterns. It can be seen that the former has a narrower transom with considerable rake, while the latter has a wider, more vertical transom with a slightly longer counter. Of course, there is a big difference in the centerboards. The Block Island has the old-fashioned

low-aspect-ratio board, but the Bermuda has a high-aspect-ratio board, which theoretically supplies more hydrodynamic lift when sailing upwind. For pure cruising, however, I tend to favor the old-fashioned board, because there is more of it in the trunk for greater strength in the lowered position.

For his long-keel boats, Tripp favored putting the propeller in a keel aperture quite far ahead of the rudder. This makes sense to me, especially on a shoal-draft centerboarder with a small, shallow rudder, because the customary aperture in the blade (or just forward of the blade) detracts

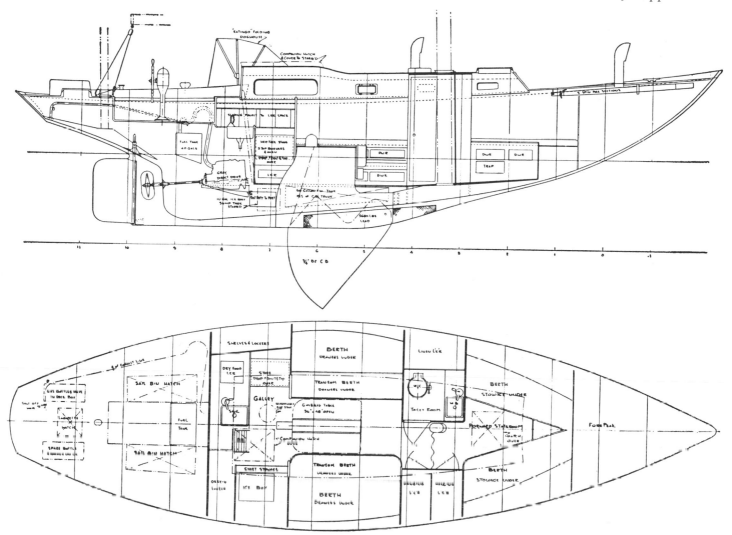

Accommodations plans of the Block Island 40, which show the centerboard trunk protruding into the cabin under the dining table. The full-width dodger labeled "folding doghouse" is now quite common on cruising boats. (Yachting)

from the rudder's efficiency. Also, having the aperture in a thick part of the keel may lessen any possible risk of cracking the keel from propeller vibration; in addition, it allows a two-bladed prop to hide behind the "deadwood" to minimize drag when under sail. A slight drawback to the arrangement is that the propeller loses a little efficiency and the rudder is farther away from the propeller wash when under power. In my opinion, however, the first priority with a centerboarder having a shallow rudder is to provide the best possible steering control under sail when the beamy hull is heeled

and rolled out, tending to lift the rudder into less dense (more aerated) water.

The Tripp centerboarders are splendid performers in most conditions. Although they need plenty of sail for light weather, they are fast on a reach and go to windward quite well. I have heard comments that the Bermuda 40 will draw a sizable quarter wave when she is driven at hull speed in strong following winds. A naval architect who owns one of these boats told me that on a couple of occasions when he was sailing in very shallow water the quarter wave actually broke into his cockpit. For an explana-

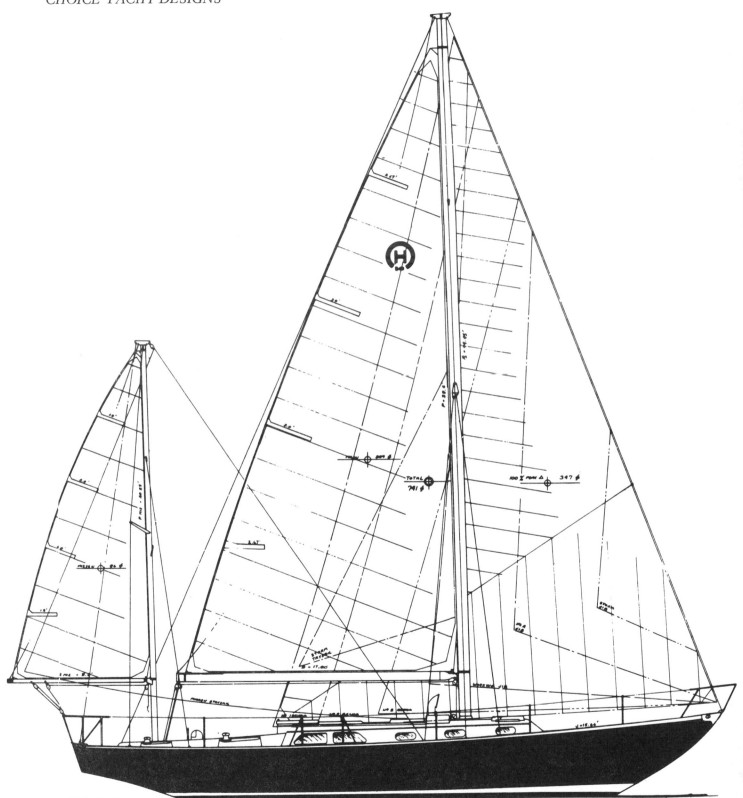

The Mark II sail plan of the Bermuda 40 seems a happy medium between the short rig of the Mark I and the high-aspect-ratio rig of the Mark III.

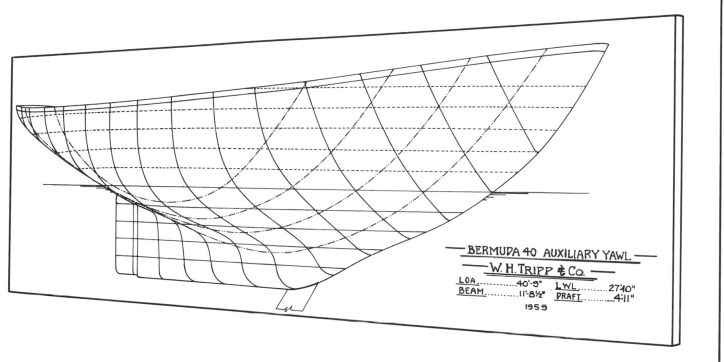

BERMUDA 40 AUXILIARY YAWL
W. H. TRIPP & Co.

LOA	40'-9"	LWL	27'-10"
BEAM	11'-8½"	DRAFT	4'-11"

1959

A. MASON, DEL. 3-7-'78

A perspective of the Bermuda 40 shows her flaring blow and rather thick keel. Not seen in this bow view are the straight, after buttock lines and the gently rounded stern sections.

Accommodation plans of the Bermuda 40. This particular arrangement shows the ice box doubling as a chart table. Notice that the high-aspect ratio centerboard can be housed beneath the cabin sole.

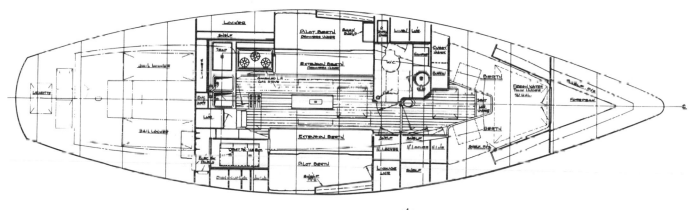

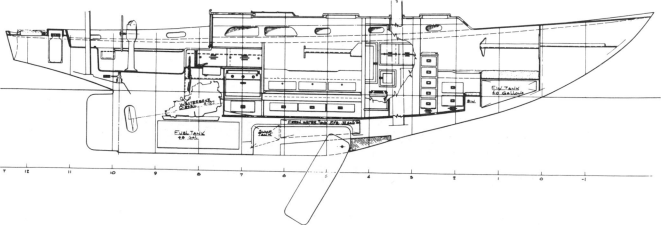

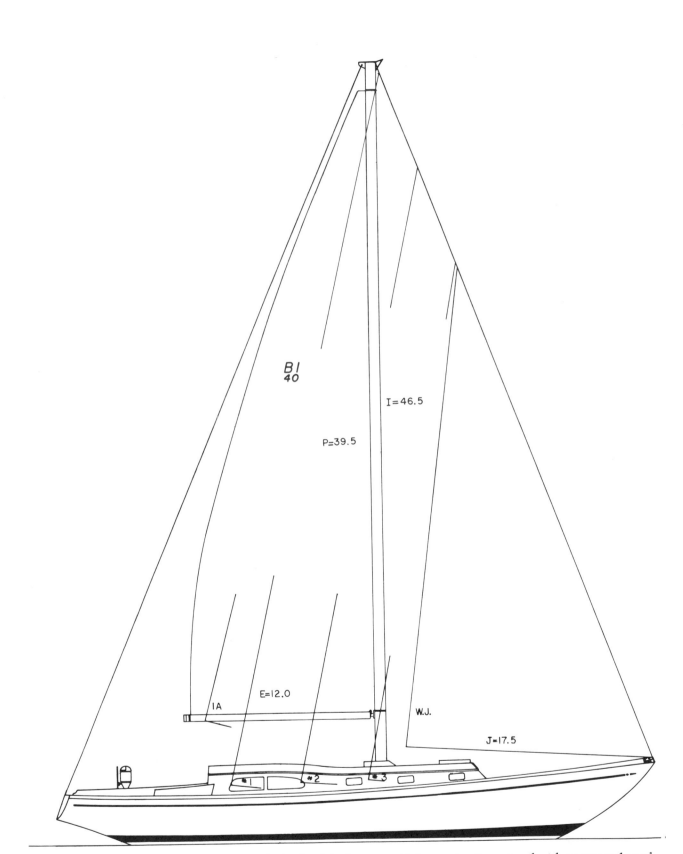

The sail plan of the Metalmast Marine Block Island 40 features a high-aspect-ratio mainsail with an unusual roach. The rail at the bow appears to sweep upward, which accentuates the sheer.

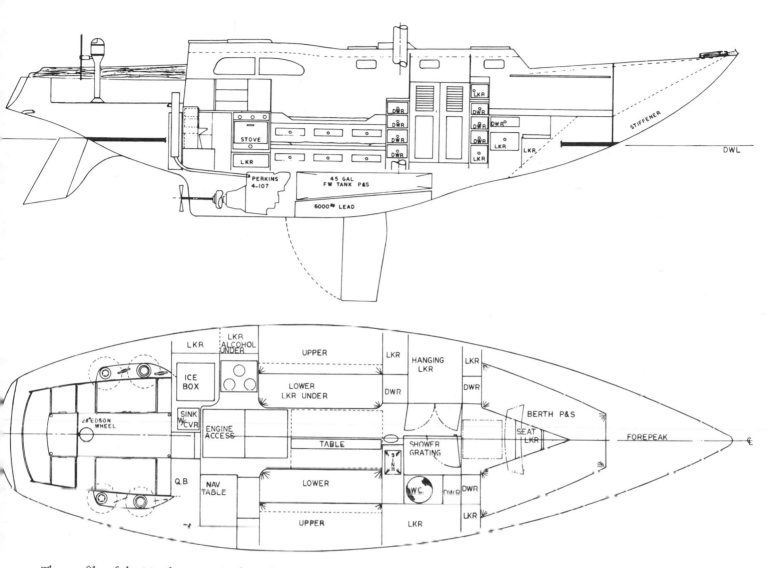

The profile of the Metalmast BI 40 shows how the original hull has been altered primarily by chopping off the end of the stern, changing the centerboard, moving the rudder aft, and cutting away the after end of the keel. Note the huge stiffener in the bow. The quarter berth/navigation table arrangement is fine, but it would be preferable to have an oilskin locker near the companionway.

tion of the hydrodynamics involved, I wrote to my friend John Letcher, a designer and hydrodynamicist who knows the Bermuda 40 very well. He replied as follows:

"I think the large wave on the B-40 is just a result of a fat hull with a short waterline being driven hard—naturally the hull wave system gets big, and the stern wave occurs not far aft of the cockpit. When a steep following sea encounters this wave, the two reinforce and interfere, and breaking can occur. My guess is a reduction of sail, reducing the speed by just a fraction of a knot, would eliminate the problem. I don't

think the boat critically lacks freeboard or buoyancy aft, though both are considerably less than the designer intended, because of the weight of machinery and tankage in the more recent boats at least. Reducing speed in a following sea to avoid waves breaking aboard is a classic storm tactic. I'm not sure it's required in a light displacement boat, which makes smaller waves and runs away from them more easily."

Both the Bermuda and Block Island 40s are heavily built, and of course, Hinckley boats enjoy the reputation of being constructed to the very highest standards. There is one aspect of

This view of the Block Island 40 Seal reveals her underwater shape. The V insignia on the mainsail stands for Vitesse, the original name for the class. (Morris Rosenfeld)

The Bermuda 40 *Jaan* with all sails set and drawing. On this occasion at least, the quarter wave seems to be well aft. (Morris Rosenfeld)

the Bermuda 40's molding, however, that puzzles me. Repeatedly advertisements have claimed the hulls are "one-piece," yet they have centerline seams. A former Hinckley employee explained to me that the two halves of the hull are laid up in separate molds. After the hull halves are cured enough so that the mating surfaces can be ground to fit, the two halves of the mold are brought together and the hull halves are joined along the centerline seam with heavy belts of reinforcement and some additional fiberglass layup. I am not sure I would call this true "one-piece" construc-

tion, but it hardly seems likely that the hull halves would ever split apart.

The original Block Island 40s and the standard Bermuda 40s have similar accommodation plans, but the latter is a bit more fancy, with a number of handsome features such as the famous Hinckley teak and holly cabin sole. In one respect I prefer the below-decks arrangement of the Metalmast Marine Block Island 40, because it has a quarter berth and a proper chart table with seat. Although I have never been overjoyed with the Bermuda 40's chart table, which is on top of the starboard-side ice box, an option on the most recent model locates the ice box on the port side outboard of the double sink. With this arrangement, the navigator need not move his charts whenever anyone wants a cold drink.

Each boat has an unusually large forepeak, which provides stowage room for a lot of ground tackle and other gear; and having the forepeak bulkhead quite far aft means that there is ample width at the forward end of the V-berths in the forward cabins. It is also interesting to see that the large forepeak in the Metalmast BI-40 allows a very large stiffener, which adds strength forward and permits carrying the headstay extra taut without any danger of bending up the bow.

The standard layout for the main saloon on both boats is a pair of pilot berths with lower transom extension berths and centerline drop-leaf tables. The Bermuda 40 has a rather ingenious way of enlarging the table by having a separate folding addition to the table attached to the main bulkhead. In the accommodations of the Bermuda 40 I particularly admire the handsome joinerwork, the attention to detail, and the numerous well-made drawers and lockers.

Rigged as yawls, these boats are quite easy to handle with a small crew. Hinckley offers a choice of three yawl rigs: the Custom, Mark II, and Mark III. The latter has a high-aspect-ratio rig and a much larger foretriangle, and it might be more suitable for racing (depending on its handicap rating). But I would prefer the less extreme Mark II, because the headsails are easier to handle and the center of effort is kept reasonably low. The Mark III version requires an increase in ballast to stand up to her tall rig, and the centerboard weight has been increased, which makes it more difficult to raise.

If I were to race the Mark II in a light air region, I might add a bowsprit and have a taller mizzen on which to hang a good-sized staysail. *Alaris,* the Block Island 40 mentioned earlier, has had success with such a rig on the Chesapeake Bay. What really intrigues me is the mizzen staysail shown on the plans of the original Block Island 40. It is a quadrilateral sail with two tacks, the lower leading to the base of a windward shroud and the upper tack held aloft by a long pendant leading to the stemhead. I don't know how legal it is for racing, but it should supply plenty of power on a reach.

Of course, not all owners or would-be owners of these boats are yawl lovers or jib-and-mizzen-thropes, as we used to call them. Metalmast offered a sloop rig, and the Bermuda 40 also can be had with one mast. There are a number of rig options. Hinckley even offers a roller-furling mainsail that winds up inside the mast, but with this rig one must compromise optimum shape, size, and leech control (since battens cannot be fitted). Regardless of the rig, though, these Tripp hulls are easily driven provided they are given sufficient sail area.

Perhaps these boats are best described with the single word "thoroughbred." According to my Webster's Dictionary, one definition of this word is: "Having the characteristics of a thoroughbred, as grace, elegance, high-spiritedness"—a good description, in my opinion, of the Block Island and Bermuda 40s.

14/ The Alberg 30

A Handsome Cruising One-Design

Length overall: 30 feet 3 inches
Length on waterline: 21 feet 8 inches
Beam: 8 feet 9 inches
Draft: 4 feet 3 inches
Sail area: 410 square feet
Displacement: 9,000 pounds
Designer: Carl A. Alberg
Year designed: 1962

For those who would like a boat similar to the Triton (Chapter 12) but slightly larger, the Alberg 30 fits the bill. This handsome fiberglass sloop designed by Carl Alberg and built by the Whitby Boat Works of Ontario, Canada, has very wide appeal because she is an all-around boat, suitable for all kinds of cruising from gunkholing to offshore passagemaking, and she is an easy-to-handle, smart sailer over a wide range of conditions. She has proven extremely popular with young families, especially those interested in organized cruising and one-design racing.

There are several Alberg 30 one-design associations, including a large fleet in Toronto, Ontario, and one on the Chesapeake Bay that has been thriving since 1965. The latter association now has 216 member boats, and it still seems to be growing. Class racing is keen, and this has attracted some of the bay's most talented sailors.

Undoubtedly there are many advantages in one-design as opposed to handicap racing. Complicated measurements and rating rules are not needed; boats will not be made obsolete by new rule-beating designs or changes in the rules; and racing is boat-for-boat, with the winner being the first one across the finish line. There is no need to wait for Monday morning's paper to see how you did in a weekend race, as is so often the case with handicap racing. On the other hand, most one-design classes are small, open boats that are often uncomfortable and unsuitable for anything but racing. To be competitive, many of these boats have to be kept out of water between races, so they can't even be used easily for informal daysailing. The perfect compromise between small boat one-design and handicap racing would seem to be racing in a cruising one-design class, such as the Alberg 30s. These boats allow keen competition but in a comfortable, more relaxed manner and with a family crew if desired. Furthermore, the races may be distant point-to-point affairs that can be mixed with cruising, rendezvous, raft-ups, and other fun events not easily done in small one-design racers.

The Chesapeake Bay Alberg 30 One-Design Association has a very active and varied schedule

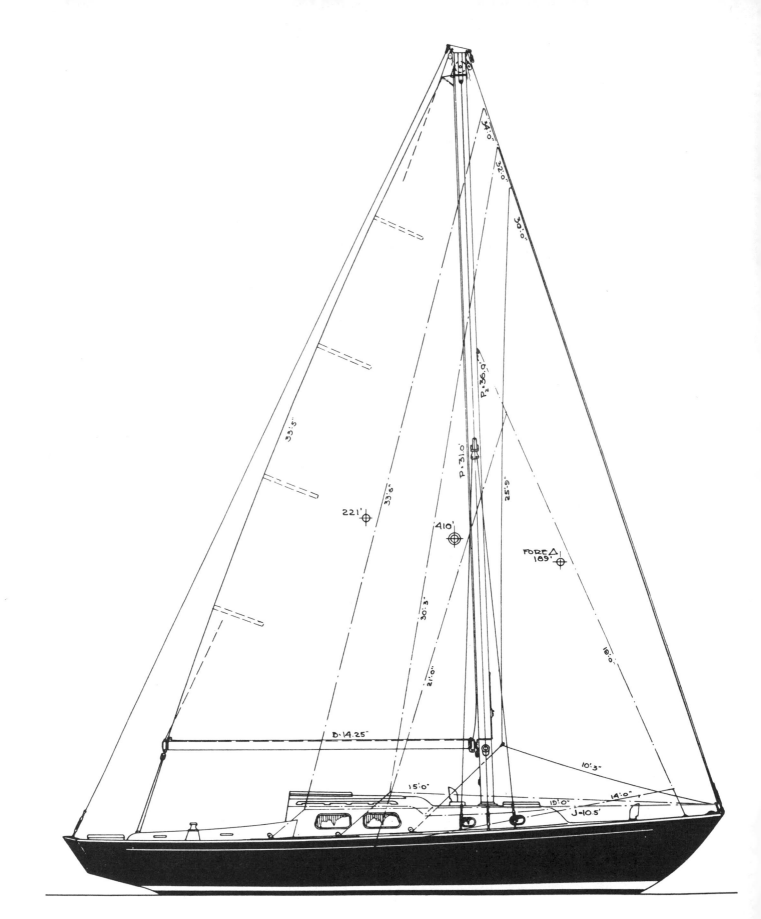

The Alberg 30 has a simple, logical rig that has proved fast and handy. About the only problem has been some sagging under the deck-stepped mast when the rigging is strung up too tight.

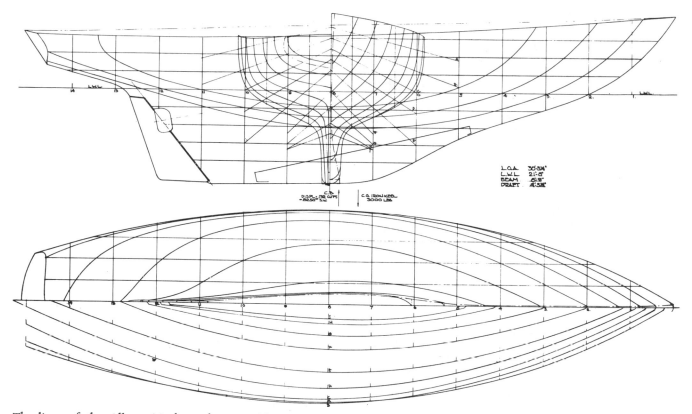

The lines of the Alberg 30 show the resemblance to her smaller sister, the Triton. On this plan the rudder has been modernized.

Notice such features in the A-30's accommodations plans as the oilskin locker and ice box, which on the earlier boats is accessible from the cockpit. It might be better if the head were raised a little, because it appears to be just level with the load waterline. (Yachting)

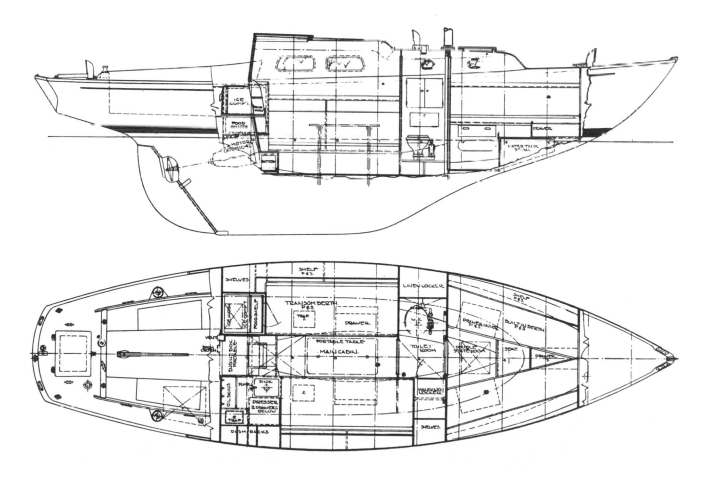

HANDBOOK

CHESAPEAKE BAY

ALBERG 30 ONE-DESIGN ASSOCIATION

1969

A sketch by the author that was used on the cover of a Chesapeake Bay Alberg 30 One-Design Association Handbook.

that includes not only a great many formal races with seasonal high point scoring, but also team races, tyro races, rendezvous, "mini" cruises, "maxi" (long distance or coastal) cruises, spectating expeditions, and so forth. It seems to me that the A-30s are especially good boats for such varied programs. They perform well enough for spirited racing, yet are forgiving and well mannered. They are sufficiently comfortable for a small family crew (without too many complaints from the first mate). They lie to an anchor well and are safe, practical boats with such desirable features as moderate draft, a protected rudder, integral keel, inboard power, and

110

A-30 one-designs use limited, all-purpose sails to reduce the cost of racing. Also, there are restrictions on expensive, sophisticated equipment, such as slotted headfoils and hydraulic backstay adjusters. (Bill Schill)

a bridge deck. In general, it could be said that the A-30 is a thoroughly wholesome boat, solidly constructed, and reasonably priced.

The associations have made a special effort to ensure that all boats will be equal for one-design racing. Alterations from the standard boat are not permitted, and there is a limitation on the sail inventory. Of course, this makes the racing as fair as possible and helps to keep the cost down.

Needless to say, A-30 racing is not always relaxed and easygoing. Whenever ultra-competitive sailors get together, some fur is apt

to fly. I recall hearing about a time when one particularly zealous sailor, whom I will call Mr. Zeal, consistently had the edge on his competition for a reason that defied any logical explanation. Good sailing was not the whole answer. After some James Bond-type sleuthing, the befuddled competitors found out that Mr. Zeal had been using a pipe and screw jack under his deck-stepped mast so that he could set up his headstay extra tight to improve windward performance in fresh winds. The secret weapon had escaped notice for a long time because it was removed and stowed out of sight after each race.

111

Eventually, the A-30 association ruled that use of the jack was not within the spirit of the one-design regulations, so Mr. Zeal was finally hoist with his own petard.

Many boats with deck-stepped masts have had a problem with sagging cabintops when the rigging is carried taut. In some cases people have been trapped in the head because the door becomes jammed by the downward thrust of the mast when the boat is strung up and sailing hard on the wind in a breeze. With the Alberg 30, however, the problem is not really serious unless the rigging is carried extra taut.

Carl Alberg wanted to specify lead for the A-30's keel ballast, and he wrote me that he was "not too happy" when iron was used. He said, "In shaping the underbody profile I was handicapped by the builder's insistence on (inside) iron keel instead of lead." Also, the early boats were a bit tender, and perhaps this was due to the higher center of gravity of the iron ballast. After A-30 number 27, the ballast was increased, and the earlier boats being raced were allowed by the Alberg association to add 460 pounds of inside permanent ballast.

Another possible drawback of iron encased in a fiberglass keel is that grounding on a hard bottom could let water into the keel, and this might cause rust. One A-30 of my acquaintance developed different steering characteristics on each tack. This mystified the owner because his mast was plumb when viewed from the bow or stern and the rudder was not warped. To my knowledge this boat was the only one of the class with such a problem. The possibility was suggested that the inconsistent steering could have been caused by rust swelling in one side of the keel only, changing the curvature slightly and thus the lift characteristics on one side. Actually, this seems doubtful, since any lack of symmetry probably would have been noticed; but nevertheless, the owner of an encased iron keel would do well to be extra careful not to run aground on a hard bottom, because water penetration and rust are possible.

I've sailed both the Alberg 30 and the Triton, and I don't think the former (even the ones after hull 27) is quite as stiff as the latter. In the early days of A-30 racing, the top skippers developed the technique of luffing their mainsails in a breeze. With the race courses having short windward legs, it seldom paid to shorten sail. I was always amazed at the A-30's speed with a flapping main. Apparently, it is important to keep the lee rail out of water even though the mainsail's drive is sacrificed. Nowadays, of course, the boats can use jiffy reefing, and the main can be reduced without undue loss of thrust in a matter of seconds.

In comparing the lines of the A-30 and the Triton, one can see the similarity. Most of the general remarks I made about the shape of the Triton could also be applied to the A-30. The greatest difference, other than the keel profile, is that the A-30's stern has been extended farther aft, and the Triton has a bit more flare forward. The flare is appropriate for a boat with low freeboard forward, and when you compare the Triton with the A-30 afloat, the latter gives the impression that she has a higher bow; but curiously enough, the lines don't show that much difference in freeboard.

Because of her larger size, the A-30 has more room below. The arrangement is basically the same as the Triton's, but there is six-foot-three-inch headroom in the main cabin, and the galley is larger. Notice on the arrangement plan that there is even an oilskin locker alongside the companionway. This is a very desirable feature that is seldom seen on this size boat. An unusual feature on the early boats is an ice box that opens through the bridge deck. This is handy for daysailing or weekending. The arrangement, however, is not helpful to the longevity of ice, especially since access to the ice box from below is a side-opening door. Every time the door is opened, the cold air, which tends to sink, escapes into the cabin.

Auxiliary power was originally supplied by Gray Sea Scout engines but now it is by the popular Universal Atomic fours. A number of boats have had problems with water getting into the engine through the exhaust line. This was caused, I understand, by an athwartship muffler that traps some water and allows it to run back to the engine when the boat is severely knocked

An Alberg 30 under sail in a fresh breeze is always a pretty sight.

down on one tack. The new owner of an old A-30 should also be warned that some (not all) of the boats had problems with galvanic corrosion due to galvanized steel tees and nipples being used with bronze through-hull valves. The steel parts should be replaced with bronze.

It is good to know that 17 years after her creation the A-30 is still being produced, and that there still is a demand for such a sensible boat. Carl Alberg is now retired, according to his letterhead, but I am sure his boats will live on and on.

15/ Ingenue

Scooning on a Beat

Length overall: 32 feet 7½ inches
Length on waterline: 27 feet
Beam: 9 feet 7¼ inches
Draft: 5 feet 5 inches
Sail area: 645 square feet
Displacement: 13,600 pounds
Designer: Edward S. Brewer
Year designed: 1962

It is something of a rarity nowadays to see a boat intended for racing with a schooner rig. *Ingenue* is a modern schooner that was eminently successful on the race courses during the 1960s, and I have been told that she is still doing surprisingly well today. Some of her triumphs are as follows: second (of 93 in her class) in the 1966 Chicago-Mackinac; first to finish and first overall in the 1966 Pensacola Race (300 miles); first in class D and fourth in fleet (127 boats) in the 1967 Tri-State; a first overall, a second to finish, a second in class, and a third in class in the next two years in St. Petersburg-Naples, Tampa-Egmont Key, and St. Petersburg-Venice Races; first in Class B in 1969 St. Petersburg-Mexico (456 miles) as well as second in fleet; and first in class in the 1974 Mystic Schooner Race.

Ingenue was designed for L. A. Wheeler by Edward S. (Ted) Brewer in 1962, and Ted told me that she was his second custom sailboat design. It can be seen from her plans that the underwater configuration is not very unusual, but the entire hull profile with its clipper bow is somewhat distinctive for a boat that is still competing in general racing events. The stern is quite wide, a feature that was encouraged (or at least not discouraged) by the last version of the CCA rule. One of the plans, however, shows a modified version (for a Dr. Millican) having a drawnout stern with more overhang and a narrower transom. This is the version I prefer for aesthetic reasons, and I think this model looks particularly handsome with her carved trailboards forward.

The keel ballast is listed at 4,000 pounds, so this gives *Ingenue* a modest ballast-to-displacement ratio of just under 30 percent. Nonetheless, the boat is quite stiff, because the ballast is low, the bilges are firm, and the center of effort of the sail plan is low. Also, her stern sections are quite powerful. Ted Brewer told me that he thinks the thickness of a keel has a great effect on speed. *Ingenue*'s keel is not very thick for a cruising boat, and perhaps this is one of the reasons she is so fast. Of course, her long sailing length gives her good speed in a breeze.

Despite not having a squared-off corner, the rudder appears to be a very efficient type with its snug fit under the counter, greatest area at

Ingenue with her modern schooner rig. Compared with the normal schooner, this boat has a larger foretriangle and taller foremast, her masts are closer together, and the aspect ratios of the boomed sails are slightly higher. Also, it is more usual to see a gaff foresail on a schooner that is not fitted with a main staysail.

A modified version of Ingenue. *The drawn-out stern and extended crane at the head of the mainmast allow a much shorter backstay boomkin. Notice the gollywobbler with its hollow leech.*

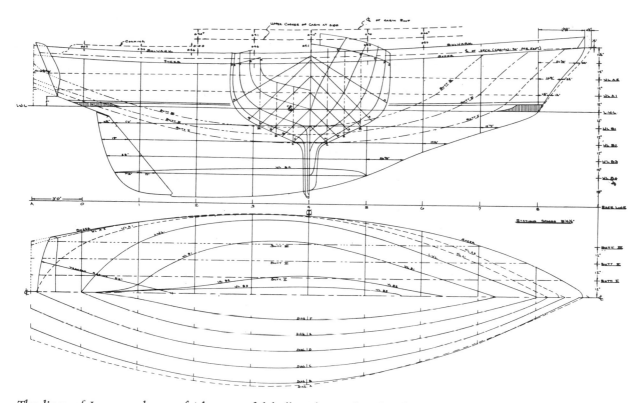

The lines of Ingenue *show a fairly powerful hull with a rather fine bow and full stern. The slightly hollow* entrance at the waterline is probably helpful in choppy head seas, since the bow seems sufficiently flared to prevent diving. (From Understanding Boat Design *by Edward S. Brewer and Jim Betts.* © *1971, International Marine Publishing)*

Sleeping at sea on Ingenue *might be easier on the starboard tack, since there are more bunks on the port side. Even if compromises were necessary in the galley arrangement, they allow a large chart table aft.*

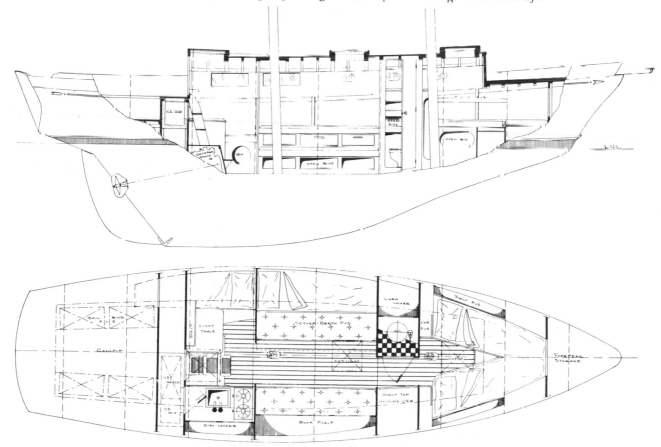

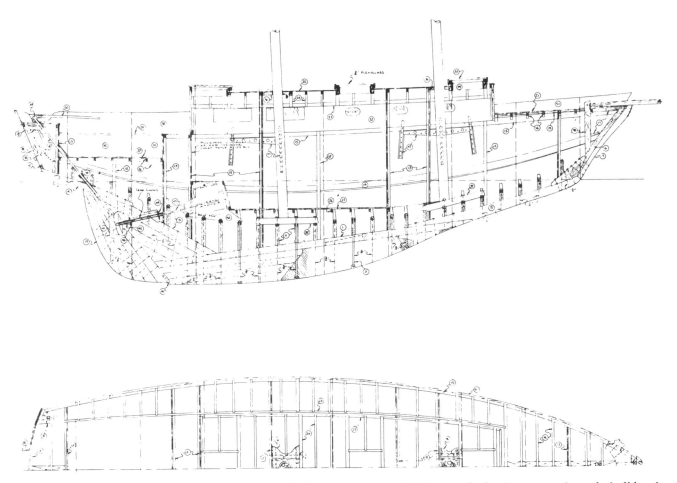

Ingenue's construction is strong but not excessively heavy. Her strip planking with glued seams and ample bulkheads allows minimal framing. Note the unusually high toe rail forward. (From Cruising Designs: Power and Sail *by Edward S. Brewer. © 1976, Seven Seas Press)*

the bottom, and aft-raking stock. This rake helps keep the side force working in a more horizontal than vertical direction when the boat is heeled. Incidentally, there is a theory that a heavy rudder with its turning axis raked in this manner will be less affected by gravity when the vessel is heeled. It is interesting that Ted Brewer reported *Ingenue* as having a little too much weather helm until he added 10 percent more area to the foretriangle. No doubt the large mainsail and sharply raked masts encouraged her ardency.

In addition to correcting the boat's balance, the large foretriangle adds sail power, of course, and the unusually tall foremast permits a size of spinnaker seldom seen on a schooner. The sail that really intrigues me, though, is the large one between the masts that I would call a golly-wobbler. This sail is shown in the striking photograph of *Ingenue* on a spinnaker reach. The golly carried by *Ingenue* is somewhat unusual in that

the luff is attached to the foremast with slides on a track, according to the specifications, and the leech is greatly curved so that it will fit under the spreaders when the sail is closehauled. The boat's wide stern makes a perfect sheeting base so that there is little negative thrust at the after end of the golly. Ted Brewer has written that the boat can carry 900 square feet of sail on a reach, which is quite a spread, and according to the sail areas listed on the plans, this does not include the spinnaker. The trick in carrying so many large sails, of course, is trimming them so that they do not overly interfere with each other, causing serious blanketing or backwind problems.

Except for the famous *Niña*, there are not many closewinded schooners, but Ted told me that *Ingenue* sails extremely well upwind. He estimates that her optimum speed made good to windward is on a heading close to 30 degrees to

118

Ingenue almost jumping out of the water with her large (for a schooner) spinnaker and huge gollywobbler. It might be good to try leading the golly sheet farther forward to help remove some of the twist.

the apparent wind in ideal conditions. It is interesting that both *Niña* and *Ingenue,* to a lesser extent, have deep drags and considerable keel slope. Aerodynamicist John Morwood wrote an interesting article in an Amateur Yacht Research Society publication (No. 66A) in which he attempts to explain the exceptional upwind ability of certain boats with this kind of underwater profile, even though they may have low-aspect-ratio keels. Mr. Morwood's theory is controversial but nonetheless interesting. He suggests that the clue to lateral resistance of a boat like *Niña* may lie in the angle of keel slope. "If the keel were horizontal," wrote Mr. Morwood,

"water would be passing below it from the lee (high pressure) side to the weather side. But, when the keel slope angle becomes greater than a critical size, the water will not flow under the keel but will flow from fore to aft, even though the yacht is making leeway."

Perhaps *Ingenue*'s keel slope is an angle that is highly beneficial to lateral resistance, but whether this is true or not, the moderately fine entrance, ample lateral plane, and considerable draft must help her climb to windward. Also, I suspect her rig may be more efficacious upwind than the average schooner's, since there are no gaffs, the foremast is so tall, and the masts are

119

quite close together. The latter feature may allow more efficient slots between the sails and minimize the harmful effects of downwash and backwind. Like most schooners, however, *Ingenue* excels when her sheets are well eased. According to Ted Brewer, the noted designer-sailor Charlie Morgan once made the comment, when he was campaigning the well-known *Paper Tiger,* that no boat under 45 feet long could hold *Ingenue* on a reach.

A fairly large crew is needed to handle all the canvas and tweak the many strings when racing, but there is plenty of room for the off watch below. There are six bunks and ample seating in the main saloon when the settee berths are not being used for sleeping. Some compromises with the galley were necessary to allow the large chart table on the port side. I am not particularly enthusiastic about the ice box arrangement, and I dislike having the stove facing aft, especially since the cook cannot stand in front of it. When possible, it is nearly always best to have a gimbaled stove facing the boat's centerline and with its axis running fore and aft.

I like the fact that the quarter berth is as far as possible from the companionway hatch so that it will not get wet from spray. Also, I'm very much in favor of a large chart table, but for some reason I feel strange working at a table when facing aft. If it were slightly smaller and mounted against the bulkhead that runs between the quarter berth and main saloon, the table would stay drier, and a naviguesser like me would feel that he were going the right way.

There is plenty of stowage space below, but perhaps there are a few too many open bins, which can sometimes spill their contents when the boat is well heeled and rolling or pitching. Although the head is small, it is completely closed for adequate privacy. The forward cabin appears to have good headroom in the after part, and I like the well-rounded corner on the starboard bunk. Ventilation is very good with the two cabintop hatches. On some boats, I don't like having a hatch close to the mast, but in this case strength is maintained with a heavy beam in way of the partners.

Ingenue is built of wood using strip planking with glued seams to provide a strong, tight hull. Since there is no need for steam-bent frames, and sheet plywood is used for the bulkheads and decks, Ted thinks the boat can be put together by an amateur builder. Specifications call for cedar or Philippine mahogany planking, white oak or yellow pine backbone, mahogany deckhouse, and bronze fastenings.

There is an old story that the word "schooner" was invented by Andrew Robinson at the launching of a vessel in Gloucester in 1713. When a spectator exclaimed, "Oh, how she scoons," Mr. Robinson responded, "Then a schooner let her be." The story is apocryphal, but there is no doubt that there are some schooners that can really "scoon" or seem to skim across the water on a reach. One of them is the trim little *Ingenue,* and she can even scoon on a beat to windward.

16/ The Cal 40

A Downwind Machine

> Length overall: 39 feet 6 inches
> Length on waterline: 30 feet 6 inches
> Beam: 11 feet
> Draft: 5 feet 6 inches
> Sail area: 699 square feet
> Displacement: 15,000 pounds
> Designer: C. William Lapworth
> Year designed: 1963

It has been said that a camel is a horse designed by a committee. It has also been said that the Cal 40 was created by a committee (consisting of three men). Indeed, the Cal 40 may have seemed as strange as a camel when she was first seen in 1963 by some conservative ocean-racing sailors. Not that she is an ugly boat; she has never been unpleasant to look at (except when she is beating you), but her underbody is somewhat like that of a flat bottomed dinghy having a streamlined fin keel and an unusual (for those times) high-aspect-ratio balanced spade rudder. This was quite a different look for a stock boat that was intended for rugged, long-distance offshore racing.

The three-man committee responsible for the boat consisted of George Griffith, who conceived of the idea; C. William Lapworth, the designer; and Jack Jensen of Jensen Marine Corporation, the builder. I have also heard that Robert M. Allan lent a few thoughts to the original conception. Messrs. Allan and Griffith owned the first two boats of the L-36 class,

Lapworth's forerunner design to the Cal 40. There is a general resemblance of a fiberglass Cal 40 to the earlier wood-built L 36, except the latter has a flatter sheer, a different keel at its after end, and a keel-attached rudder with conventional rake. I have read that George Griffith talked Bill Lapworth into giving the Cal 40 its free-standing spade rudder, which became almost a trademark of the Cal boats during the middle and late 1960s.

Of course, the Cal 40 went on to become about the most winning ocean-racing class boat of all times; and with the possible exception of the yawl *Finisterre,* it has been the greatest influence on modern American yacht design. Some fleet victories of various Cal 40s are: the Bermuda Race, Annapolis-to-Newport Race, the Southern Ocean Racing Conference (in 1964 and 1966), Whitney and Ahmanson Series, Northern Ocean Racing Championship, and the Transpac Race (in 1965, 1967, and 1969). This does not begin to cover the numerous class wins and fleet victories in less important events. Some of the

121

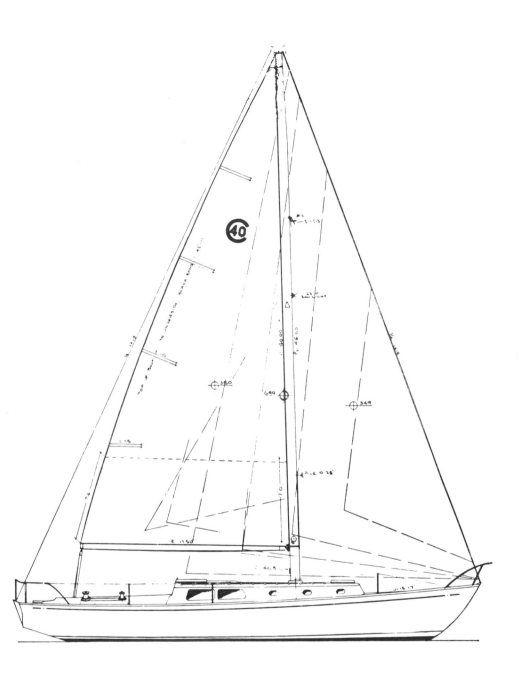

The Cal 40 has a moderate sail plan of medium aspect ratio. Sail area is on the small side considering her wetted surface, but the area is ample considering her displacement. The long main boom nicely balances a spinnaker or poled-out jib when the boat is running. (Yachting)

more famous Cal 40s are: *Conquistador, Vamp X, Lancetilla, Thunderbird, Psyche, Tangent, Holiday Too,* and *Argonaut.*

I am most grateful to Bill Lapworth for allowing me to reproduce the Cal 40's lines. To my knowledge they have never before been published. Undoubtedly, the most striking characteristic is the boat's lack of deadrise. Even when you see the actual hull out of water, it is not always obvious that the bilges are almost completely flat, but the lines on the body plan show this feature most dramatically. They reveal a very powerful hull with a lot of waterline

beam and a rather sharp turn of the bilge. This gives the boat her ability to carry her sail well in a breeze. The flat sections increase wetted surface, but the moderately short keel assures that drag from this source will not be excessive. I see from the plans that the wetted surface area has been figured at 325.19 square feet. With a sail area of 699 square feet, the sail-area-to-wetted-surface ratio comes to about 2.15. This measure of light air performance does not indicate excellence in drifting conditions, but the ratio is quite reasonable for light winds when you consider that that boat's displacement is rather

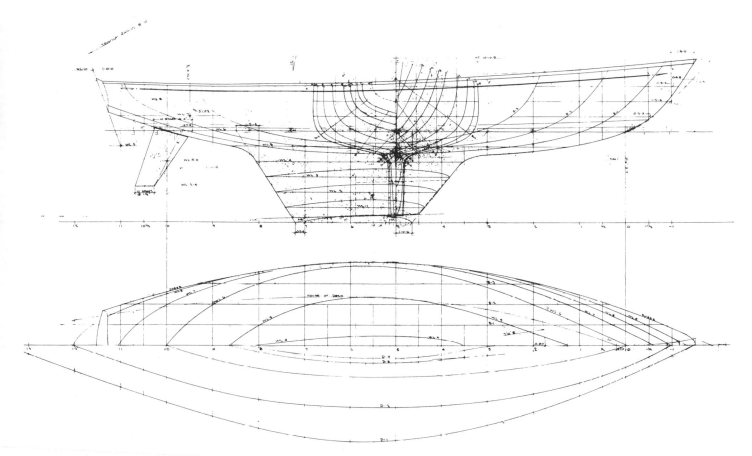

The heretofore-unpublished lines of the Cal 40. Note the extraordinarily flat bilge and great beam near the load waterline. The hull is not as full aft as one might expect for a downwind machine.

Although the Cal 40's accommodations might be criticized for having too many bunks, the arrangement makes sense for ocean racing, because the off watch can sleep aft on the low side.

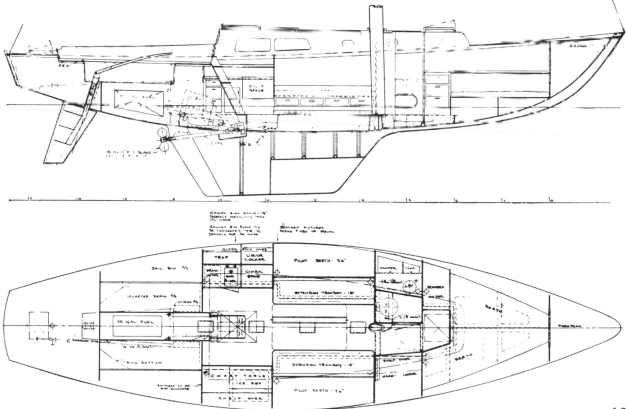

light. Her sail-area-to-displacement ratio (sail area in square feet divided by the cube root of displacement in cubic feet squared), another measure of performance, is 18.3, which is considerably higher than the CCA ideal of 15.4 for sloops of all sizes.

For a boat designed to excel when running in fresh winds, the Cal 40 has a surprisingly symmetrical hull with a somewhat narrow stern and full bow by modern American standards. One might think that a boat with the Cal 40's ability to surf would have a run that was wider and flatter, but one of the virtues of this boat is that her stern is not so buoyant nor her bow so fine that she will tend to root or dig in when running before large following seas. The moderately full bow does detract somewhat from upwind performance in light winds with choppy seas, but it tends to lift rather than bury. Her flat bilges and lightish displacement provide the ability to surf; while the well-balanced ends, having the right amount of buoyancy, help assure that she will not easily broach to or be pooped and that the helm will not be difficult to handle.

The Cal 40 is so well mannered that she can easily be steered with a tiller. Of course, the spade rudder with its leading edge forward of the rudder stock allows the water flow to assist in turning the rudder. For wild runs downwind, many sailors prefer a tiller to a wheel because it avoids arduous spoking and allows a quicker response. In conditions where the boat is threatening to broach, immediate helm response is very important. The spade rudder has been severely criticized, and many sailors (myself included) prefer a skeg forward of the rudder to give it protection and to delay stalling. Bill Lapworth seems to be one of the few designers to have had real success with the spade. One world-famous naval architect tried a Lapworth-type rudder on a new design, and the boat steered so atrociously that he decided never again to use another spade (or so the story goes), and thereafter he used only skeg or keel-attached rudders.

There are several possible reasons why Lapworth rudders succeed when others fail. First of all, they are deep, high-aspect-ratio types and properly streamlined to delay stalling and produce high lift with low drag. Second, they are not located so far aft that they are apt to seriously ventilate or suck air down from the surface. Third, the rudder stock is not excessively raked forward, which practice, when carried to the extreme, can cause the side force on the rudder to act in a more vertical than horizontal direction when the boat heels. The Cal 40's rudder appears to have considerable rake, but the actual stock on which the rudder pivots is not raked very much. Another theory explaining the efficiency of the Cal-type spades is that they are fairly broad at the top and fit close to the counter so that the hull acts as an end plate to reduce turbulence.

Perhaps the main reason for the Cal 40's fine steering characteristics, however, is that her hull has intrinsic good directional stability. Designer Halsey Herreshoff attributes the Cal 40's steering control at least partially to the fact that "they have relatively long keels fore-and-aft, compared to the newest hot boats." Of course there are other reasons for directional stability, such as a long waterline, moderate beam, reasonably balanced ends, moderate body depth, and a center of lateral resistance that is probably abaft the center of gravity. Nevertheless, the particular trapezoidal shape of the Cal 40's keel, being fairly long at the top, helps make the boat track exceedingly well.

Just to show that there is very little that's totally new in yacht design, I've included here the profile of *El Chico* designed by Nathanael Herreshoff in 1892. Of course, there are many differences between this boat and the Cal 40, but they both have free-standing balanced spade rudders and trapezoidal fin keels. A major difference in the keels is that *El Chico* has a thin fin with a bulb of ballast at its bottom. She needs this for stability, because she does not have such a powerful hull form as the Cal 40. The latter has a more hydrodynamically ef-

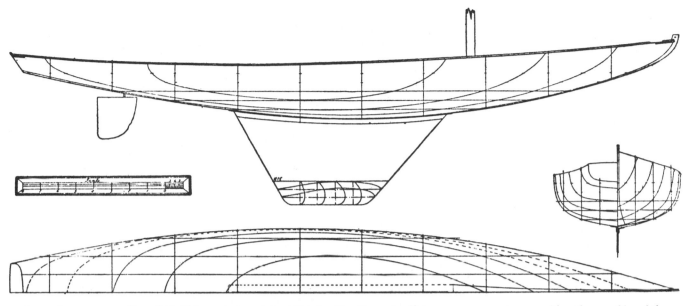

The underwater profile of El Chico, *designed in 1892 by Nat Herreshoff, in some respects resembles the profile of the Cal 40. (From* The History of American Sailing Ships *by Howard I. Chapelle, © 1935, W.W. Norton)*

ficient keel, since it avoids the drag of a bulb and can be streamlined from bottom to top.

Bill Lapworth was one of the few American designers advocating light displacement for ocean racers in the late 1940s. The design that first brought him wide recognition was the extremely light (for those days) sloop *Flying Scotchman* that sailed in the 1950 Bermuda Race. At that time, I was somewhat of a light-displacement enthusiast myself, having heard many glowing reports about foreign boats of that type, such as the British *Myth of Malham* and *Gulvaine* and the Dutch Van de Stadt creations. Just prior to the race, I had the opportunity to see the *Flying Scotchman* sailing around the harbor at Newport, Rhode Island, under jib alone. She darted to and fro through the crowded waters with the maneuverability and acceleration of a dinghy. That experience almost totally converted me to light displacement, but I'll have to admit that now I lean to medium displacement as a good compromise between the responsiveness of light boats and the easy motion and power of heavier boats.

The Cal 40's weight is not extreme. She is light, but she is not a ULDB (ultra light displace-ment boat). Personally, I dislike the trend toward extremely light ocean racers. Although they are quick to surf downwind, performance is apt to suffer upwind in rough seas; and many of these boats lack strength for the heaviest weather offshore, while some of them even lack sufficient ballast. The ULDB named *Pi*, for example, capsized a few years ago, which led to the death of two crew members. Of course, there are a number of recent examples of ultra-light ton cup boats with serious hull failures and lack of reserve stability in heavy weather.

In contrast, the Cal 40 has ample ballast and she is built to withstand considerable punish-ment. She may pound when going to windward, but she has repeatedly proven she can take it. In 1967 the Cal 40 *Lancetilla* smashed her way to victory in the Annapolis-Newport Race when a northeast storm turned the event into one of the most rugged of all upwind legs. Thirty-seven percent of the fleet dropped out, and many boats were damaged, but *Lancetilla* suffered little more than some slack rigging.

Almost the only major failure of a Cal 40's hull I have heard about is the mysterious leak that led to the foundering of *Tangent* in 1972. I

The light-displacement racing-cruiser Flying Scotchman, *which first brought Bill Lapworth wide recognition, was occasionally called a blown-up International 14 dinghy. (Beckner Photo Service)*

won't go into the details of her sinking, but I wrote a short article about the incident for *Yachting* magazine (March 1972) based on the Coast Guard's investigation. It seems that *Tangent* had been driven very hard in quite a number of long-distance ocean races, including two Transpacs and a Tahiti Race; and later she had lain ahull in a Force 12 cyclone for five days in the South Pacific. This Cal 40 (hull number 11) had been subjected to stresses few stock boats experience, and she had not been given an out-of-water survey after the cyclone. Still, her sudden sinking in San Pedro Channel, California, while under sail in fair weather cannot easily be explained, since there had been no collision or grounding, and all the through-hull fittings appeared to be sound.

Tangent took about an hour to sink after her crew had noticed the bilge being flooded from a leak near or abaft the after end of the keel. In my article, I suggested as one possible explanation that vibration from a partially open folding propeller might have caused the leak. This is pure speculation, but the possibility occurred to me for the following reasons: first, vibration of this kind can and has cracked fiberglass stern tubes, and Jensen Marine posts warnings on their boats about hung-up folding props; second, the Cal 40 has a V-drive with the propeller shaft running through the top of the keel's trailing edge, near where the water was seen coming in; and third, *Tangent* had a badly vibrating hung-up prop that had been fouled with kelp on the very day of the accident. Whether or not this vibration could have been the ultimate cause, probably no one will ever know, for *Tangent* sank in about 400 fathoms.

With the exception of *Tangent*, Cal 40s have had no structural problems to my knowledge. These boats have proved time and again that they can take tremendous punishment. I only mention *Tangent*'s accident to alert any Cal 40 owner who might be planning a tough offshore passage. It would be a very good idea to inspect the hull and keel carefully, especially in way of the propeller shaft. Of course, folding propellers on any boat should be stopped from turning immediately when one blade fails to open.

Although the Cal 40 is primarily a downwind racing machine, she is quite a respectable performer on all points of sailing, and some sailors like her below-decks layout for offshore cruising as well as racing. She has lots of bunks, so there is almost always a place to sit or sleep on the low side, and the two comfortable quarter berths are located near the pitching axis so that motion is minimized. One boat of my acquaintance has ports in the cockpit well to give the quarter berths light and air when the boat is moored or at anchor in fair weather. The standard main cabin is more or less conventional, with two berths on each side. Some seamen prefer this arrangement to the deep dinette, because it is difficult to sit facing fore and aft when the boat is heeled. There is a practical drop-leaf table mounted between two vertical pipes that also serve as grab posts in rough weather. A rather handy feature is a long gimbaling (actually pivoting) shelf or stowage bin above the table between the two pipes. The galley is adequate, but I would prefer one that is U- or L-shaped for more counter space and also so that belts can more easily be rigged and the sink can be located close to the boat's centerline. In addition, I prefer a chart table that has a permanent seat.

Since the advent of the Cal 40 and boats of her type, there has been some rumination on the definition of seaworthiness. I think most modern ocean-racing sailors consider the type *seaworthy* (provided it is well built), but it really cannot be called *seakindly,* because a light, flat hull will inevitably pound when beating into a head sea. To some extent compromises are always necessary in yacht design, and the Cal 40 trades some seakindliness for performance downwind. But a thrilling performance is possible when conditions are right.

I know no better way to conclude this chapter than to quote from an article called "The Surfing Boat," written for *Yachting* (June 1971) by Frank E. Bilek. It described his sail to Hawaii in the 1969 Transpac Race aboard the Cal 40 *Montgomery Street.* Mr. Bilek claimed that on one occasion the boat momentarily surfed at speeds in excess of 25 knots, since the

Aerial view of a Cal 40 on a quartering reach. These fine boats are nearly always used for the annual Congressional Cup match race series in California, and this picture shows the 1969 winner Madrugador of the U.S. Navy Yacht Club, skippered by Henry Sprague III. (Long Beach Promotion, Inc.)

sails collapsed and filled backwards in a 25-knot following wind! His description is as follows:

"Imagine if you can, the starboard bow wave dousing the spinnaker pole ten feet above the deck, and to port a solid wide stream of water slamming into the mainsail higher than the first reef points with such force and volume that there was danger the main would be torn from its slides. No, the main was not reefed. It was held in place by the boom vang almost 90 degrees from the centerline.

"On these occasions, we on watch found it impossible to contain ourselves. With sheer exhilaration we screamed, pounded the deck, and yelled 'Faster, Faster, FASTER.' Even the watch below, although disgruntled at being awakened, looked at the companionway and joined in with 'GO, GO, GO.' "

17/ The Vega 27

"A Jolly Fine Boat"

```
Length overall: 27 feet 1 inch
Length on waterline: 23 feet
Beam: 8 feet
Draft: 3 feet 8 inches
Sail area: 295 square feet
Displacement: 5,062 pounds
Designer: Per Brohall
Year designed: 1964
```

For a small offshore cruiser having durability, comfort, and speed, the Vega 27 is hard to beat. At least, that's my feeling about this sensible Swedish design, and a great many sailors must agree, for at this writing almost 3,500 Vegas have been built. There are Vega class associations all over the world, and these fine little sloops have made a great number of distant blue water passages.

Perhaps the best known Vega voyage was made by John Neal, who did extensive cruising in the Pacific, because John wrote an account of his adventures in a fairly popular little book called *Log of the Mahina.* Other outstanding but lesser known cruises were made by the likes of Dima Grinups, who circumnavigated the world in his *Sandra II,* and by Pelle Norclius, who set a transatlantic speed record for small boats in his *Little My III.*

Mr. Grinups set out from Sweden and followed the east-to-west trade-wind route around the world via the Panama Canal. Off Madagascar, according to a Slocum Society report, he was severely injured by a blow from the main boom.

This report said that the voyage was ended by the accident, but I understand from Vega agents that *Sandra II* eventually completed the circumnavigation. It was said that she passed around the Cape of Good Hope, crossed the South Atlantic to Brazil, sailed up to the West Indies and Florida, then crossed the North Atlantic to England, and returned to Sweden.

Little My III crossed the Atlantic from the Cape Verde Islands to Barbados in 14 days and 16 hours, which is truly remarkable time for a boat only 23 feet on the waterline. She made several runs of over 160 miles per day, and her crew reported that she would often surf at 10 to 13 knots. Yet she was said to be dry and comfortable running before the boisterous trade winds. One of the crew, Mats Fagerstrom, wrote: "It was a bit hard for us to see this cruise as any form of a record. We never had to struggle. Sometimes it was a bit inconvenient, as always when you sail a small yacht in high sea and can't find a peaceful harbor. But in general, life on board was comfortable, and sometimes even luxurious . . . ."

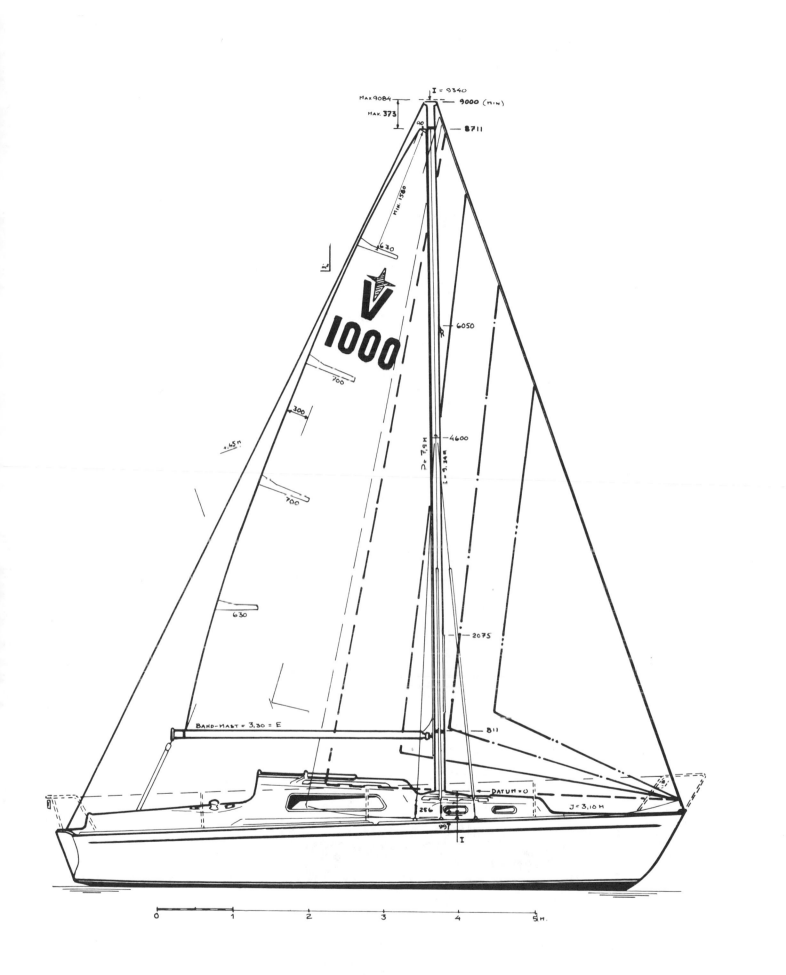

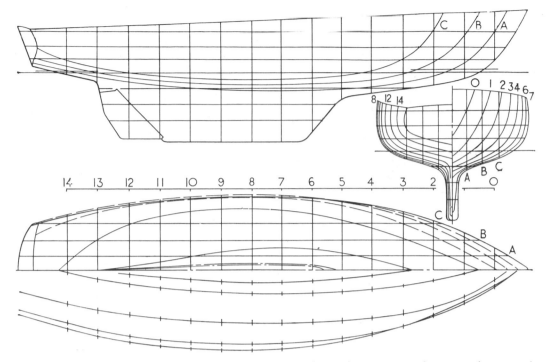

The Vega's lines indicate good balance and directional stability. One would expect her to sail downwind very well, but her upwind performance is somewhat surprising, considering her shoal draft. (Yachting World)

Many of the Vega's unique accommodation features cannot be shown in a standard arrangement plan, but several of them are apparent, such as double faucets in the galley, the sliding head sink, and the trash container under the bridge deck.

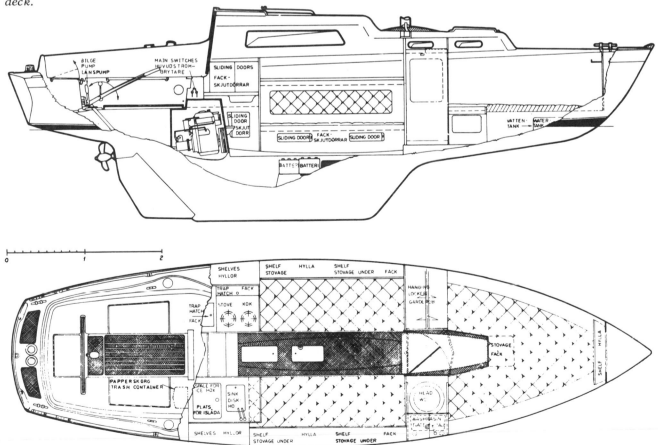

Her lines give us a clue as to why the Vega is so fast and well mannered when running off in fresh winds. Her flattish run and low deadrise encourage surfing; her bow is nicely flared to keep it from burying; there is little forefoot to root; and the keel is fairly long and shallow to encourage directional stability. Then too, her moderately light displacement helps keep her on top of the water.

One would not expect such a hull to be very good against the wind, at least not in rough seas, but she does surprisingly well on a heavy-weather beat. After Peter Richmond sailed one of these boats, *Eva*, across the notoriously rugged North Sea, he wrote, "The most impressive feature of our Vega was its ability to beat to windward under rather adverse conditions for a 27-foot boat." To be sure, the boat pounded some with her flattish bilge, but according to Richmond, she had plenty of power to drive to weather, and she stayed on top of the seas rather than plowing into them. It was said that *Eva* averaged over four knots on the rugged beat.

A speed curve published by the producers of the Vega shows that her best speed made good to windward in 16 knots of true wind occurs at a heading of around 42 degrees, which seems a bit optimistic to me. I'm sure this angle between the true wind and heading presupposes very smooth water, because when I sailed one of these boats into a short chop, I needed to crack off quite a lot to keep her footing.

The Vega's beam is somewhat modest by modern standards, and this detracts slightly from initial stability. John Neal almost always sailed with a reefed main in the South Pacific, and he eventually bought a small roachless and battenless sail with the equivalent area of a normal single-reefed main. Of course, this was strictly a cruising rig that was primarily for the purpose of simplifying sail handling with a small crew. I don't mean to imply that the Vega is tender, because she has ample reserve stability with her 40 percent ballast-to-displacement ratio and her short rig. As Peter Richmond put it when describing his North Sea crossing, "While her angle of heel was considerable, such that

maneuvering below was rather tricky, her lee deck was never buried, and once she settled her shoulder she became very stiff."

One of the nice features about the Vega, to my way of thinking, is the shallow keel. It is deep enough to ensure sufficient reserve stability and reasonable windward performance in almost all conditions, yet it permits gunkholing without the need for a centerboard, which can sometimes be troublesome. Draft is a mere three feet eight inches, and that allows access to most harbors anyone would want to visit.

Designed by the Swedish yacht architect Per Brohall in 1964, the Vega was intended to be a go-anywhere family cruiser with the accent on safety and comfort without significant sacrifice to sailing performance. Some of the safety features are sturdy construction, a bridge deck, high cockpit coamings, wide side decks (for a small, narrow boat), four hand rails on the cabintop, and a particularly wide foredeck that provides security when handling headsails. With the high coamings, the crew feels well protected in the cockpit, but I would prefer a clearing port or two in the after end of the coaming to reduce the volume of water the cockpit could hold in the event a large sea should happen to break aboard.

The foremost requirement of a safe boat is sound construction, and the Vega is well put together. According to the builder, Albin Marine Inc., she is built to Swedish specifications that are similar to Lloyd's. The solid (nonsandwich) fiberglass hull is said to vary in thickness from ¼ inch at the upper topsides to ½ inch in the bottom and keel area. The hull and deck are well bolted together, and even the main bulkhead is secured in place by bolts to a frame or flange rather than being secured with minimum fiberglass tabbing or tape, as is the case with a great many boats. About the only flaw I noticed in the Vega's construction is the inadequate support for her deck-stepped mast. Indeed, John Neal reported that his *Mahina* had a troublesome weakness in this area: he noted sagging beam, split post, and bulkhead warp in way of the mast.

The Vega Windward sailing on Lake Michigan. The sail symbol, of course, stands for the star Vega, which is so familiar to celestial navigators. (The preferred pronunciation, incidentally, is Veega, not Vayga.)

The stern view of Windward *emphasizes the height of the cockpit coaming aft. This gives the crew a great feeling of security, but it would be preferable to have a couple of freeing ports in the after end of the coaming.*

Comfort features include a standard dodger that gives the helmsman good protection when sailing with the wind forward of the beam. Incidentally, a dodger can also increase ventilation below by sucking air out of the companionway or by forcing air down it when the boat is anchored by her stern. The dining table can be set up in the cockpit for meals on deck, and the 6½-foot-long cockpit seats allow sleeping topside in fair weather.

There is a special ventilation system below that uses the cold hull's side as part of a convection cycle. Advertising literature describes the unique system as follows: "Ventilation is effected by the 'cold wall' principle. Fresh air is drawn in an air duct from the cockpit along the cold bottom of the hull where moisture is condensed. The air which then enters the cabin and forecastle contains no excess moisture." An impartial boat test report (*Yachting World*, January 1970) said that this method of ventilation "noticeably lowers the temperature in the cabin on a hot day." The intake duct is in the side of the cockpit well, so the vent should be closed when underway in the very heaviest weather.

Some other unusual features below are a dining table that swings out of the way, a galley sink with both fresh and sea water foot-operated pumps, a sliding hatch to the stowage space under the cockpit seat where a rubbish bucket is placed, and a forward wash basin that slides over and drains into the head. The standard arrangement has four berths, two in the forward cabin and two in the main cabin, and there is even an option of additional folding upper berths aft. I can't imagine, however, wanting to cruise on a 27-foot boat with six people.

When the Vega was examined by British judges at the *Yachting World* rally for small cruising boats in 1969, she was given top marks for performance under power. In fact, she was said to be the fastest boat in the power trials. Curiously, though, I have some friends, Barbara and Tom Moore, who are not entirely satisfied with the performance of their Vega under power, although they are tremendously pleased with the boat in every other way. The Vega tested at the rally was fitted with an Albin 0-22 gasoline engine, while the Moores' boat is fitted with a 10-horsepower diesel engine, a Volvo Penta MD 6A. It is my understanding that the newest Vegas have 13-horsepower Volvos, and so perhaps performance under diesel power has been improved. The batteries are under the cabin sole, but I take a rather dim view of this location, because there is always a possibility that the bilge could become filled with water. Sea water and charged batteries can form deadly chlorine gas, and there is also a danger of hydrogen accumulating in a poorly ventilated space.

The propeller is somewhat unusual in that it is installed abaft the rudder and its pitch is variable. Although the after location of the prop may detract from maneuverability when moving ahead, because wash cannot be directed against the rudder, control in reverse should be improved because the upper part of the rudder does receive some propeller wash when the boat is moving astern. Also, the propeller location

The nearly straight sheer of the Vega gives her a slightly hogged appearance from the windward side when she is heeled, but a straight (or reversed) sheer helps keep the lee rail clear of the water.

allows a slightly off-center installation so that the stern will not be pulled to one side as a result of torque. The ability to vary the blades' pitch allows non fail, complete feathering for low drag when the boat is under sail. A single lever control operates forward, reverse, or full feathering, and the engine speed.

The anodized aluminum spars are made by Proctor, and the masts on the Vegas I have been aboard are fitted with through-mast roller reefing. Nowadays, jiffy reefing seems to be favored in the United States, but some Europeans prefer roller reefing, especially the type that cranks from the forward end of the mast. Champion sailor and expert sailmaker Bruce Banks has described through-mast roller reefing as "the most important gear development in recent years." Of course, roller reefing allows sail reduction that is infinitely variable, and the through-mast system obviates the need for setback at the tack, since the gears are housed inside the mast. A word of caution, though: anyone near the mast should station himself where he could not possibly be hit by the spinning handle when the reef is shaken out.

At the *Yachting World* rally mentioned earlier, when a group of expert judges picked their favorite small cruiser, the Vega finished a close second, beating out 20 well-known boats. The rally was not just an evaluation of speed and comfort, for it considered the combination of all characteristics, including construction, looks, handling qualities, seaworthiness, and workmanship. One of the judges made the comment that the Vega is "a highly professional piece of production with a good performance." The editor of *Yachting World* called her "a jolly fine boat," and I think that just about sums her up.

18/ Aleutka

We've Been to Alaska

> Length overall: 25 feet 6 inches
> Length on waterline: 22 feet 6 inches
> Beam: 7 feet 2 inches
> Draft: 2 feet 9 inches
> Sail area: 250 square feet
> Displacement: 5,000 pounds
> Designer: John S. Letcher Jr.
> Year designed: 1965

The naval architect often refers to the design compromises he is forced to make as "trade-offs." He trades one desirable attribute for another or perhaps accentuates one at the expense of the other in order to make his creation most suitable for her intended purpose. *Aleutka* is a rather specialized boat in that her designer, John S. Letcher Jr., has said that "her ultimate purpose is to carry her crew of two safely and inexpensively on long voyages of exploration." For this work the boat has proven a great success. She has sailed about 18,000 miles and easily managed such passages as one from California to Hawaii and another from Hawaii to Alaska. In addition, she has crawled innumerable ditches and explored many a coast off the beaten track.

Yet John is the first to admit that trade-offs were necessary. He had to compromise some sailing performance, especially the ability to excel upwind, for such features as shoal draft, directional stability, and the ability of the boat to stand upright when grounded. John estimates that *Aleutka* is 20 to 30 percent slower than the typical MORC racer in speed made good to windward, but he wrote, "An important note is that in Alaska, where we never saw another sail, we always believed her performance was sterling." This reminds me of a remark attributed to the skipper of a famous old Chesapeake bugeye called the *Brown, Smith and Jones*. When her skipper was asked by a yachtsman how his boat performed, the old waterman replied. "Well, when she's all by herself she's fast as hell, but when she's alongside another boat she ain't worth a damn." Of course, that story is not meant to imply that *Aleutka* is slow. In conditions for which she was designed, John's boat would give a very good account of herself alongside the vast majority of boats her size. In fact, John has written: "All by herself on the deep ocean, running or reaching in the trade wind toward some island landfall, she will be a delight, for that is what she is built to do. And then she will have left 99 percent of those lovely, tall, long-legged racing boats far, far behind."

Some of the differences between *Aleutka* and a typical American stock boat of her size are: a

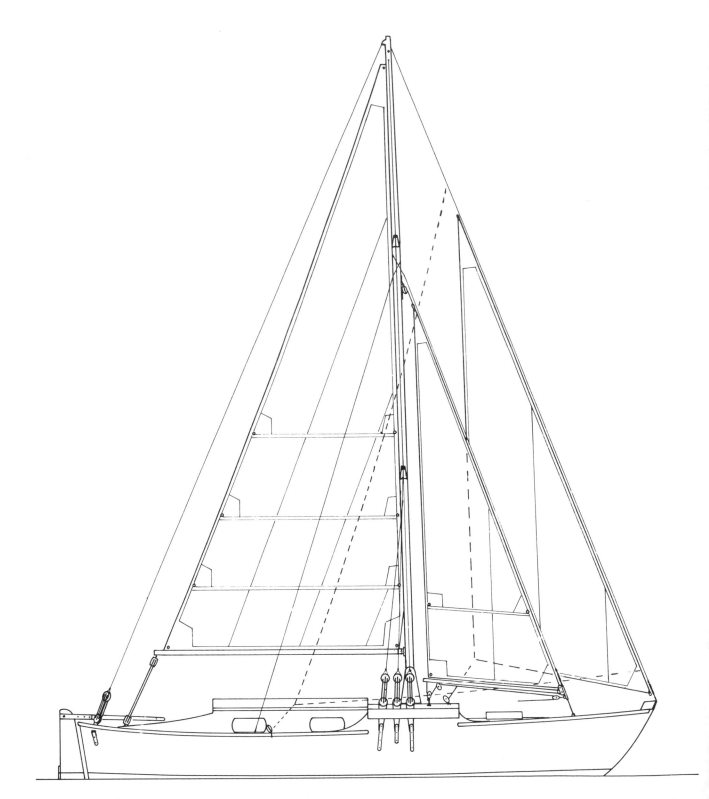

Aleutka's rig has many interesting features, such as the tabernacle, twin poles for the twin running headsails, and deadeyes and lanyards in lieu of turnbuckles. The mainsail's slightly hollowed leech obviates any real need for battens, but still they would give better assurance against leech curl and flutter.

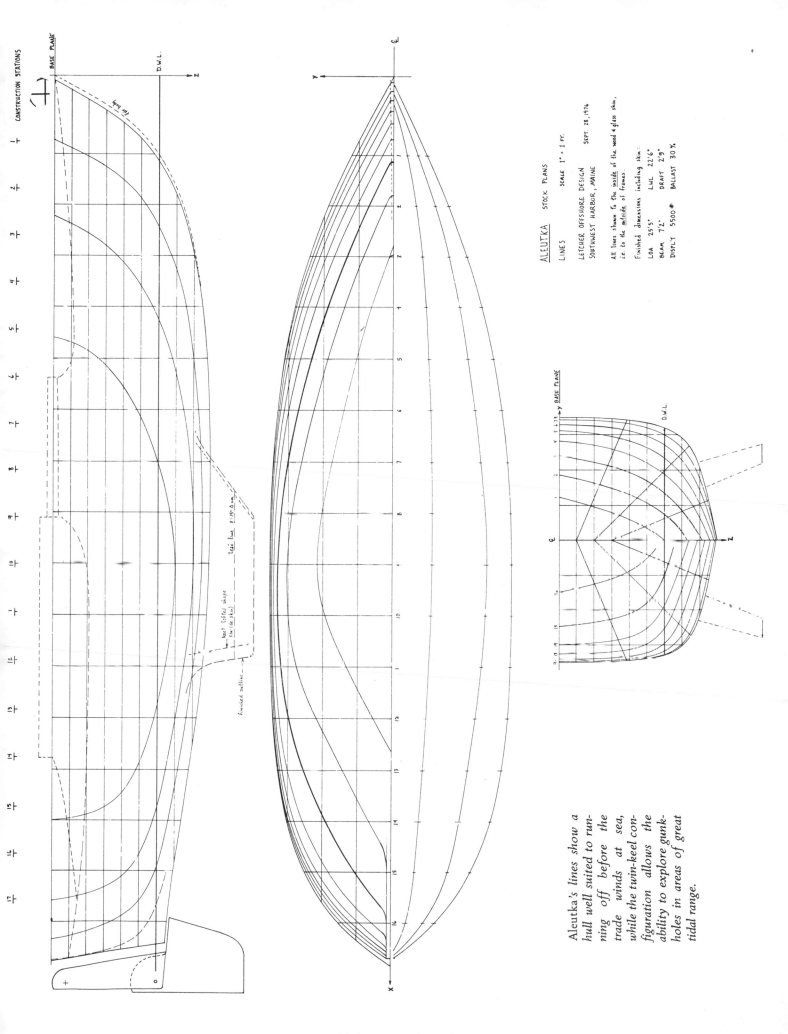

Aleutka's lines show a hull well suited to running off before the trade winds at sea, while the twin-keel configuration allows the ability to explore gunkholes in areas of great tidal range.

ALEUTKA   STOCK PLANS

LINES   SCALE 1" = 1 FT.

LETCHER OFFSHORE DESIGN   SEPT. 28, 1976
SOUTHWEST HARBOR, MAINE

All lines shown to the inside of the wood & glass skin,
i.e. to the outside of frames.

Finished dimensions including skin:

LOA 25'5"   LWL 22'6"
BEAM 7'2"   DRAFT 2'9"
DISPL'T 5500#   BALLAST 30%

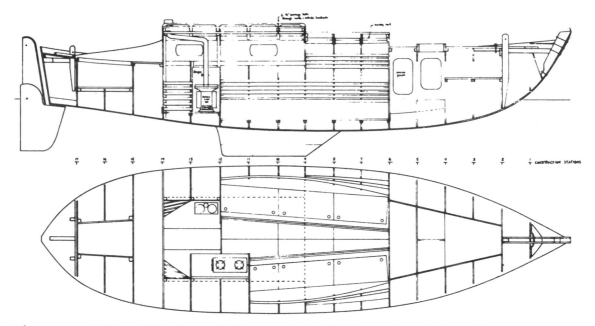

The accommodations of Aleutka *are highly customized with the extra long bunks and huge stowage area forward. Not shown is a very short bunk on the port side for the Letchers' young daughter Lucy.* (Cruising World)

double-ended hull with less than normal beam, a tiny cockpit well, an unusual raised-deck/cabin-trunk combination, twin keels, a fold-down mast hinged on a tabernacle, cutter rig with permanent twin headsail booms, outboard chain-plates with deadeyes and lanyards, flotation, a breakaway rudder, enough stowage space for skis and two disassembled bicycles. I could go on and on. John Letcher is a very original thinker, and he's practical, too.

The reason for the twin keels is that they enable *Aleutka* to sail in less than three feet of water (when she is unheeled) while providing reasonable stability and the ability to remain upright when grounded in areas with extreme tides. There are several advantages to the boat's being able to stand on her keels: She will not fall on her side when the tide leaves her high and dry, maintenance of her bottom is possible without the expense of slipping or lifting with a crane, and overland transporting or deckloading on a ship is simplified. *Aleutka* was moved on a truck from California to Seattle, Washington (with all of the Letchers' possessions piled into the unfinished hull), and later she was transported across Mexico on a flatbed railroad car to

avoid using the Panama Canal. Another advantage of twin keels is that they tend to dampen rolling when running before sizable seas. I recall Maurice Bailey telling me about the downwind characteristics of his twin-keel *Auralyn,* which was eventually sunk by a whale, forcing the Baileys to spend 118 days in a life raft. Maurice said that the boat rolled much less when running in the trades than his single-keel replacement boat, *Auralyn II.*

The principal disadvantage of twin keels is that there is nearly always some sacrifice to windward performance, despite some propaganda to the contrary from certain British enthusiasts. Another problem is that unless there is a skeg, the rudder is quite vulnerable to being damaged by flotsam, since there is no keel directly forward of it to give protection. A skeg just ahead of the rudder would afford protection, of course, but at the cost of extra wetted surface, which is already considerable on a twin-keeler.

John solved the problem in a rather unique way, with a breakaway (or, as he calls it, a "pop-out") rudder. The lower part of the outboard rudder's blade (which is balanced, incidentally) fits into a slot between cheeks, and the blade is held in place with a wooden pin. If the rudder should happen to strike an object, the pin will break and the blade will depart, although not permanently, because it is attached to the boat with a lanyard. John told me that he has lost the rudder on five occasions. Usually the cause was kelp that engaged the rudder, but once he hit a rock that passed between the two keels. Although John is not entirely satisfied with the arrangement, it serves the purpose of preventing serious damage to the rudder or stern post. An obvious difficulty is rehousing the blade after it has popped out, especially if instant maneuverability is needed.

Aleutka's lines show a long, narrow hull that gives the appearance of being quite symmetrical, but maximum fullness of the underbody is quite far abaft amidships. These characteristics, together with her straight sides and low angle of deadrise, make for good performance downwind. Indeed, John speaks highly of the boat's ability to track and surf in blusterous downwind conditions. In a recent letter he wrote: "My most exciting memories from *Aleutka*'s cruises came from strong winds. There were the northerly fall gales off northern California in which we found how sweetly the light double-ender would run before the big seas, surfing often." The waterlines and sections forward show a certain fullness, and there is little forefoot, so the bow has no tendency to root. The stern sections from amidships to station 15 are more U-shaped, thus enhancing the ability to surf. The merits of a pointed stern are somewhat controversial, as I've said before, but *Aleutka*'s stern is certainly handsome; it appears to have ample buoyancy; and, of course, there is no flat counter to slam. The plans also show the unusual skegless outboard balanced rudder, although the one illustrated seems to be the kick-up type that pivots on a permanent pin.

Some other seagoing characteristics of *Aleutka* are her small cockpit well with bridge deck and high coamings, low cabin trunk with small windows, and strong construction. The twin keels don't provide quite the ultimate stability of a single deep keel, but *Aleutka* should have a greater stability range than a typical shoal-draft centerboarder. Furthermore, John gave the boat a narrow beam partly to ensure prompt self-righting in the improbable event of a capsize.

Certainly the boat is well proven in heavy weather. Not only has she come through a number of gales at sea, but she also has experienced some williwaws and other unusually strong offshore winds. There was the time, for instance, when John and his wife, Pati, sailed in the Gulf of Tehuantepec. He wrote me the following account:

"During the winter months the atmospheric pressure over the Gulf of Mexico is usually considerably higher than over the eastern Pacific. This causes very strong winds to blow through the narrow notch in the Continental Divide and out over the Gulf of Tehuantepec. It was February when we were there, and we had to reach Salina Cruz at the head of the Gulf, to get on the railroad for our portage to the Gulf of Mexico. During January and February the wind at Salina Cruz *averages* Force 7, and reaches Force 12 an average of six days a month. From Puerto Angel, where you turn the corner, it's 75 miles to Salina Cruz. This took us seven days. When the wind would ease up so we could stand up to it with deep-reefed sails, we would beat into it, keeping always within half a mile or so of the beach. When it would pipe up we would run quickly in close to the beach and anchor in 2-3 fathoms, where we always found a good sand bottom; then we would go for a swim, or swim ashore to walk on the beach, or hole up below to wait for the shrieking of the rigging to drop below C above middle C, when my perfect pitch would tell me it was time to give it another go."

Although John makes no promises about *Aleutka*'s ability to claw off a lee shore in a gale, he guesses that the light, narrow hull with low windage "would come through all right." Her experience beating into the Gulf of Tehuantepec would seem to indicate this is true. One feature that would give me some misgivings for heavy weather sailing, however, is *Aleutka*'s companionway hatch, which is quite far off-center.

This close-up view of Aleutka *under sail shows a lot of the details on deck. The partial raised deck, sometimes referred to as a hunting cabin in the old days, adds some character and individuality. (John S. Letcher)*

John admits that this is a trade-off to allow for stowage of an eight-foot dinghy on the cabintop. He told me that he sails with the companionway slide in when it is blowing hard.

The reason it is important for *Aleutka* to carry a dinghy is that she has no engine, and usually it makes sense to anchor out in a harbor and use the dink for transportation to and from the shore. I'm not so sure I wouldn't prefer an inflatable dinghy that could be folded over in order to allow an on-center companionway, but inflatables don't row well and the constant need to pump them up is a nuisance. For locomotion in calm weather, *Aleutka* is provided with what John calls a "two oarspower auxiliary." In other words, she is rowed with two eight-foot oars. Oarlocks are fitted into ports on the rail, and the rower sits on the bridge deck facing aft. John claims the boat is quite easy to row in smooth water and that it only takes about a sixteenth of a horsepower to keep her moving at 1½ knots. Would you believe the Letchers have taken the boat through almost the entire length of the east

coast's Intracoastal Waterway under sail and oars?

John and Pati sailed into our home port at Gibson Island, Maryland, in the fall of 1978, and my wife, Sally, and I had the pleasure of paying them a visit aboard *Aleutka.* I was amazed to see how easily they could live on such a small boat, even though they had along their 2½-year-old daughter, Lucy, who had numerous toys as well as a pet cat. There is plenty of sitting headroom below, and the cabin is surprisingly bright because there are deadlights in the deck. John is built like a basketball player, so the bunks are much longer than those on the average boat. There is an ample galley and a huge stowage area forward; but what impressed me most was the little woodburning stove (a Fatsco "Tiny Tot") for heating the cabin on cold days and making it cozy as a bear's den.

Aleutka's rig is easy to manage, for the total sail area is small, it is divided into three sails, and the center of effort is low. One might question the value of a cutter rig on such a small boat, for it might be a bit cumbersome in crowded waters; but bear in mind that *Aleutka* was designed for going to sea and sailing off the beaten track. The sail plan shows her twin headsails and permanent booms secured to the mast just below the spreaders. These sails, of course, are for running in the trades or whenever there is a steady following wind. They are excellent sails for self-steering. Incidentally, *Aleutka* is fitted with a small self-steering vane on her rudder head, but John says that for about 11,000 miles of her voyages he has used sheet-to-helm self-steering (i.e., methods of connecting a sheet and elastic cord to the tiller so that when the boat strays off course, the appropriate line pulls on the helm to make the course correction). As for John's preference for deadeyes and lanyards, they are cheaper, add much character, and are not subject to metal fatigue. The tabernacle allows the mast to be folded down so that *Aleutka* can pass under low bridges or be transported overland. The arrangement also facilitates spar and rigging maintenance.

Aleutka is a one-off fiberglass boat, and she was built by John, with some help from Pati, using the batten-mold method of construction. Almost the entire mold, which consists of plywood cross-sections "planked" with long fir battens, is incorporated into the finished hull. The cross-sections act as frames or bulkheads, while the battens act as stiffening stringers. Of course, there are many layers of fiberglass (mostly woven roving) on the outside of the stringers to form a strong, composite structure. The method is inexpensive and quite suitable for home building. Construction details and complete plans of the boat can be obtained from Letcher Offshore Design, P.O. Box 369, Southwest Harbor, Maine 04679. In a recent letter John wrote: "We sold 35 *Aleutka* plans the first year, and they're still going at the rate of about two per month. The first boat I know to be completed is supposed to be launched this weekend at Freeport, Maine. I'm working on stock plans for a little larger version (29' x 8' x 3' draft) right now." Incidentally, I know of one *Aleutka* that is being home-built by the Seemann C-Flex method of construction.

Aleutka sailing in a moderate breeze looks very salty with her "tanbark" main, radar reflector, and self-steering vane. (John S. Letcher)

What tremendous satisfaction it must have given John to design and build his own special boat and then use her to fulfill his dreams of adventurous voyages. *Aleutka* might at times seem a bit disappointing for ordinary use in crowded waters, but she has character and distinction. John has written that when he is beating to windward in the company of typical MORC racers, "They eat us up, pointing higher and footing faster, and all I can say to poor *Aleutka* is, 'To hell with 'em, old girl. You and I have been to Alaska.' "

19/ The Redwing 30

Handsome is. . .

> Length overall: 30 feet 3½ inches
> Length on waterline: 21 feet 9 inches
> Beam: 8 feet 9½ inches
> Draft: 4 feet 6 inches
> Sail area: 404 square feet
> Displacement: 7,458 pounds
> Designer: Cuthbertson & Cassian
> Year designed: 1967

Eight years ago, I wrote an article about the Redwing 30 in which I expressed my admiration for her looks and decried the general trend toward ugliness in many of the new racing-cruisers. I still haven't changed my opinion very much. Perhaps some transoms have grown smaller since the advent of the International Offshore Rule, but all too often freeboard is too high, sheerlines are ungraceful, cabin trunks are weirdly shaped and/or defaced with huge picture windows, while bows on some racers are so low and fine that the boats look as if they could submarine in a seaway. But what I most dislike aesthetically is the prevalent trend toward truncated reverse transoms. We used to own a boat with such a stern, and I never could quite get used to it. I liked the boat, and she was handsome in most other respects, but her stern looked as though it had lost an argument with a guillotine.

Not so the Redwing 30; this pretty little sloop has her stern drawn out nicely to match the bow's overhang. Of course, I am familiar with the argument that small boats should not have long overhangs because this could result in a tendency to hobbyhorse. Perhaps the Redwing 30 could stand a slightly shorter stern, but I really don't think the overhang aft is extreme, and the boat doesn't seem to pitch to any great degree unless she happens to meet seas that exactly correspond to her waterline length or she carries too much weight in her ends. Of course, the overhangs add waterline length when the boat heels, and they provide some reserve buoyancy.

Other features that enhance the boat's appearance are moderate freeboard, a graceful sheer with the bow considerably higher than the stern, and a well-shaped cabin trunk with small, tasteful windows. It is amazing that, although the boat is only about 22 feet on the waterline, she has full headroom in the main cabin without the need of a high cabin trunk or a lot of freeboard. This was accomplished with a high crown to the top of the cabin trunk, and also the hull is fairly deep amidships, which allows a low cabin sole.

With her long ends, low silhouette, and lack

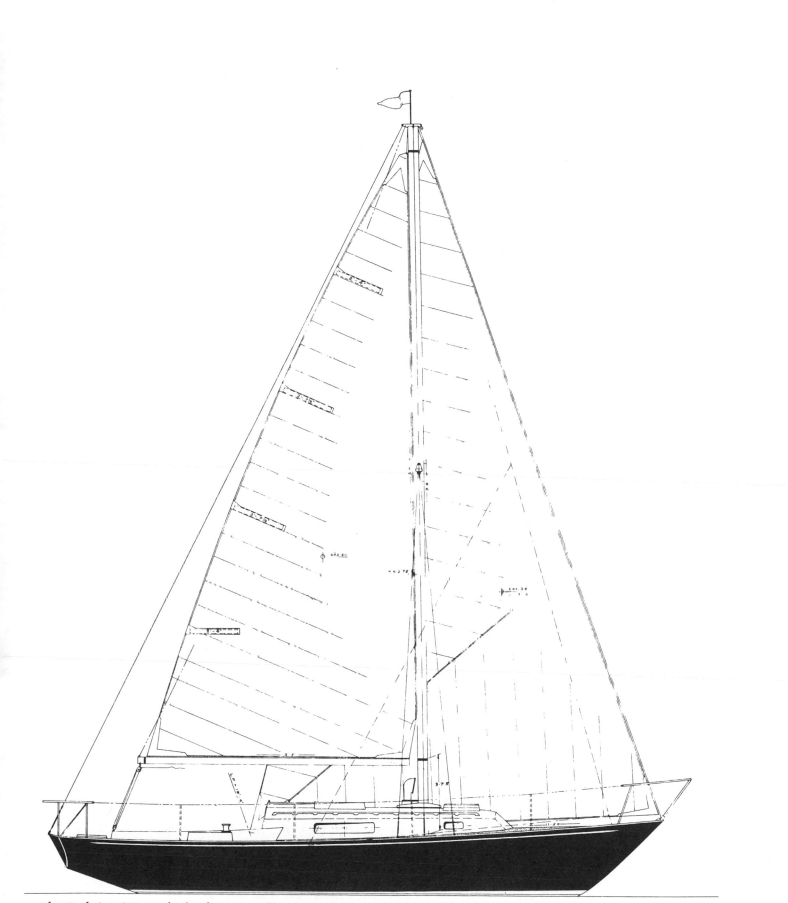

The Redwing 30's rig looks short, but the boat moves exceedingly well in light airs, and she is apt to be somewhat overburdened under full sail in fresh winds with a taller rig.

145

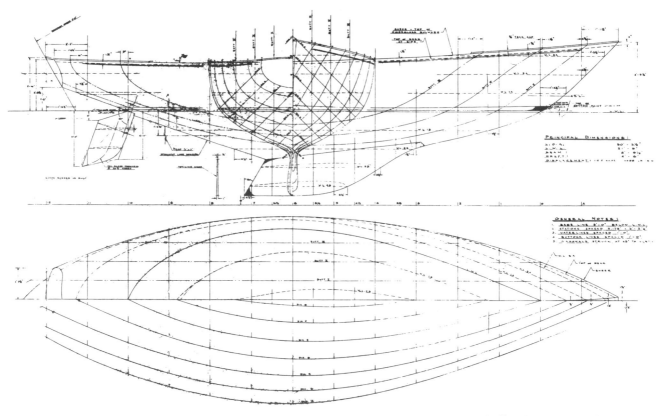

Lines of the Redwing 30 show her slack bilges and rather narrow waterline beam. The hull is fairly wedge-shaped, even though the stern has been drawn out to match the bow overhangs.

For a boat that's less than 22 feet on the waterline, the Redwing 30's main cabin is surprisingly roomy and quite comfortable for harbor living.

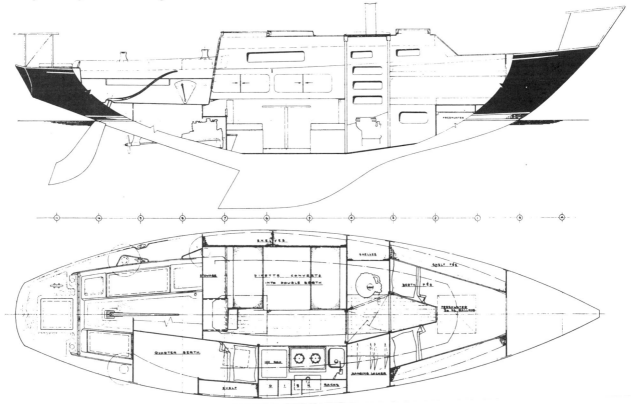

The Redwing 30 *Au Lieu,* owned by Parker Matthai, makes a pretty sight as she runs up the Chester River on Maryland's eastern shore. This boat has a mast one foot longer than standard.

of chubbiness, the Redwing 30 looks like a scaled-down model of a larger boat. Indeed, it has been said that she is a smaller version of the well-known 40-footer *Red Jacket,* which was designed by Cuthbertson & Cassian of Ontario, Canada, in 1966 to challenge the racing supremacy of the Cal 40s. *Red Jacket* was eminently successful, and so was a very similar C & C production design called the Redline 41. More often than not, the scaling of a boat up or down in size does not work, but an exception is the Redwing 30, although she is certainly not an exact scaled-down model. She simply bears a

strong family resemblance to her larger sisters. At any rate, this 30-foot version by C & C has proven tremendously successful not only as a club racer but also as a small family cruiser.

Her lines, drawn in 1967, show surprisingly slack bilges and narrow waterline beam, which would indicate some lack of stability; however, she has a high ballast-displacement ratio of 49 percent. Her low-aspect-ratio rig is also helpful to stability. A friend of mine added a taller rig to his Redwing 30, and the boat goes like a scalded cat in light airs, but she is a trifle tender in a breeze, even though only one foot was

147

The successful C&C-designed Red Jacket, *which inspired the design of the smaller Redwing 30. (Dan Hightower)*

added to the mast. The slack bilges help prevent pounding in a seaway, and they also minimize wetted surface.

The keel is a thin metal fin bolted to the hull, and the salient part is not very deep, but the turn at the garboards has a small radius that increases the effective area of the fin. Abaft the midship section, the keel is considerably thicker at the bottom than at the top. This slope to the side of the fin may help prevent the decrease in side force as the boat heels.

The hull appears deeper in profile than it does in the body plan. This is because there is an unusual thin, shallow skeg attached to and integral with the upper trailing edge of the keel. This feature probably helps alleviate cross-flow from the leeward to windward sides. Also, it may be somewhat helpful to directional stability, although a skeg just forward of the rudder would undoubtedly be more effective. Directional stability is not really a problem with this boat, however, because her ends are so well balanced and the keel is fairly long by modern standards.

The original rudder was a narrow scimitar-type spade, but the lines plan shows a much greater blade width with both edges parallel. Actually, there was an intermediate rudder too, which was a wider version of the original (see the accompanying photograph). I sailed on a Redwing 30 with the original rudder and then on the same boat after the intermediate type was installed. In my opinion, the original stalled out quite easily, but there was a noticeable improvement after the change to the intermediate. Presumably the third version is still more effective in preventing what the modern sailor calls a "wipe out," or an inadvertent rounding up on a spinnaker reach as a result of a stalled rudder.

The layout below is best for cruising in protected waters where the boat is anchored or moored every night. I say this because the dinette has seats that face fore and aft only, and the galley is not well arranged for cooking or washing dishes while heeled under sail. Nevertheless, the accommodations are splendid for

harbor living, and occasional overnight sailing with a small crew certainly imposes no real hardship.

There are several modifications I would make before taking the Redwing 30 offshore. First and foremost would be a substantial weather board or lower slide in the bottom of the companionway, since there is no bridge deck and the sill is less than six inches above the cockpit sole. Without a weather board, the cabin could be flooded by a boarding sea or possibly by an extreme knockdown in rough waters. Also, I would change the location of the bilge pump, which is normally installed inside a cockpit seat locker. Opening the locker to operate the pump in heavy weather could admit more water to the bilge than the pump could remove. Another improvement would be to round off the sharp corners on the cabin table and elsewhere below to minimize the risk of injury to the crew in rough weather. In addition, whether or not the boat will sail offshore, I would raise the head above the level of the waterline so there would be no danger that the boat would sink from a faulty check valve. It would not be a bad idea to install a vented loop on the discharge line to prevent the head from overflowing when the boat is heeled.

A lot of details of the Redwing 30 are highly commendable. Among these are recessed engine controls, proper seacocks, adequate hand rails above and below deck, toggles on all shrouds and stays, an S-curved tiller to minimize interference with the legs of crew members sitting in the cockpit, fiddles larger than those on many boats, more than two dozen stowage compartments, gasoline fill pipe on the side deck rather than on the cockpit sole, and a wet locker abaft the dinette. In regard to the latter feature, I would certainly recommend a waterproof material on the dinette seats to protect them from the wet foul-weather gear. Also, the quarter berth might be covered with the same material, since it is subject to some rain and spray coming down the companionway.

Construction is light but strong, and the workmanship by Hinterhoeller Ltd. of Ontario,

This is the second version of the Redwing 30's scimitar rudder.

Canada, seems to be superior to that of many cheap stock boats made in the U.S. The fiberglass hull is molded in one piece, which eliminates the centerline seam. When the keel is an integral hollow fin, I prefer that the hull be molded in two halves, because it is difficult to properly lay up the laminate inside a deep, narrow cavity; but the Redwing 30 presents no such problem, because her keel is a metal fin bolted

on. One trade-off for this arrangement is no bilge-water sump; thus, special attention should be paid to keeping the bilge dry. Decks have a core of end grain balsa for stiffness, lightness, and insulation.

The Redwing 30 is a sparkling performer. Although she is better, perhaps, in light than heavy airs, she is an all-around boat with a balanced performance on all points of sailing. Furthermore, she is easy to handle because of her well-balanced helm, fine maneuverability, and small rig. On the race course in the days of the CCA rule, she was almost always a threat, and she is still competitive under certain local rules and Performance Handicap racing. The Redwing 30 may even become a contender against some of the IOR boats under the new Measurement Handicap System (MHS) if that form of handicapping becomes widely accepted.

Some years ago when our handsome Ohlson 35 was beaten by a newer fast but ugly boat, my cousin, who was crewing for me, declared in utter disgust that his next boat was going to be the ugliest one he could find. Isn't it a shame that some of us now tend to identify speed with ugliness rather than beauty? There is nothing that would please me more than to see a pretty boat like the Redwing 30, under the MHS or any true handicap rule, take the measure of the ugly pumpkin seeds with their graceless sheers, bloated hulls, and butchered sterns.

20/ The Ohlson 38

A Boat for All Reasons

Length overall: 36 feet 8 inches (conventional stern)
37 feet 3 inches (reverse transom)
Length on waterline: 26 feet 6 inches
Beam: 10 feet 3 inches
Draft: 5 feet 6 inches
Sail area: 560 square feet
Displacement: 15,000 pounds
Designer: Einar Ohlson
Year designed: 1967

During World War II, the GIs would have elections periodically to determine the favorite pinup girl with whom they would most like to be marooned on a desert island. The ruminations involved were a popular pastime, but the choice among the likes of Grable, Hayworth, and Turner were difficult to say the least. It would be equally difficult for most yachtsmen to pick an all-time favorite boat, because there are so many beauties abounding with desirable features. Such a choice would not be easy for me, but if I had to pick one boat to own and sail for the rest of my life, it would most probably be the boat I now own, an Ohlson 38.

By no means have I sailed them all, but of the boats I am familiar with (and there are more than a few), the O-38 is my favorite. Of course, there are some boats that are faster, a few that are prettier, others that are more comfortable, still others that are easier to handle and maintain, and some that are better built and more seaworthy; but there are none I'm familiar with that have such a favorable combination of all these features.

Perhaps the most attractive feature of the O-38 is her sailing ability. She is responsive, beautifully balanced, and fast, especially when beating to windward in a moderate to fresh breeze. She is also the kind of boat that is very forgiving. When beating you can crack sheets a bit and bear off and foot, or you can strap in tight and pinch a little without much affecting the speed made good. Even with the sails not perfectly trimmed, the O-38 is fast, and many a time when we have sailed past other boats, we have noticed their crews looking us over and then checking the trim of their own sails.

It is a real pleasure to take experienced sailors out for a first sail on our O-38, *Kelpie* (named after the Alden yawl in Chapter 1), for they are invariably impressed. For example, this past summer we took out sailmaker Jim Allsop, *America*'s Cup 12-meter sailor and a former World's Champion in Star boats. Jim had been sailing on the hottest ton cup boats, and he was impressed with *Kelpie*'s stability. "In a ton cupper," he said, "we would have to shift to a smaller jib." Then when I left the wheel

There are several rig options for the Ohlson 38, including a high-aspect-ratio racing rig with inboard shrouds, but the rig shown here is the one the author prefers for cruising, and it has even proven fast on the race course.

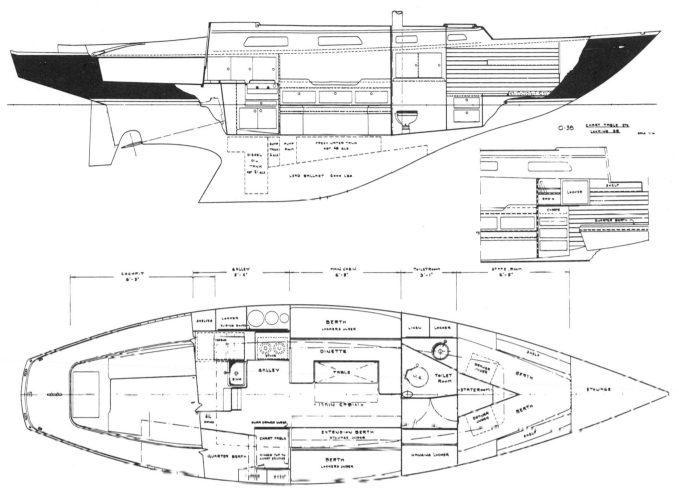

With her splendid galley, chart table, oilskin locker, dinette, roomy head, private stateroom forward, and numerous bunks, the O-38's accommodations satisfy just about every possible need. One could only ask that the W.C. be raised above the load waterline.

momentarily to go below and get a couple of beers, Jim was amazed at the way *Kelpie* steered herself with no one at the helm. He also admired her speed and lack of leeway. He carefully studied the wake and noted that it was dead aft, and there was not a trace of a slick to windward, indicative of leeway, which is sometimes noticeable on ton cuppers with extremely short keels. But I guess my cousin best summed up the O-38's performance when, after his first race aboard our boat, he wrote, "she is the sweetest boat I have ever sailed." About her only real weakness under sail is in very light airs. With moderate wetted surface and a sail-area-to-displacement ratio of about 15, she is no ghoster, but given two knots or so of breeze, she

comes to life in the most delightful way. Furthermore, her reasonable sail area and moderate displacement make her easy for one or two people to handle but without undue sacrifice to performance.

Designed in 1967 by the Swedish naval architect Einar Ohlson, the O-38 gives a hint of meter boat influence. Of course, Ohlson was a leading designer of 5.5-meter boats in the 1950s and early 60s, and the O-38 bears some superficial resemblance not only to his own meter boats but also to the famous Stephens-designed 12-meter *Intrepid*. Whether Mr. Ohlson was influenced by *Intrepid* or whether he anticipated that kind of configuration I cannot say, but the underwater profiles are not too dissimilar, with

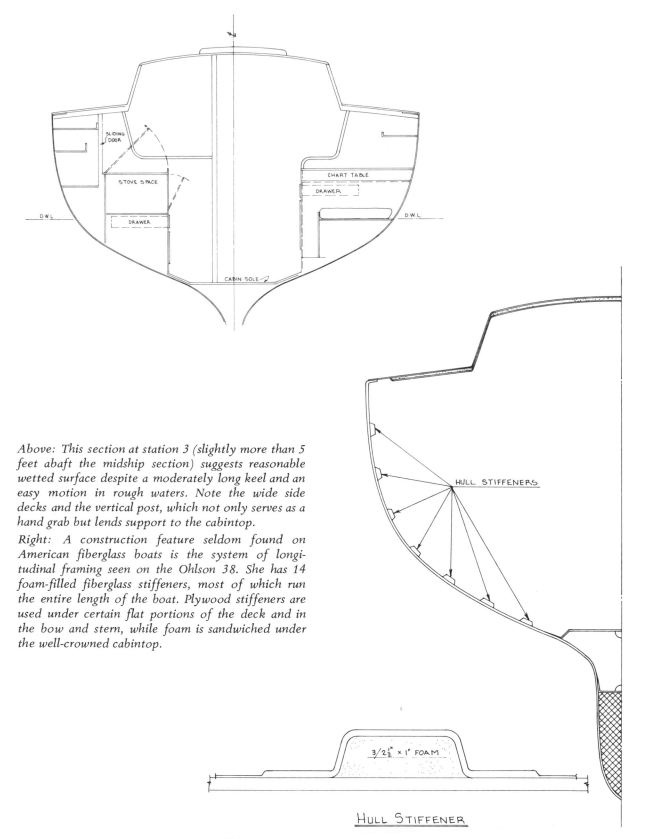

Above: This section at station 3 (slightly more than 5 feet abaft the midship section) suggests reasonable wetted surface despite a moderately long keel and an easy motion in rough waters. Note the wide side decks and the vertical post, which not only serves as a hand grab but lends support to the cabintop.

Right: A construction feature seldom found on American fiberglass boats is the system of longitudinal framing seen on the Ohlson 38. She has 14 foam-filled fiberglass stiffeners, most of which run the entire length of the boat. Plywood stiffeners are used under certain flat portions of the deck and in the bow and stern, while foam is sandwiched under the well-crowned cabintop.

A windward-side view of Kelpie in calm waters slipping along under her number one genoa. Her speed is deceptive because of her smooth wake. (Rip Henderson)

each having a swept forefoot, shark fin type of keel, kicker skeg abaft the keel, and small rudder. Each design also has a bustle, although the O-38's is less prominent. The analogy between the two boats cannot be carried too far, however, because the O-38 is obviously a relatively beamy cruising boat.

For about 10 years we owned a handsome Ohlson 35 (Mark I). This was Einar Ohlson's first ultra-popular cruising design, and it brought him wide recognition among U.S. cruising yachtsmen primarily because of the boat's outstanding racing successes. A further development of this hull was the Ohlson 36, which also had a great racing record in the early and middle 1960s. The only trouble with these boats was that they were built of wood and therefore were more expensive to maintain than fiberglass over a long period of time. A number of Ohlson enthusiasts requested fiberglass versions, and finally, in late 1967, the fiberglass 38-footer was introduced. An advertising brochure explained it this way: "For years now we have been asked why we have not brought out the well known and highly successful Ohlson 36 in fiberglass. If we did, we knew we would be backlogged with orders, because this lovely vessel proved itself a top racing winner and also a wonderful cruising boat. However, Mr. Ohlson, its designer in Sweden, resisted this temptation because he knew that as a result of his newest world-championship 5.5 meters and other recent successful racing boats, he could now design an even faster and more powerful hull. And so he held off until now, conducting further tank tests and carefully, meticulously developing and refining this new hull form to create an outstanding boat. The Ohlson 38 is the result."

The fiberglass hulls are molded by the highly respected Tyler Boat Company in England, and they are built to Lloyd's standards. I visited the Tyler Yard at Tonbridge, Kent, in 1975, and was most impressed with the operation. The O-38's hull is laid up entirely by hand, and clear gel coat is used on the bottom to give the laminator good visibility, thus helping prevent the entrapment of air in the laminations. According

to chemists used by Tyler, the lack of pigment also prevents adulteration of the resin and provides better protection against permanent immersion.

The O-38 hulls are made tremendously rigid with the use of 14 foam-filled fiberglass longitudinal stringers that run the full length of the boat or nearly so. Additional rigidity at the bow and stern is provided by glassed-in plywood vertical stiffeners to ensure that stays can be set up extra taut without distorting the hull. Further strength is provided by three full bulkheads and five half-bulkheads (made of Thames Marine plywood) and three fiberglass tanks (a 48-gallon water tank, 21-gallon fuel tank, and 8-gallon ice box sump) bonded in the hull and keel.

After completion of the molding, the hulls are shipped to a finishing yard, normally either Broderna Ohlson (Ohlson Brothers) in Sweden or Alexander Robertson & Sons Ltd. in Scotland. *Kelpie* was finished at the Swedish yard, and her wood interior of African mahogany is superb. There is very little wood above decks on our particular boat, because her cabin trunk and decks are fiberglass, but the O-38 can be had with a mahogany cabin trunk and teak decks if the owner does not object to having some extra maintenance.

Unfortunately, Einar Ohlson would not release the O-38's lines for publication, but he was kind enough to send me the drawing of a section that is located slightly more than five feet abaft amidships, plus the midship section. Also, a number of photographs showing the O-38 out of water give the reader a fairly good idea of her underwater shape. The slackish bilge with easy curves at the garboards and at the turn of the bilge reduces wetted surface, thus overcoming the frictional drag of a fairly long keel. The easy sections (together with moderate displacement) help give the boat a comfortable motion with minimal pounding and without the jerkiness so often experienced on beamy boats with hard bilges. A large radius at the turn of the bilge suggests some lack of power, and the O-38 heels fairly easily up to about 25 degrees, but then she

The author's O-38 Kelpie *under sail with her 150% genoa. The after window appears shorter than it really is because the sunlit companionway is seen through the after end of the window. (Fred Grell)*

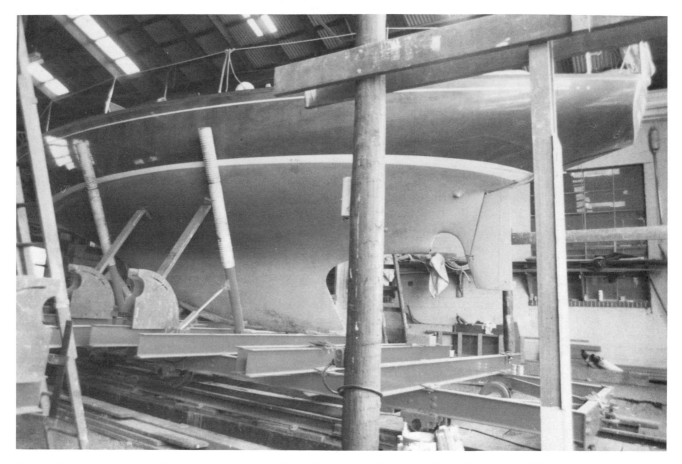

Kelpie *hauled out soon after she was purchased by the author. Note the shark-fin keel and kicker skeg, which help reduce cross flow. The small bump near the top of the rudder is the fathometer's transducer.*

becomes exceedingly stiff and rarely dips her rail.

To my way of thinking, the O-38 is extremely handsome. Her sheerline is fairly flat, but it gives the boat a sleek appearance, and it provides adequate freeboard amidships to help keep the rail out of water in a fresh breeze. Her overhangs may look old-fashioned to some, but to me they are very attractive, and they make sense. They not only supply a reserve of buoyancy at a boat's ends, but they allow a reduction of wetted surface when the boat is upright in light airs and an extension of sailing length when the boat is heeled in a breeze. I regret the modern fetish of reducing weight in a boat's stern at any cost, and I think the effectiveness of this practice in reducing pitching is somewhat over-rated. I remember racing our Ohlson against a

bobtailed competitor during an overnight race. We were closely matched until the increasing wind kicked up a nasty chop. The masthead light of our competitor took on the appearance of a metronome as she began to hobbyhorse, but our motion was much easier. We soon left our rival behind, pitching like that well-known robin that went "bob-bob-bobbin' along."

Other features that enhance the O-38's appearance are her moderate freeboard with bow definitely higher than the stern, her low cabin trunk sans doghouse, smallish cabin windows, and attractive cockpit coamings that curve around to meet a dodger coaming on the cabintop. The dodger coaming is not only attractive and useful in keeping water away from the companionway hatch, but it also adds strength to the cabintop.

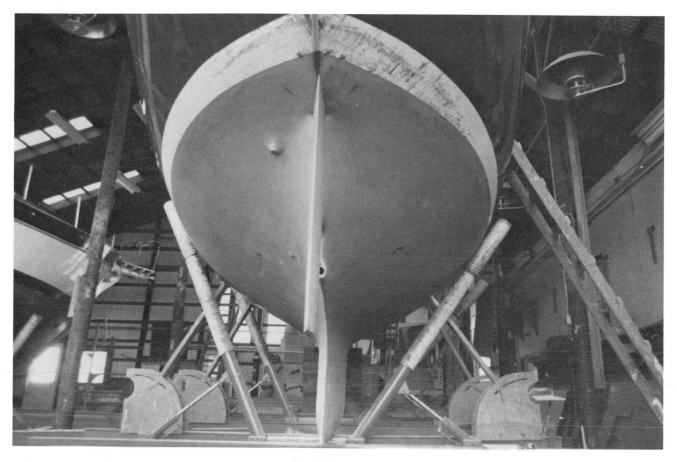

The stern view of Kelpie *shows her thin keel and the slightly swollen bustle area just forward of the rudder. Who forgot to clean off the boot-top!*

There are seven berths below, and these are more than what are needed on this size boat, but this gives great versatility to the accommodations. For instance, the after bunks can be used in rough weather at sea, and there are always two or three bunks to leeward when the boat is heeled. At anchor, the forward bunks afford good privacy in a well-ventilated stateroom. Two bunks in the main cabin are pilot berths, and these are handy for sail stowage when they are not needed for sleeping. The pilot berths are quite narrow (one is sliding), and they still leave room for a dinette to port, which converts to a bunk, and a sliding transom berth on the starboard side. I particularly like the sliding transom, because it allows variable width for the most comfortable sitting, sleeping in port, or sleeping at sea when narrow width is desirable. A quarter berth on the starboard side makes a splendid sea berth, or it can be used for stowing sails.

Unlike many boats of her size, the O-38 has a large chart table that can be used standing up or sitting down, and on the boat's opposite side is a fine U-shaped galley that allows the cook to be securely belted in during heavy weather. The galley has a three-burner stove with oven, a large stainless steel sink near the boat's centerline, and a three-compartment ice box that holds 125 pounds of ice. The O-38 has a large enclosed head that allows use of the full width of the boat if desired. There are numerous shelves throughout the boat and a total of 36 lockers, including a large hanging locker and one for oilskins near the companionway.

Auxiliary power is supplied by a 15-horsepower, two-cylinder Volvo diesel. Ours has proved reliable and amazingly economical. We are very much comforted by the safety of a diesel.

The Ohlson 38 may be had as a sloop or yawl, but I prefer the sloop, which is the way *Kelpie* is rigged. Not that I don't like yawls, but *Kelpie* is perfectly balanced, and I think the addition of a mizzen might cause a bit too much weather helm at times unless the main boom were cut off to make an extremely high-aspect-ratio mainsail, which would be less desirable, in my opinion. There are two sloop versions, the original with a low-aspect rig and outboard shrouds, and a modern version with tall rig and inboard shrouds. Of course, the modern rig allows close pointing, 67 degrees between tacks in a 12-knot wind according to advertising literature, but judging from the upwind performance of *Kelpie,* which has the outboard shrouds, I don't think her speed made good would be very much improved with a closer sheeting angle. We have found it seldom pays to strap the genoa in extra tight.

In 1975 my family (son, daughter, wife) and I sailed *Kelpie* from the Chesapeake Bay to the Azores. We experienced some very heavy weather, and this is when I learned firsthand that the O-38 is a splendid sea boat. During the heaviest gale we ran off under bare pole and then lay ahull for 15 hours. Our experience was described in my book *East to the Azores,* published by International Marine Publishing Company, Camden, Maine.

I was very interested to read of Clare Francis'

heavy-weather experiences aboard the Ohlson 38 *Robertson's Golly* when she crossed the Atlantic alone via the northern great circle route in the 1976 singlehander's race. Miss Francis encountered several gales, including a Force 10 screamer with 35-foot seas, and she, too, successfully lay ahull. Although some seamen disapprove of hulling in severe weather, I think a boat like the O-38 is quite well suited for the tactic in all but perhaps the most extreme conditions with very confused seas having spilling breakers. This suitability is due to the boat's having a low center of gravity and thus a good range of stability; the ability to self-right; a small cockpit well; a low, strong cabin trunk with small windows; some initial tenderness to allow heeling from wind pressure on the bare mast; and the kind of keel that allows considerable leeway when there is no forward speed so that the boat can retreat from beam seas without tripping.

At any rate, because of all the aforementioned qualities, the Ohlson 38 is my favorite boat. I have often said there is no such thing as a perfect boat, but the present *Kelpie* comes very close. Of course, there is no such thing as a perfect woman, either; but if I were to choose, like those World War II GIs, a favorite from the opposite sex (hmmm), I guess I'd stick with my wife. After all, she is probably the only one who could really endure and put up with all of my idiosyncrasies over the long haul. I'd better say so anyway, because she may get around to reading this.

21/ The Morgan 30

A Touchstone Boat

Length overall: 29 feet 11 inches
Length on waterline: 24 feet 2 inches
Beam: 9 feet 3 inches
Draft: 3 feet 6 inches
Sail area: 466 square feet
Displacement: 10,500 pounds
Designer: Charles E. Morgan Jr.
Year designed: 1967

Back in the late 1960s and early 1970s on the Chesapeake Bay, a group of Cal 2-30s had some keen racing against a group of Morgan 30s. As the skipper of one of the Cals, I developed a lot of respect for the M-30s. I was especially impressed during an overnight Cedar Point Race that involved a long beat down the Bay. Working the shore too closely, the leading Morgan ran aground and jammed her board when it was almost fully up. After she got free of the bottom, her board remained jammed, yet she still continued to sail upwind, and she hung on to us amazingly well all through the night.

The ability to make progress to windward without the help of a centerboard is a definite asset, in my opinion, because boards can jam, and on rare occasions they have even fallen out of their trunks. Furthermore, there should be sufficient depth of keel to ensure a reasonable range of stability and to allow ample rudder depth.

The Morgan 30, designed by Charles Morgan and produced by the Morgan Yacht Corporation, comes from a long line of centerboarders

beginning with the famous yawl *Paper Tiger*, which won the Southern Ocean Racing Conference in 1961 and 1962. This 40-foot yawl was the first complete boat that Morgan designed entirely on his own, and he had no more formal training in naval architecture than a few weeks in a correspondence course. Although she stirred up some controversy, *Paper Tiger* turned out to be an outstanding boat. She was soon followed by *Sabre*, the Columbia 40, and a smaller model called the Tiger Cub. From the *Tiger*'s offspring came such popular stock designs as the Columbia 31 and Morgan 34. With this ancestry, it is little wonder that when the Morgan 30 appeared in 1968, she was a highly developed centerboarder.

There are some differences between the M-30 and her forebears. The most obvious is that the keel is a bit shorter, and the rudder is a spade type. Normally, I prefer that the rudder be attached to the keel or to a skeg; but in the M-30's case, the free-standing spade does allow the rudder to be placed as far aft as possible, allowing minimal wetted surface with good rudder depth,

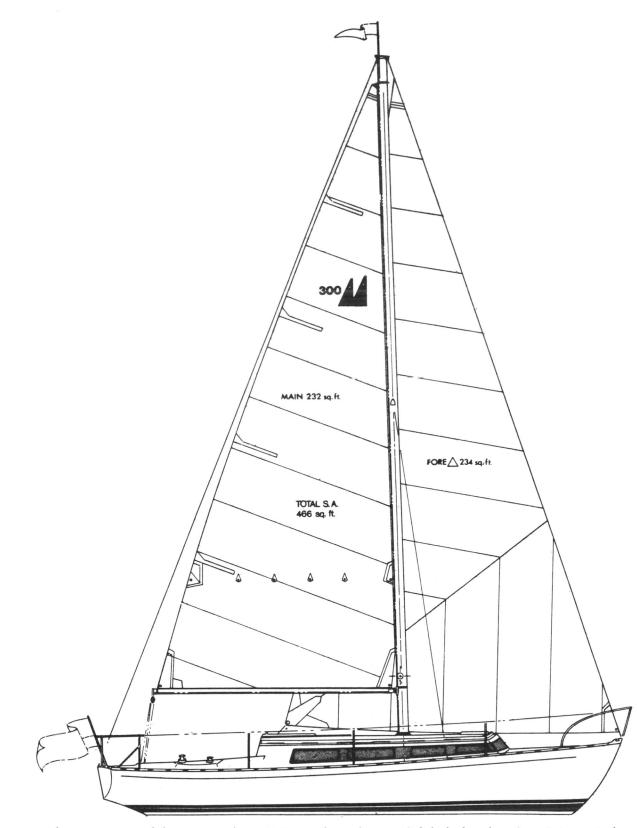

MAIN 232 sq. ft.

300 **M**

FORE △ 234 sq. ft.

TOTAL S.A.
466 sq. ft.

The aspect ratio of the Morgan Classic 300's rig, shown here, is slightly higher than that of the original Morgan 30. This is not helpful to stability, but there are advantages in light airs, and the main boom will now clear the backstay during a so-called Chinese jibe.

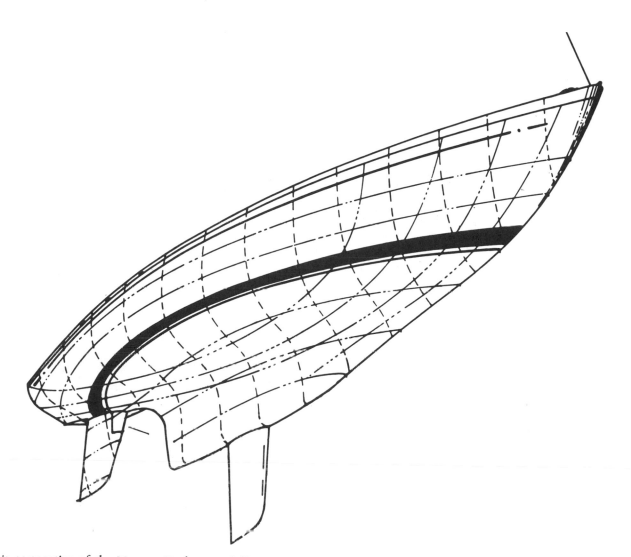

This perspective of the Morgan 30 shows a different spade rudder. On the actual rudder, the upper trailing edge is cut away, presumably to discourage ventilation.

and a powerful turning moment. At any rate, the rudder seems to work well, and when I sailed the boat one day in a light to moderate breeze, the helm had a good feel.

If the Morgan 30 has any fault under sail, it is that she is a trifle tender. When we raced her in our Cal 2-30, she would normally have to reef sooner than we when it breezed up. The M-30 has a reasonably high ballast-displacement ratio of almost 43 percent, but her beam is fairly modest for a centerboarder of her size, and her moderately shallow draft gives her a slightly higher center of gravity than a normal deep-keel, non-centerboard boat. Of course, her draft allows her good access to many attractive gunkholes. One of the boats we raced against eventually took off for the Bahamas, where she must have been ideal with her thin water suitability

combined with sufficient seaworthiness to cope with a chop or "rage" (breaking seas) kicked up by a norther.

With a sail area of 466 square feet (100 percent foretriangle), the M-30 has ample power in light airs. The sail plan shows a very long main boom, which gives the boat reaching power and balances the spinnaker on a run, thus avoiding any need for a cumbersome blooper. I would prefer, however, that the boom be just a little shorter, so that it would clear the permanent backstay in the event of a Chinese jibe. If you lay a pair of dividers along the boom (with one point at the gooseneck and the other point at the boom's outboard end) and swing the outboard point upward, you will see that the boom does not have to ride up very far to strike the backstay.

163

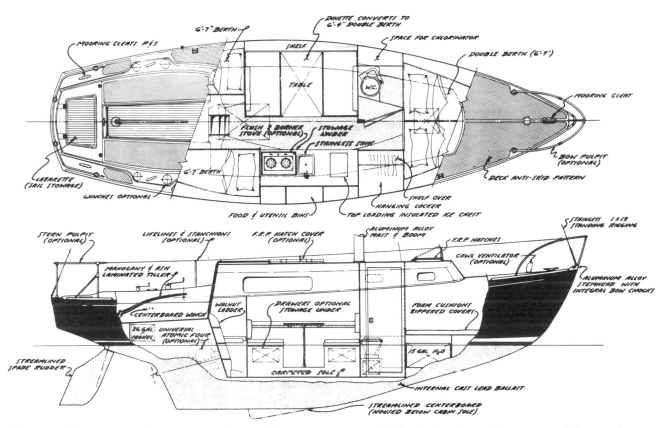

The original Morgan 30 has accommodations that are quite suitable for harbor living by a crew of four or less. A traditionalist might prefer the windows on the M-30 to those on the Classic 300.

The boat is quite attractive looking, even if she is not beautiful. Her bow is a little too snubbed for my taste, and the transom might be raked just a bit more; but the freeboard is moderate, there is some overhang aft, she has some sheer, and the cabin trunk is low. The windows on the original M-30 are not bad, but I'll have to admit that I dislike the extremely long look of the many windows on the latest version, which is called the Morgan Classic 300. They are made to look like one continuous stripe, which seems more appropriate for an automobile or an airplane. Perhaps I am old-fashioned, but there is little doubt that sailboat styling is getting rather "far out"—in some cases, perhaps, out of this world altogether, for recently I saw a radical new half-tonner with the hailing port "Krypton" painted on her stern. Unless I have forgotten my comics, that is the planet from which Superman came.

But back to the Morgan 30. She is a comfortable boat below with full headroom and four permanent bunks plus the ability to convert the dinette to an additional double berth. As I've opined before, a dinette that has only fore-and-aft facing seats, as on the original M-30, is not the most practical arrangement when the boat is heeled; so I would prefer either the L- or U-shaped dinettes offered on the Morgan Classic 300. On all M-30 arrangement options, the galley runs entirely along the starboard side, and this makes cooking difficult at high angles of heel, especially since the sink cannot drain on the port tack, and it may flood and overflow without a check valve on the outlet line. Nevertheless, the galley is adequate for harbor use or level sailing. The after galley option on the Classic 300 gives more sitting room in the main cabin, but there are several advantages in the midship galley: it is more convenient to the dinette, the ice box is

This view of the Morgan 30 under sail shows the well-rounded curve of the transom, which enhances its appearance.

more accessible, and the ice is farther away from the engine's heat. One feature of the accommodations that I particularly like is the completely enclosed head. On most boats of this size the head can only be closed off from the after cabin. Another attractive feature is the unusually large hanging locker for this size boat.

The quarter berths detract from stowage space under the cockpit seat lockers, but there is a fair-size lazarette aft. If I owned one of these boats, I might look into the possibility of enlarging the forward hatch, since it is a bit small for use as an alternate exit and also for accepting bagged sails being passed from the forward cabin to the foredeck. The companionway sill is very low, so a weather board should be fitted when the boat is sailed in exposed waters.

Despite some minor faults, many of which can be corrected, the Morgan 30 is an all-purpose vessel. She is fast, easy to handle, comfortable, inexpensive, and not bad looking. I have always considered her a touchstone boat—one that serves as a standard of comparison for any centerboard cruiser of her size.

22/ The Swan 43

An Adaptable Sloop

Length overall: 43 feet
Length on waterline: 31 feet
Beam: 11 feet 8 inches
Draft: 6 feet 8 inches
Sail area: 807 square feet
Displacement: 19,850 pounds
Designer: Sparkman & Stephens
Year designed: 1968

About the last thing I'd want to do would be to sail a stock boat having an IOR configuration to within less than 10 degrees of the North Pole. But if I were determined to attempt this feat in such a boat, the one I most probably would choose would be a Swan 43. This is the boat that carried E. Newbold Smith to the far north in 1976 and earned for him the Blue Water Medal awarded by the Cruising Club of America.

Smith's boat, appropriately named *Reindeer*, sailed from Newport, Rhode Island, to Newfoundland; then to Iceland and Norway via the Faeroes; and finally to Moffen Island off the northern coast of Spitsbergen, a point closer to the pole than any other American yacht had yet ventured. The return route passed through the notoriously stormy Denmark Straits to the ice-filled waters of southern Greenland. Although *Reindeer* was fortunate not to experience exceedingly bad weather in the Denmark Straits, she withstood some contact with ice, and underwent a grounding and inadvertent careening to a heeling angle of 65 degrees in Prins Christians

Sund, Greenland. Early in the voyage, she was given a dusting by four full gales but was only obliged to heave to for seven hours. At any rate, *Reindeer* was well tested, and she came through her rugged experiences with flying colors.

Actually, the Swan 43 should not be considered a true International Offshore Rule boat. I only said she had an IOR configuration, and at one time she did extremely well racing under that rule. She made her debut just before the advent of the IOR, but her designer is Olin Stephens, the rule's principal architect, who had some inkling of the kind of boat that would be well treated by the rule when the 43's lines were drawn. IOR type or not, though, the Swan 43 is a moderate boat with many wholesome features as compared with many of the latest IOR boats. For example, she has a relatively full bow, a bit of sheer with some freeboard forward, slackish bilges, moderate beam, some overhang aft for reserve buoyancy, and a rig that is not exceedingly tall. Although the keel is short, it has a raked leading edge to lessen damage from con-

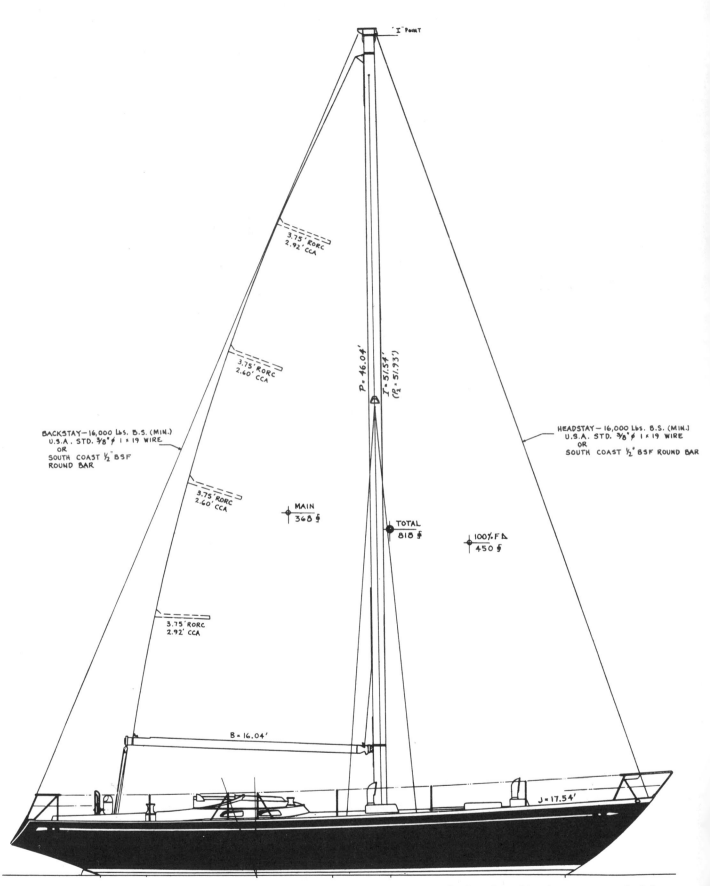

The aspect ratio of slightly less than 3 to 1 for the mainsail seems just about right for a boat like the Swan 43, which has good stability and is used for racing as well as cruising.

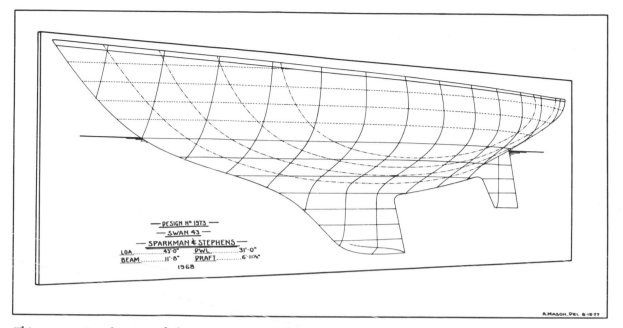

This perspective drawing of the Swan 43 shows her V'd sections abaft the keel, wide beam just above the LWL, and tumblehome amidships.

The accommodations of the Swan 43 offer plenty of bunks on the low side and also, of course, on the high side when it is necessary to satisfy the whims of a gung-ho racing skipper who insists on putting the off watch up to windward.

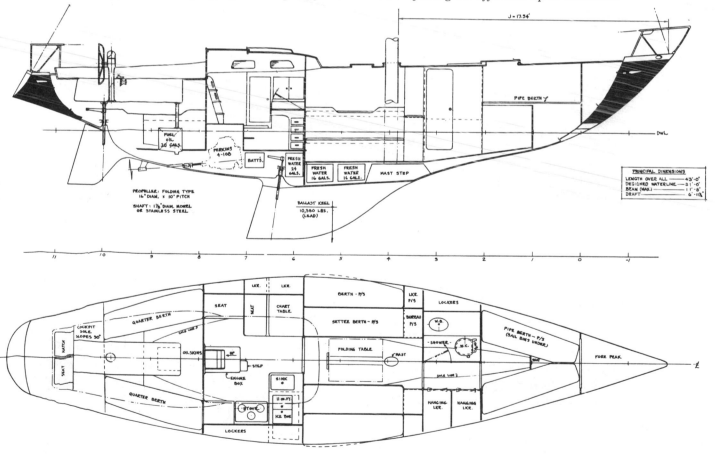

tact with flotsam, and the boat has rather deep V'd sections abaft the keel and a skeg to help provide directional stability.

Furthermore, the Swan 43, sold as the Palmer Johnson 43 in America, is exceptionally well built by Nautor Ky of Finland. Nautor has a reputation for tremendous pride in craftsmanship, and the company is extremely anxious to please. In a *Yachting* magazine article about Nautor (November 1974) it was written that Rod Stephens was inspecting the plug for the deck mold of an early Swan design, and he was not convinced that the winch pads were in the best possible location. Within several hours, the pads were cut off and relocated, whereas another builder had refused to perform a comparable relocation job because "it would cost thousands." The Swan hulls are built of fiberglass to meet or exceed Lloyd's standards, and for the most part they are fitted with extensive stiffeners that are quite often foam-filled to provide great strength and rigidity without excessive weight. As one might expect, the wood finish and joinerwork are superb. The 43's cabin sole is made of teak and holly, the cabinets are of teak and exotic koto wood, while the deck is teak notched into a king plank and laid over fiberglass.

An unusual feature shown on the plans of the Swan 43 is the trim tab at the trailing edge of the keel. This device is similar to a flap on an airplane wing, and its main function is to enhance the lift characteristics of the keel and thus improve windward ability. Lift is improved because the tab can increase the angle of attack at the keel's after edge, and it will add some camber so that the water flow will speed up and lower the pressure on the keel's windward side. The trim tab also can correct helm balance, especially on a reach when the sails' center of thrust is far outboard of the hull's center of resistance, creating a long moment arm that tends to turn the boat into the wind. Some designers feel that using the tab to correct for balance is inadvisable, because it costs too much in drag, yet it can relieve the helm when

cruising. Rod Stephens told me that he thinks the trim tab is an unnecessary complication, but on the other hand, he concedes that it might be handy for emergency steering, since the tab is controlled by a wheel next to the main steering wheel. Most of the tabs are now fixed in place so they can never be used, primarily because racing skippers don't think the tabs are worth their cost in rating and complication, and when this is the case, a rudder deeper than the original is recommended.

There is no doubt that Swan 43s and PJ 43s are fast. Their victories have included class wins in such prestigious events as the Bermuda Race, Chicago-Mackinac, Annapolis-Newport, and Marblehead-Halifax Races. Furthermore, these boats have been used in the Admiral's Cup series, the well-known international team races for offshore boats.

Sailing across the Atlantic from the Bahamas to England for the Admiral's Cup races, *Firebrand II,* a PJ 43, ran into extremely heavy weather in the notorious Bermuda Triangle. For more than two days she encountered gale force winds with gusts higher than 60 knots; yet her crew never felt obliged to heave to. Part of the time they ran off under reduced sail at speeds often exceeding 10 knots, and once they were pooped by a huge sea. It not only filled the cockpit, but torrents of water cascaded down the companionway, despite the fact that the boat has a high bridge deck. No real damage was inflicted during the lengthy gale.

Windward performance of the boat is unquestionably excellent, yet this type of hull with its moderately narrow V'd sections aft has been criticized by at least one leading designer as not having the best form for running off in fresh winds. Compromises, of course, are always necessary, and it is true that the Swan 43 may give up a little off-the-wind ability in exchange for excellence on a beat. Nevertheless, the experience of *Firebrand II* shows the boat is surprisingly manageable downwind even when scudding before a heavy gale. The moderate bustle helps tame the stern wave, and it adds

The go-anywhere Reindeer after finishing a Bermuda Race. Her retroussée stern is much more handsome than many, because there is some overhang aft and the slope of the transom is not extreme. (Bermuda News Bureau)

some buoyancy aft, which is helpful to the downwind performance of boats with fine sterns.

I like the height of the rig as shown in the accompanying sail plan. Unlike many of the most modern IOR boats, the original Swan and PJ 43s don't have extremely tall rigs, which can often cause tenderness and handling problems, yet there is sufficient height for power in light airs and efficiency to windward. The mainsail has an aspect ratio of approximately three to one, and it seems to me this is quite appropriate for a stiff racing-cruiser of this size. There is sufficient luff length to provide high lift, and the boom is sufficiently short to allow an ample roach without its fouling the backstay; yet the boom is long enough to allow a mainsail foot length that will balance the spinnaker on a run reasonably well and thus obviate any real need to set a blooper. Another argument against extremely high aspect ratio sails is that they are difficult to make, and they are not easy to control in terms of achieving optimal shape for all conditions. The largest headsails are not easy for a small crew to handle, but the boat is sufficiently smart that she can be sailed quite effectively with smaller jibs.

There are plenty of bunks in the Swan and PJ 43s. With two pipe berths forward, two pilot berths and two settee berths in the main cabin, a quarter berth on the port side aft, and an optional quarter berth to starboard, a good-size crew can sleep comfortably under almost any condition. Many boating writers, including myself, have criticized boat producers for trying to cram an inordinate number of bunks into a small hull. However, it makes sense for an offshore boat to have ample berths aft and on both sides, because it is safer and more comfortable to sleep on the leeward side and as close as possible to the boat's pitching axis when under sail at sea.

The cabin trunk is very short, which prohibits trunk windows in the main cabin, but plenty of light is provided by numerous deck prisms. As is customary on S&S yachts, there are a lot of hatches and Dorade vents to provide fresh air below, but surprisingly, the accompanying plans don't show a vent from the head. Comfort and convenience features include a hot and cold freshwater pressure system, a shower in the head, a heating stove in the main cabin, and a large chart table with navigator's seat. There is a splendid galley with deep stainless steel sink, an ice box of approximately 11 cubic feet, and a three-burner stove with oven. Lockers abound, and low ones that could be wet by bilge water are watertight.

Not long ago I saw *Reindeer* at a Cruising Club of America get-together on the Chesapeake. During a race prior to the rendezvous, she showed her heels to some fine ocean racers, and she turned out to be the overall winner. I could not help but admire this handsome vessel that had previously sailed to within 45 miles of the polar cap. She seemed remarkably adaptable to any environment—from the warm, calm waters of the Chesapeake to the hostile, ice-packed seas of the far north.

23/ Amee

An Innovative Ketch

> Length overall: 37 feet 5 inches
> Length on waterline: 31 feet 6 inches
> Beam: 11 feet 4 inches
> Draft: 4 feet 1½ inches
> Sail area: 700 square feet
> Displacement: 14,800 pounds
> Designer: Edward S. Brewer
> Year designed: 1968

We have a dog named Amee that I call a double-ender, because she greets us with a licking tongue and wagging tail. So how can I resist writing about a double-ended boat named *Amee*? Actually, this boat is not a true double-ender, because she has a round rather than a pointed stern. At any rate, she is a most unusual boat, and I think she adds more than a little variety to this book.

Some of her unusual features, aside from the distinctive stern, are: the snubbed clipper bow; flaring topsides; unique underbody; bow cockpit; asymmetrical center cockpit; a steering pedestal that includes controls for three movable appendages and a remote crank for the sheet winches; an unconventional ketch rig for racing with some offbeat details such as a folding spinnaker pole; trailboards with a small figurehead; a unique layout below that includes such innovations as a saloon table that is raised and lowered with a winch and V-berths with hinged bottoms giving access to sail bins; and last but not least, double trim tabs on the keel so that both of its ends can be moved.

Amee was designed in 1968 by Ted Brewer for John B. Lawson, who had a lot of special requirements. Mr. Lawson is quite an original thinker who invented many of the unique mechanical devices used aboard the boat. His requirements included shoal draft, ease of handling for a small crew, comfortable accommodations with maximum privacy, the ability to cruise almost anywhere, sufficient speed for occasional racing, and a handsome if somewhat unconventional appearance.

In my opinion, this boat is about the minimum size for a center-cockpit/double cabin trunk arrangement. The usual purpose of this arrangement is to afford maximum privacy for two couples or perhaps one couple with children; but on a smaller boat, privacy is difficult to achieve no matter what the plan, especially if there is only one head, and the disadvantages of the center cockpit outweigh its advantages. Some of these disadvantages are: detraction from the boat's appearance due to having a large cabin trunk aft, poor visibility from the helm, and often cramped accommoda-

Amee's ketch rig may not be the most efficient to windward, but it provides plenty of sail area while keeping the center of effort low, and, of course, individual sails are easy for a small crew to handle.

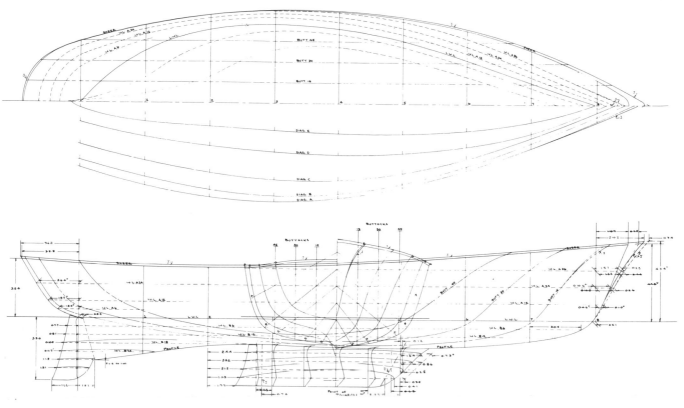

Lines of Amee show her shallow hull with full stern and unusual (for a sailboat) flaring sections forward.

tions because the cabins are in the relatively narrow ends of the boat rather than near her point of maximum beam. Another problem with the center cockpit is that it is very often wet, and the after companionway can be soaked from spray blowing aft when sailing upwind.

On *Amee* the problem of the cramped after cabin has been alleviated without the need of a large, ugly cabin trunk or a huge transom by using the round stern, which affords both volume and good looks. Ted Brewer has at least partially solved the wet cockpit problem with the flaring topsides, especially the considerable (for a sailboat) flare at the bow.

My only real objection to *Amee*'s arrangement is that the after head is not enclosed. It seems to me this might be possible with a slightly longer cabin trunk, elimination of the wash basin, and a different berth arrangement. Also, I would prefer a vertical (rather than raked) forward end of the after cabin trunk, for the rake

must add to the difficulty of keeping rain out of the companionway.

Amee has sufficient beam that there is not a problem with cramped accommodations in the saloon. The deep U-shaped dinette with its unusual crank-down table is a comfortable and cozy arrangement in the harbor, although it might be difficult to use at sea when the boat is heeled. Ordinarily, I don't like a galley for offshore use that runs fore and aft on one side of the boat, but *Amee*'s is better than many, because it is slightly indented between lockers so that a cooking belt can be rigged. There seems to be ample capacity for ice, since there is a box in the cockpit as well as one in the galley. A highly desirable feature is the chart table, but it is a folding type, and I presume it limits use of the berth under it. I'm very much in favor of the oilskin locker near the companionway, although it is important to have a really waterproof cover on the seat in front of the locker.

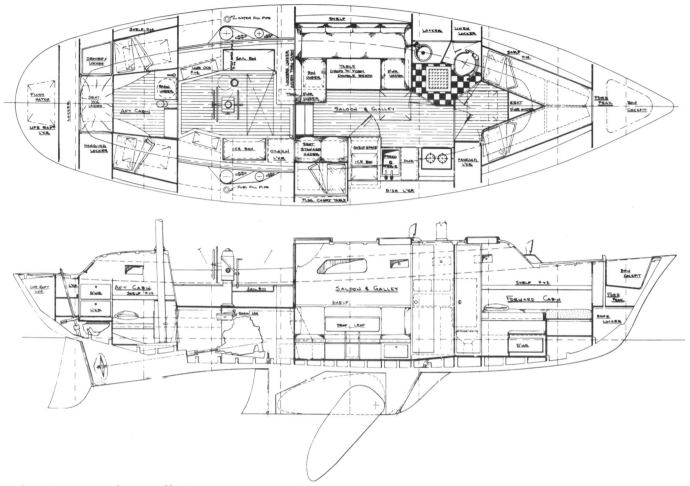

Amee's accommodations afford maximum privacy for a boat of this size. The profile plan shows several unique features, such as the bow cockpit and articulated keel.

The forward stateroom affords almost as much privacy as the after cabin, because it has its own door to the large head, and the door to the saloon can be kept closed, if desired, without restricting ventilation to any great degree. The forward cabin has its own Dorade vent and cabintop hatch, while the saloon has a similar means of ventilation in addition to the companionway hatch. The forepeak/rope locker arrangement is quite unusual, especially with the bow cockpit well above. I suppose the main value of the well is for stowing an anchor and/or lowering a headsail into the well.

The lines show a rather shallow hull with little deadrise and the maximum fullness well abaft amidships. It might seem that with the full buoyant stern, fine entrance, and clipper bow

with little overhang, the boat might tend to root or bury her bow in certain conditions, but the great flare forward gives her reserve buoyancy. Ted Brewer holds with the theory that the wedge-shaped hull with fine bow and full stern is far more resistant to pitching than a symmetrical hull, because the forward end of the wedge is less prone to excitement, while there is a damping effect aft. If this theory is true, and I haven't much doubt that it is if the hull form is not extreme, *Amee* must behave well in a seaway and show little tendency to hobbyhorse, provided excessive weights are not allowed to accumulate in her ends.

Of course the unique feature of *Amee's* underbody is the shoal-draft keel with double trim tabs. Some years ago designer Halsey Herre-

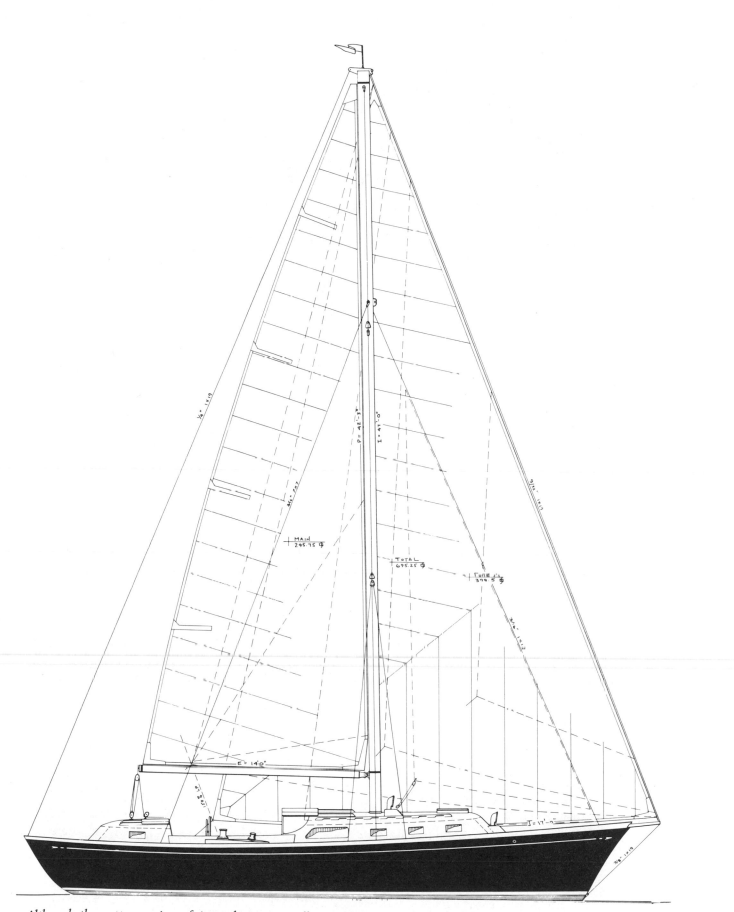

Although the cutter version of Amee has a very tall rig, stability should not suffer very much, because she has been given a deeper keel, which will lower the hull's center of gravity for a given weight of ballast. She might be more tender initially but will pick up stability at increasing angles of heel.

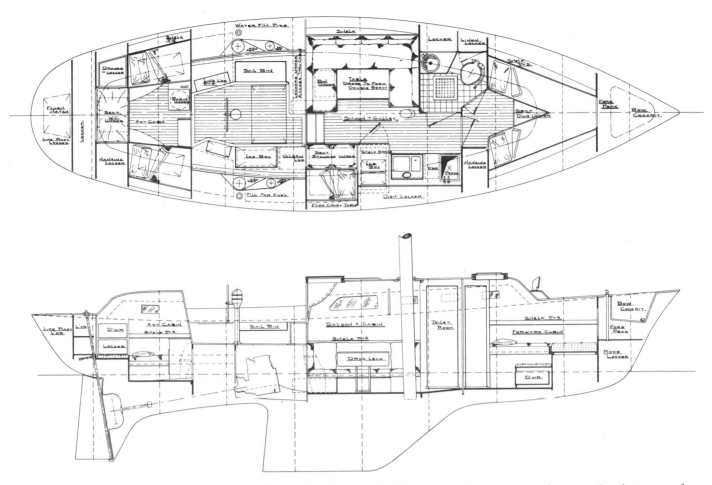

Accommodations of the cutter do not differ greatly from the ketch version of Amee *except for some details in way of the mainmast and the galley arrangement. The cutter's different rudder and skeg should improve steering, although the rudder would probably be even more effective for sailing with a smaller propeller aperture.*

shoff had great success using a double-tab rudder, which he called an articulated rudder, so I suppose it could be said that *Amee* has an articulated keel. The main purpose of the tabs is to give the keel some camber for added lift to prevent excessive leeway. My understanding is that the forward tab is turned to the same side as the after tab, but it is not turned as far. One might think the tabs would be more effective on a high-aspect-ratio keel, but if the boat had deep draft, the articulated keel would not be needed. I asked Ted Brewer if the tabs really worked, and he assured me that they did, but he said they were later fixed because of a severe penalty under the Mark II version of the International Offshore Rule. Nevertheless, *Amee* is a belt and suspenders boat, in that she has a centerboard as well as the trim tabs. When more lateral re-

sistance is needed in deep water, the board can be lowered, and the tabs are not really necessary.

There is also a deep-keel version of *Amee* that was designed for William D. Kinsey in 1975. This boat is cutter rigged, and her plans are also shown. She has a very tall rig but can stand up to it well because of her powerful sections, broad beam, and hard bilges. Then too, the deep keel, which increases the draft from 4 feet 1½ inches to 5 feet 7½ inches, lowers the ballast and thus the center of gravity. For extensive offshore work and/or racing, I would prefer the deep keel for the best possible performance to windward and the highest range of stability.

Both versions carry ample sail, about 700 square feet, but obviously the high-aspect-ratio cutter rig will be more efficient to windward.

Amee boiling along on a quarter reach. Notice that the mizzen has been lowered to avoid blanketing the mizzen staysail.

Still, the ketch-rigged *Amee* is no slouch, and Ted Brewer tells me she can pass smart-sailing 40-footers on a reach. Of course, the ketch rig divides the total sail area into smaller individual sails, but there are a number of disadvantages to the normal ketch. Aside from the fact that the mizzen is backwinded when sailing to windward, the mainsail is often blanketed by the mizzen when running. In fact, Eric Hiscock once noted that the main on his *Wanderer IV* was becoming badly chafed on the shrouds from being alternately filled and then blanketed by the mizzen when the wind was on the quarter.

Amee's ketch rig is not entirely typical, however, partly because her mizzen is slightly smaller than the norm. She is almost a yawl with the mizzen pushed forward, and therefore she does not have quite the same problems of the typical ketch, at least not to the same degree. Also, she has an unusually large foretriangle for a ketch. This allows big headsails and a well-shaped spinnaker, so that the mizzen can be lowered without undue sacrifice to sail area when there is harmful interaction between the mizzen and main and/or it is desirable to move the center of effort forward.

There are good arguments against bowsprits, but they are often preferred on boats with clipper bows, if only for aesthetic reasons. Of course, the main objection is lack of security for the crew handing a jib; however, the sprits on *Amee* and her cutter-rigged sister are not at all the long variety commonly referred to as "widowmakers." One nice feature of a bowsprit is that it is handy for catting a fisherman's anchor. I notice that *Amee* has a chock just abaft the stem. This is fine for a dock line, but I prefer that the anchor rode be led to the end of the bowsprit when possible, so that it will not chafe on the bobstay.

The original *Amee* was built of wood with a laminated mahogany keel and white pine strip planking covered with fiberglass. The newer deep-keel version, however, was built of fiberglass over Airex foam.

This design concept might not be every sailor's choice, but it offers great versatility, and the unusual details alone make it worthy of careful study. As an old-timer once said about a particularly innovative boat, "She has more wrinkles than an elephant's trunk." The same could be said about *Amee*.

24/ The Ranger 26

Not Much to Hold Her Back

Length overall: 26 feet 3 inches
Length on waterline: 21 feet 9 inches
Beam: 8 feet 8 inches
Draft: 4 feet 4 inches
Sail area: 322 square feet
Displacement: 5,860 pounds
Designer: Gary W. Mull
Year designed: 1968

After racing from Newport, Rhode Island, to Bermuda and back in a Ranger 26, William G. Homewood proposed an amusing plan for a home study course to prepare greenhorns for offshore sailing. Parts of the program are described as follows:

"First, at home, you should go into the bed room fully dressed and pour a bucket of water over your head. Put on your foul weather gear and harness. Prop up one side of the bed to an angle of 20 degrees, then pour a bucket of water over the pillow and bedding. . . . Engage the services of a forklift (and operator) who will lift one corner of your house up into the air six feet and then let it drop down with a bang. He should do this all night long, intermittently without warning. Now go to bed. After one hour of sleep it will be time to get out of bed, open the sliding door to balcony, and peer out (checking the sails). At this moment a friend, well-hidden, should throw a bucket of water onto the back of your head. Your jacket hood must be in the off position, as this will allow the water to run down your neck. . . . As you turn to go back

into the bedroom another well-hidden friend should club you over the head with a two-by-four. This simulates head blows from bulkheads. . . ."

Judging from Bill Homewood's training program, it seems that his Ranger 26, named *Union Jack*, was a rather wet and uncomfortable boat on her Bermuda trip. But let us consider the conditions. For two and a half days, Force 7 winds, gusting above 40 mph, were on the nose or forward of the beam, and the seas were described as being "reminiscent of the Swiss Alps." *Union Jack* was driven hard under a double-reefed main with a 90 percent jib and later a 50 percent jib. Homewood said his boat would repeatedly shoot up a wave and land with a resounding crash on the other side. *Union Jack* was leaking quite a bit at the hull-deck connection, but when you consider that the Ranger 26 is a moderately light fin-keeler (weighing less than 6,000 pounds) that was never intended for rugged passages offshore, she did amazingly well. She not only held together and proved easily manageable by a crew of one; but also she

181

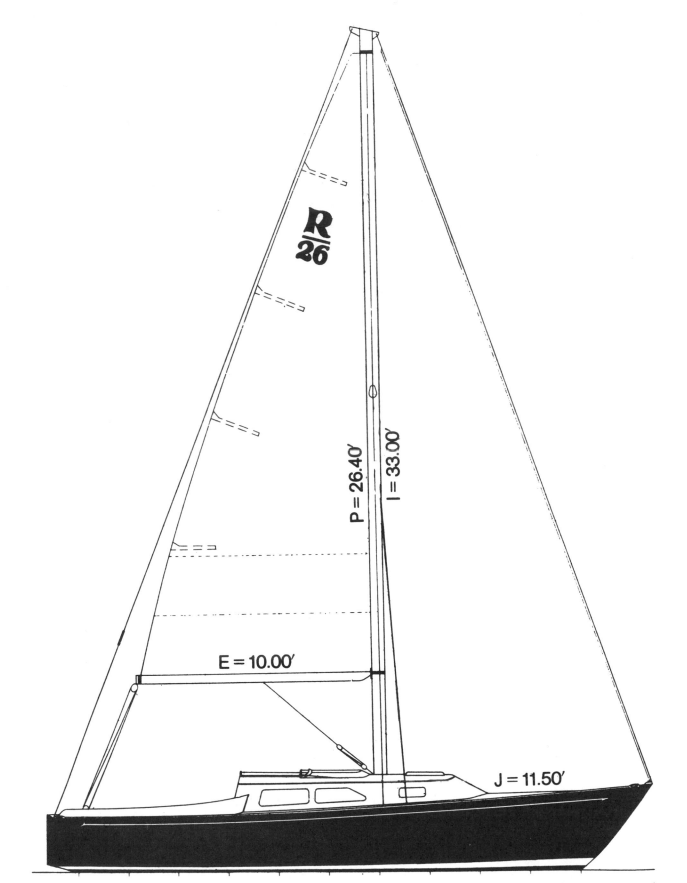

The sail plan of the Ranger 26 shows the unusually high main boom, which helps the rating a bit and enables the effective use of a permanent vang. The high boom also helps prevent the crew from getting beaned, but Bill Homewood might think an occasional blow from the boom would be good training for ocean racing.

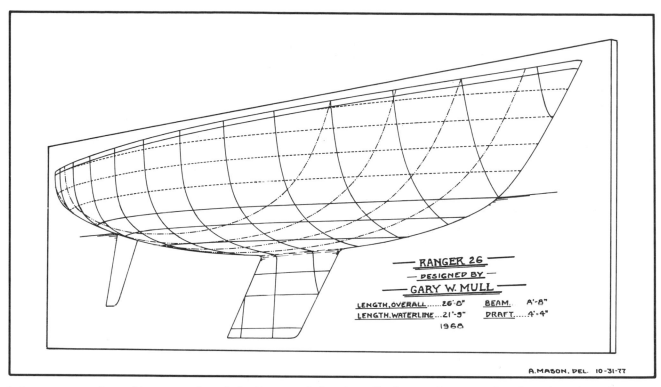

RANGER 26

DESIGNED BY

GARY W. MULL

LENGTH. OVERALL......26'-0"   BEAM.   8'-8"
LENGTH. WATERLINE...21'-9"   DRAFT.....4'-4"

1968

A. MASON. DEL. 10-31-77

It is easy to see from this perspective of the Ranger 26 that she will ride over the seas rather than plow through them.

showed remarkable speed in completing the singlehanded leg to Bermuda in 5 days, 7 hours, 47 minutes, and completing the doublehanded leg returning home in 5 days, 15 hours, 55 minutes. Her respective finishing positions for the two races were second in class/third in fleet and first in class/second in fleet.

Designed by Gary W. Mull in 1968, the Ranger 26 is built in Costa Mesa, California, by Ranger Yachts. An article in *Yachting* magazine (February 1969) related that Gary Mull was the first designer to have one of his model yachts surf in the Stevens Institute testing tank. The Ranger 26 has this unusual ability to surf or at least surge, and yet she is an all-around performer with upwind as well as downwind excellence. One of the many successful Ranger 26 skippers, John Tsirimokas (otherwise known as John X), described the performance of his boat as follows: "She's very good in light stuff, holds her own in medium winds, and comes alive again in heavy wind."

Bill Homewood wrote me that his Ranger 26 is well balanced and handles very well in most conditions, but that it is important to properly match her sail to the wind conditions. Over-canvasing even moderately can cause her to knockdown or broach to.

Bill wrote that he is *"very, very* pleased" with *Union Jack*'s performance, but he is not overjoyed with her construction. Her main problems on the Bermuda trip came from the leaking hull-deck joint and a weak main bulkhead. For such rugged sailing, she seems to need more than the numerous self-tapping screws that hold the deck and hull together. Personally, I would prefer a bonded and bolted joint. Homewood says he knows several Ranger 26 owners who have had trouble with the bulkhead that supports the mast. He recommends reinforcing the bulkhead with a stainless steel girder. As I said before, the boat is not really intended for distance ocean racing, but I would like the reinforcement even for sailing in sheltered waters, for there is always the possibility of being caught by a bad squall, and any kind of serious racing can subject a boat to a lot of stress.

A glance at the perspective drawing of the Ranger 26 shows why she is so fast. There's just not much under water to hold her back. Her

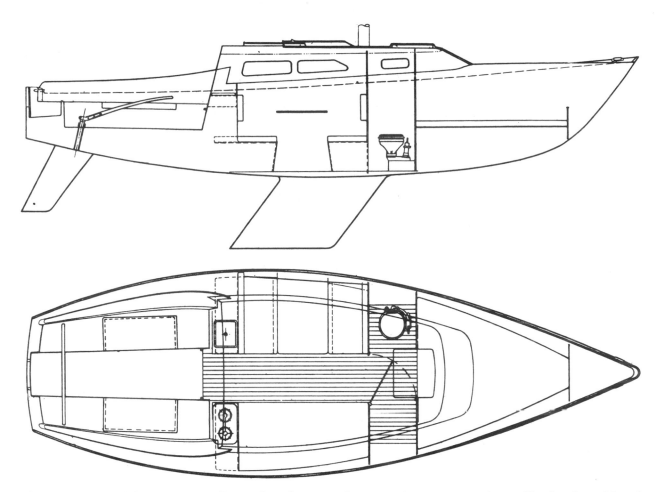

The ample beam of the Ranger 26 allows a lot of room in the main cabin. Notice on the profile plan that, although the spade rudder is swept back, the rudder stock is nearly vertical.

shallow bilge, wide beam, and flat run aft help give her the ability to surf. Given the right conditions, it seems that the boat can almost plane, for Bill Homewood reported a 24-hour run of 183 miles, which is truly remarkable for a boat with a waterline length of less than 22 feet. There is no skeg to help the boat track, but the bolted-on fin keel is fairly long at its bottom, and this may very well be helpful to directional stability. Incidentally, the keel shape allows more or less constant curvature on each side for reasonable lift with minimum draft, and of course the long bottom keeps the center of gravity low. The free standing spade rudder is quite swept back, but the rudder stock is nearly vertical, and my feeling is that this is helpful to steering control when the boat is heeled.

The Ranger 26 carries ample sail for a boat of her displacement. The main boom is unusually high, and this feature seems counter to modern theory as seen on the latest 12-meter boats. The *America*'s Cup racers have their main booms so low that the deck acts as an end plate to inhibit air flow under the boom from the sail's high pressure side to its low pressure side. On the other hand, there is another theory that when a boat is heeled, the windward rail causes much turbulence, and a high boom is preferable to keep the foot of the mainsail in clear air. At any rate, the high boom on the Ranger 26 prevents the crew from getting "beaned" when tacking or jibing, it enables an efficient on-center boom vang to be permanently rigged, and it helps keep the rating reasonable.

Another possible benefit of the high boom is that it sometimes allows effective use of a staysail under a large jib. One of the most successful R-26 skippers, Walter Fink, frequently used a double-head rig on his Ranger 26 *Kalkun.* An overlapping staysail can easily be carried under a

184

A Ranger 26 running off under radial head spinnaker and tallboy staysail. Even though she is moving very fast, the quarter wave seems to be quite flat.

high clewed reaching jib, and occasionally the staysail is even effective under a genoa, due in part to the high boom, which minimizes the harmful effect of backwind against the mainsail. The height of the mainsail allows a low-cut staysail to be sheeted well inboard to open up the slot between the two headsails. Incidentally, Bill Homewood carries a double grooved headstay, and he has worked out a system whereby he can change jibs quite easily singlehanded.

In addition to being fast, the Ranger 26 is also a comfortable boat. There are two cabins with a large double berth forward and a four-person dinette on the port side aft with a berth opposite on the starboard side. Seats for the dinette face fore and aft only, so they are difficult to use when the boat is heeled on the port tack; nevertheless, the table can be lowered quite easily so that the dinette can be converted to a berth, which makes a better seat when there is a considerable angle of heel. It would be nice if the head could be completely closed off from the forward cabin, but that is a lot to ask for a boat of this size. At least there is a door between the two cabins, and this makes the head private with respect to the after cabin. For a 26-foot boat, the galley is sizable, with a reasonable ice box, stainless steel sink, and two-burner stove. Although the stove faces the "wrong way" so that it can't gimbal properly, a one-burner Sea Swing stove can be mounted.

The cockpit is comfortable, and there are ample lockers under the seats for stowing sails and other gear. The well is self-draining but the companionway sill is quite low, so it should be fitted with a heavy lower slide for any offshore work. The boat is powered with an outboard motor. A small cutaway in the transom allows the outboard to be mounted low enough to properly submerge the prop and there is a safety well just forward of the transom to give protection from following seas. For the most rugged sailing, however, I might want a filler piece to close off the cutaway, because, even though the safety well has drains, its forward end is considerably lower than the top edge of the transom.

All told, the Ranger 26 is a remarkable little boat. She is not only fast, handy, and comfortable, but she is also quite attractive to the eye. Although she may have some construction weaknesses for offshore sailing, she can be beefed up. At any rate, *Union Jack* was strong enough to withstand the rugged trip to Bermuda. Bill Homewood certainly had complaints, but his problems were not really grave with respect to safety. According to his unpublished, jauntily written account of the passage, the boat was wet and uncomfortable during the worst weather, but he implied that there was no more serious problem than when the zipper on his fly rusted shut. I suppose that can be serious enough.

25/ The C & C 35

Bridging the Rules

Length overall: 34 feet 7 inches
Length on waterline: 27 feet 6 inches
Beam: 10 feet 7 inches
Draft: 5 feet 3 inches
Sail area: 575 square feet (MK I)
Displacement: 10,500 pounds (MK I)
Designer: Cuthbertson & Cassian
Year designed: 1969

Back in the early 1970s, when the International Offshore Rule replaced the Cruising Club of America rule as the principal method of handicapping the larger boats racing on U.S. waters, there were not many boats that could successfully bridge the two rules. Almost overnight, many racing-cruisers were made obsolete for competition by the rule change. The C & C 35, however, is one of the few hot CCA boats that was able to continue her winning ways for quite a while under the IOR.

When Cuthbertson & Cassian designed this boat in 1969, they certainly knew that the IOR was coming, but rather than try to anticipate loopholes in the rule, they apparently decided to create a fast, wholesome racer that could sail to her rating under any reasonably fair handicap system. To the regret of many owners of old boats, the IOR turned out to be somewhat more of a development rule than a handicap rule, and thus any boat specifically designed to IOR parameters had a distinct rating advantage. Nevertheless, the C & C 35 turned out to be such

a fast boat that she could not be overly subdued by an unfavorable rating.

The C & C 35, originally called the Redwing 35, is not the type of boat I would prefer for extended offshore cruising, because she is quite light, with an abbreviated fin keel and spade rudder. These characteristics produce quick motion with steering that may demand too much attention for shorthanded voyaging. Furthermore, the free-standing spade rudder is not as well protected as most rudders attached to skegs or keels; and the particular shape of the fin makes drying out (for bottom cleaning) and hauling (or slipping, as the British say) a difficult operation in boatyards that are off the beaten track and that do not have TraveLifts or large cranes. Nonetheless, the C & C 35 is great for racing, inshore cruising, and even coastal passages. Although lightly built, she is strong; her accommodations are comfortable; she is delightful to sail; and she will get you to your destination in a hurry. With this kind of boat, beating away from a lee shore in heavy weather

187

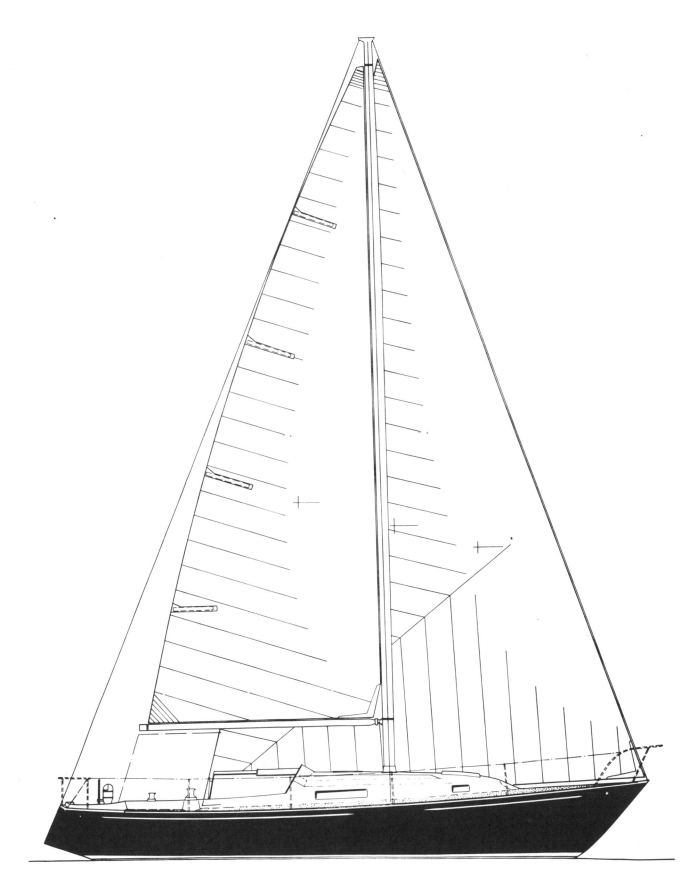

Although the original rig of the C&C 35 looks a bit short by today's standards, it is ample to drive the light hull exceedingly well in all conditions except perhaps in the lightest airs.

188

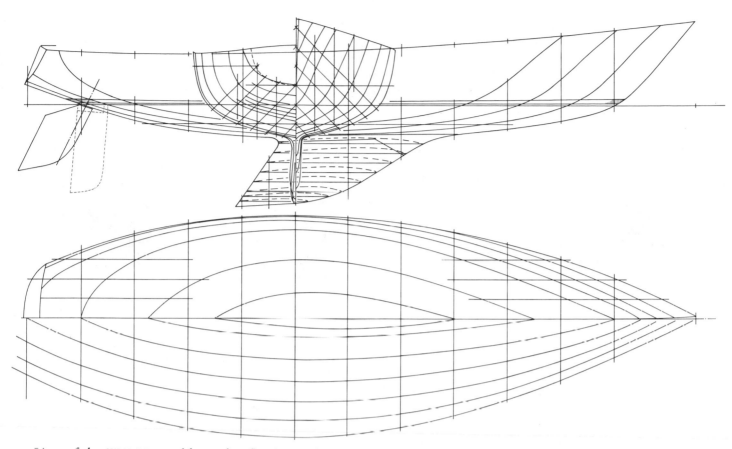

Lines of the C&C 35 reveal her rather flat, beamy hull with well-rounded bilges. Note the deep, full sections abaft the keel which add some buoyancy to the stern and may move the quarter wave farther aft.

should be no problem, and of course, a good turn of speed extends the cruising range when time is a limiting factor.

I am very pleased that C & C Yachts of Ontario, Canada, has agreed to release this boat's lines for publication. It can be seen that she has quite a powerful hull with little deadrise but with somewhat rounded bilges. The large radius at the turn of the bilge, together with the cutaway fin keel and lack of skeg, keep the wetted surface low, even though the underbody is fairly flat and beamy. The round bilge is also helpful to sea-kindliness and hull rigidity. The hull is moderately wedge-shaped, but the ends are not extremely unbalanced. For reserve buoyancy and dryness, there is some flare forward. While there is no true bustle, the after sections are rather wide, and they are slightly V'd forward of the rudder in such a way as to deepen the hull profile and thus bring some volume aft. The buttocks are quite straight and easy, giving a hint of the boat's speed downwind in a fresh breeze.

As mentioned before, the keel shape adds to the difficulty of hauling on a marine railway, but in many ways it is a good shape for this boat. Because of the keel's considerable rake, it provides some fore-and-aft length for directional stability, and this may be desirable on a boat with no skeg. Furthermore, I like the slope to the leading edge, which serves as protection against fouling with seaweed, lobster pot lines, and the like. The all-metal, bolted-on fin does not allow space for tanks or even a small bilge water sump, but it is thin and thus reduces head resistance and assures that keel damage will be minimal in the event of a grounding on a hard bottom.

The keel shape may not provide the lift of the high-aspect-ratio, so-called Peterson-type keels, but it does create minimal drag. C.A. Marchaj, the world-famous aero-hydrodynamicist, has written: "Theory says that very little side force is supplied by the area of keel behind the maximum draft and almost all the side force is produced by the part of the keel behind the

189

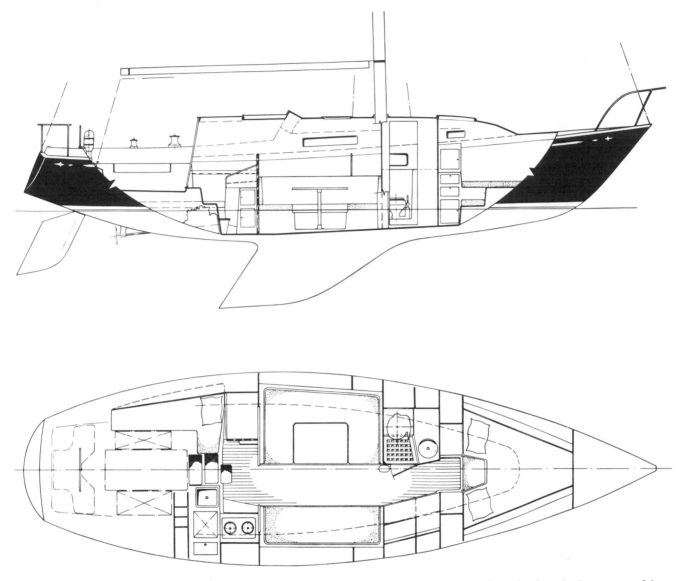

The adequate accommodations of the original Redwing 35, later the C&C 35. About the only thing lacking is an oilskin locker, but this might be worked in between the quarter berth and companionway steps.

leading edge. So the possible evolution of the keel proper would be toward the shark fin profile. . . ." The C & C 35's profile is close to the shark fin, and the raked trailing edge cuts away a lot of area that would be adding wetted surface without contributing much to side force.

Notice that the plans show two rudders. The shallow aftermost rudder was the original design. It is interesting to follow the evolution of C & C rudders. The early rudders were scimitar-shaped spades, and apparently George Cuthbertson and the other designers at C & C had a theory that

differed considerably from that of Bill Lapworth (of Cal boats) in regard to free-standing rudders. The Cal-type rudders are more balanced, and they have the greatest area up high, with the top fitting as tight as possible against the counter so the hull forms an end plate. The early C & C rudders, however, are not balanced, and the top after edge is considerably cut away. Presumably, the reason for this cutaway is to get the greatest amount of the blade into solid, less turbulent water and to get the rudder as far aft as possible without the danger of air injection, which could

190

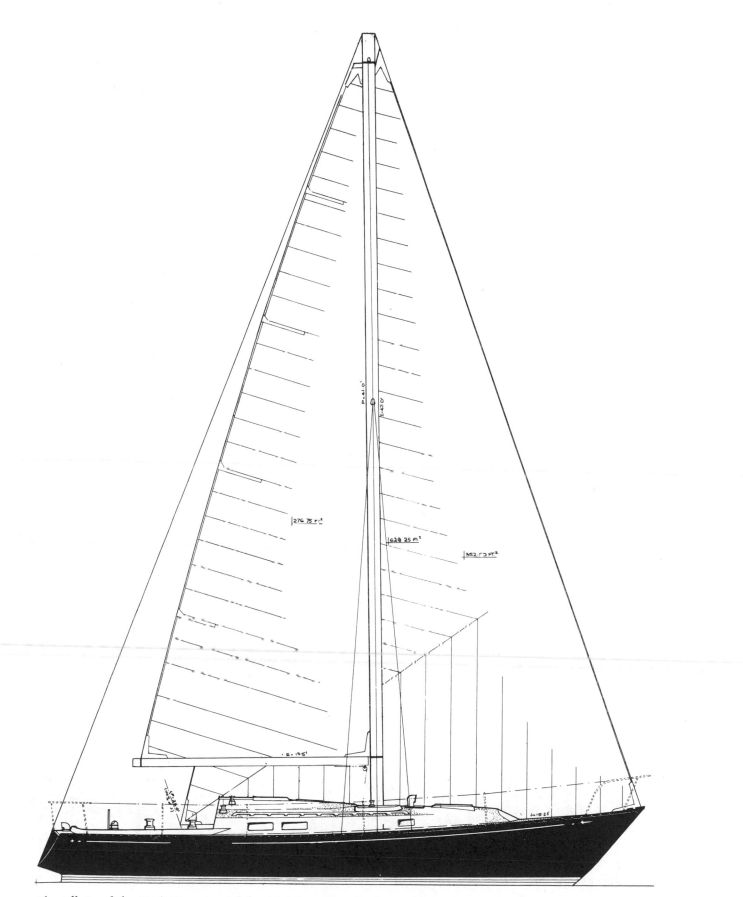

The tall rig of the Mark II version of the C&C 35. Ballast has been added to compensate for the higher center of effort of the newer sail plan, and some additional freeboard has been added to compensate for the loss of freeboard caused by the extra ballast.

Jack Quinn's C&C 35 Banshee, *a boat the author had the pleasure of sailing on occasionally.*

cause the rudder to ventilate. The newer type of C & C spade, however, is a deep, high-aspect-ratio type with a more constant fore-and-aft width. The change was made to improve steering on heavy-air spinnaker reaches when the boat sometimes had a tendency to broach. The greater rudder depth seems to help, and in my opinion, the more vertical axis gives better control when the boat is heeled.

Two sail plans are shown, the original short rig and a tall rig for the Mark II version drawn in 1973. The new rig increases the sail area from about 575 to 629 square feet, but ballast (and hull weight) has been increased to compensate for the higher center of effort of the tall plan; so the sail area-displacement ratio hasn't changed a great deal. In light-air conditions where there is more breeze aloft, of course, the taller rig is more advantageous, but from what I have seen, the original boat seems to be just as competitive in almost every other condition. For cruising shorthanded, I would prefer the smaller rig, which has ample sail area considering the boat's displacement of 10,500 pounds (for the Mark I hull).

The helmsman's position is extremely far aft. This has advantages for racing, as it keeps the crew out of the helmsman's way; the skipper, who is usually at the helm, can see what his crew is doing; and the after location provides good visibility to leeward. There is a disadvantage for cruising in that the helmsman is far from the companionway and the protection of a dodger, but the rudder stock head is forward of the wheel pedestal, and therefore the emergency tiller can be rigged to put the helmsman farther forward. Incidentally, there is what appears to be a prominent dodger coaming (and cabintop stiffener), but it is so far forward that the normal dodger will not cover much of the cockpit.

The helmsman's well has a high coaming aft, and it should have holes or be partially cut away to meet ocean racing requirements for cockpit volume. I would prefer a bridge deck or higher companionway sill, but the sill is not unreasonably low for normal sailing. For heavy weather

offshore, of course, a weather board is needed.

Below decks, the C & C 35 is roomy and comfortable, with berths for five or six in a pinch. Many seamen prefer a transom-pilot berth arrangement to the dinette for offshore sailing, but this particular dinette is U-shaped, and it allows a couple of occupants to sit facing athwartships. Also, the outboard seat may be used as a single berth on the starboard tack without the need to lower the table. The original boats had a chart table and quarter berth on the port side with the galley to starboard, but the Mark II version has the chart table to starboard with the galley to port. The latter arrangement provides more room and security for the cook, but at some sacrifice to the size of the navigator's niche and the width of the quarter berth.

I would definitely prefer a porthole in the head even though there is a deadlight in the cabintop for light and a small ventilator for air. Both the head and galley sinks are located close to the boat's centerline so that they will not overflow during a knockdown with the outlet valves open. There are fine dressers, lockers, and drawers in the forward cabin, but at some sacrifice to bunk length. Ventilation below is not entirely adequate for southern waters; so I would add two Dorades on the cabintop and a Dorade or removable vent on the foredeck.

The C & C 35 is certainly light, but it was quite well built by Hinterhoeller in Ontario, Canada. Construction is fiberglass with considerable use of end-grain balsa core for rigidity and lightness. The workmanship in the bilge in way of the keel bolts is somewhat crude looking but strong. I would be sure that the ends of the transverse plywood floor timbers were well covered with epoxy or some other coating to guard against delamination. Also, plenty of bedding and sealer should be used where fittings go through the balsa core to assure there will be no rot.

When Charlie Stein sold his Owens cutter, *Snallygaster,* he looked long and hard for a replacement boat. Charlie is one of the few successful racing skippers who believes in hanging on to the same boat for a good length of time. He finally decided on a C & C 35, and I don't think he has ever regretted the choice. He has won plenty of races in the new *Snally,* and he is still doing remarkably well with her, despite numerous rule changes. Undoubtedly, the greatest amount of publicity for Charlie came when he won a 150-mile sail training race competing against some so-called "tall ships," including the *Pride of Baltimore,* a full-size replica of a Baltimore clipper schooner. In the light headwinds that prevailed, of course, *Snallygaster* walked away from the big, rakish schooner. Any sailor would expect as much, but the press made a great fuss about the affair. It was almost as miraculous as David slaying Goliath. At any rate, the *Pride* is still a proud ship, but she gained a touch of humility from the speedy little C & C 35.

26/ The Whitby 42

Life Should be a Reach

Length overall: 42 feet
Length on waterline: 32 feet 8 inches
Beam: 13 feet ½ inch
Draft: 5 feet
Sail area: 875 square feet
Displacement: 23,850 pounds
Designer: Edward S. Brewer
Year designed: 1971

A racing sailor once said, only half in jest, that if he wanted a room full of silver trophies he would buy a Whitby 42. This remark was intended to raise some eyebrows, and it did, because the Whitby 42 is strictly a cruising boat. In fact, she is really considered an 80/20 motorsailer. Nonetheless, she sails surprisingly well and is certainly capable of collecting considerable silver under a true handicap rule in reaching events.

Indeed, the Whitby 42 *Revelation*, owned by William O. Fordiani of Santa Ana, California, has been doing extremely well on point-to-point races in the PHRF (Performance Handicap Racing Fleet). A few examples are: first in class and second overall, 1975 San Diego to Ensenada (65 miles—80 boats in fleet); first in class and first overall, 1976 Catalina to Newport Beach; first in class, 1976 Newport to Dana Point; second in class and second overall, 1976 Newport to Ensenada (125 miles—434 boats in fleet); first in class8 and third overall, 1977 San Diego to Guadalupe Island and return (450 miles); first in class and first overall, 1977 Pacific Cup; and

second in class, 1977 Marina del Rey to San Diego.

Mr. Fordiani writes that he doesn't want to tout his boat as a racer, but he says that in the more than 6,000 miles he has cruised and raced *Revelation*, she performs "amazingly well." With her shoal draft and ketch rig, the Whitby 42 obviously will not go to windward like a single-masted racer, but she points well, and as the skipper of *Revelation* put it, "We have no problem sailing higher and faster than boats of the same type." Mr. Fordiani went on to say: "There are so many of the recent wave of cruising boats that just won't sail well, and I guess I had to prove that the Whitby was different and capable of good performance. We also got tired, in our early days of racing, while grinding over a competitor, of being asked, 'Are you racing?' They don't ask anymore!"

It's not surprising that the Whitby 42 is so fast on a reach. She has a 33-foot waterline and carries a lot of sail. Then too, there is a definite bustle aft to smooth the flow and extend the sailing length, while the keel, which is not

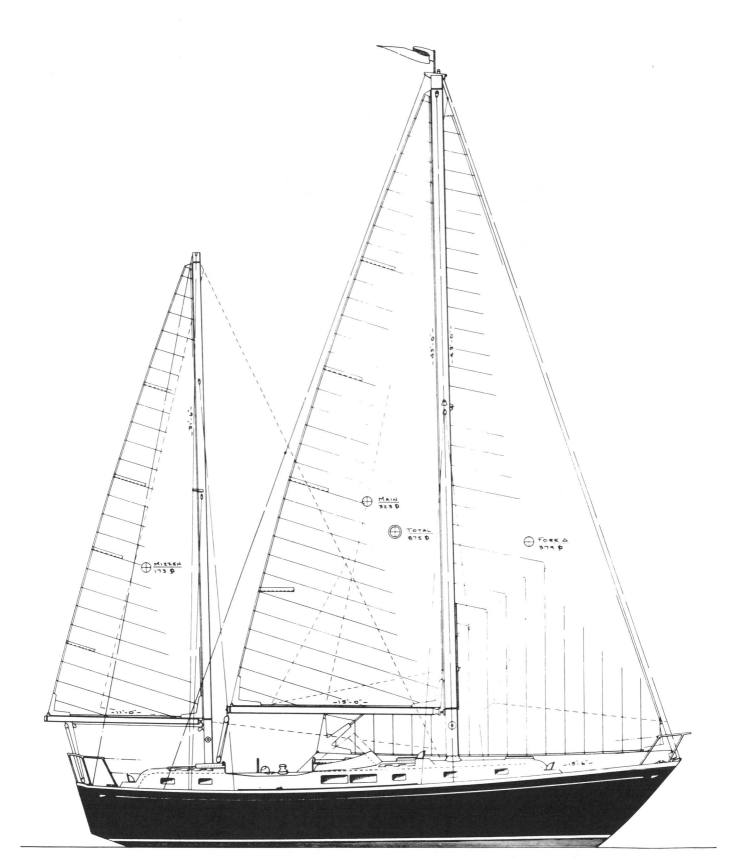

The high-aspect-ratio rig of the Whitby 42. Use of the Alberg 30's mainmast for a mizzenmast on the 42 is largely an economy measure, but it affords plenty of effective sail area on a reach.

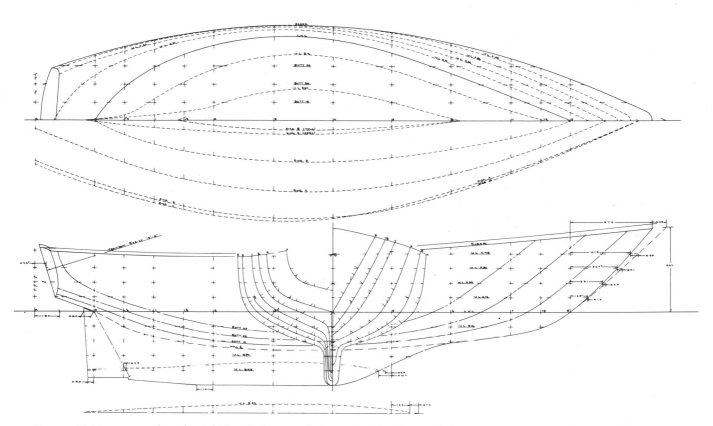

For an 80-20 motorsailer, the Whitby 42 has a rather cutaway forefoot and fine entrance with slightly hollow waterlines below the load waterline. The well-flared bow gives her a reserve of buoyancy forward.

The Whitby 42's accommodations are luxurious and very private for two couples. The high freeboard and flared bow help keep the center cockpit dry.

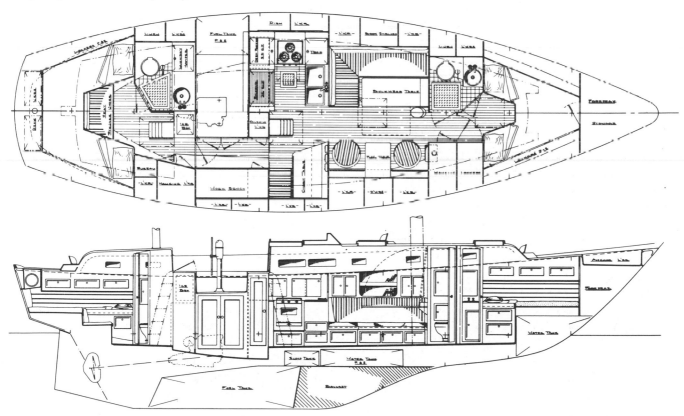

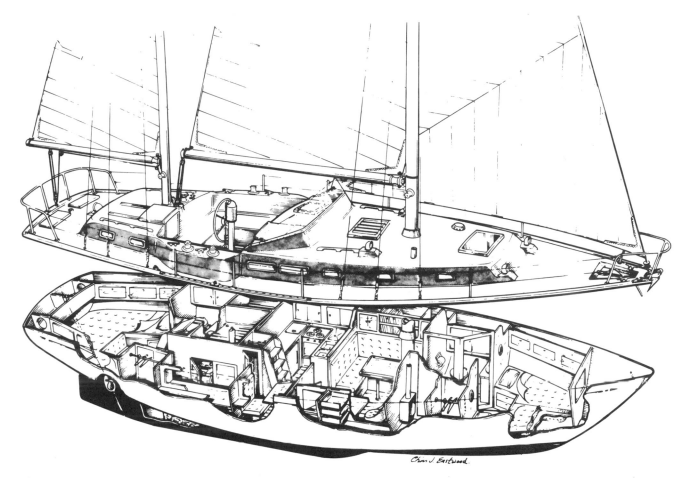

This exploded drawing of the Whitby 42 shows a lot of her details above and below decks. (From Cruising Designs: Power and Sail *by Edward S. Brewer. © 1976, Seven Seas Press)*

extremely thick for a boat of this type, does not cause much head resistance. Although the keel is fairly long, wetted surface is not great because of the keel cutaway forward, shoal draft, and somewhat rounded sections. Ted Brewer, the Whitby's designer, told me that he would have preferred another keel cutaway just forward of the rudder in the manner of the Cabot 36 (Chapter 29) but the builders, Whitby Boat Works, Ltd., of Ontario, Canada, thought this would cause unnecessary construction problems. Although the boat certainly performs the way she is, the after cutaway would have reduced wetted surface slightly, and, more important, it would have made the helm a bit more responsive and the boat quicker in stays.

The Whitby 42 does not run quite as well as she reaches. Aside from the usual difficulty that

any ketch encounters with blanketed sails when the wind is aft, this particular boat can have some minor steering problems in quartering seas. Although this was never apparent to me when I took an easy-going week's cruise on a Whitby 42, I've heard several owners complain about steering before a fresh following wind. Mr. Fordiani put it this way: "The sequence is that a wave picks up the stern and drives the boat in its direction . . . because of the tracking of the full keel, it's hell to get the boat out of its track and back on course . . . by the time you do get it out, you have oversteered and it starts all over again."

Several owners have expressed the opinion that the Whitby needs a larger rudder. It is interesting that the lines plan and the accommodation profile plan show slightly different

A Whitby 42 hard on the wind. Beating is not this boat's strong point, but it is surprising how well she goes to windward considering her shallow draft and high freeboard. (Robert K. Berry)

rudders. The actual boats I have seen out of water have the type of rudder seen on the latter plan, with the bottom of the blade sloping upward rather than being horizontal. Of course, the sloped-up blade will be better protected during a grounding, but I would prefer a horizontal bottom, which gives the blade more area and yet is sufficiently high above the bottom of the keel for reasonable protection.

Basically, though, the boat sails remarkably well when you consider that she is a go-any-place, shoal-draft cruiser with great emphasis on live-aboard comfort. She is well balanced, directionally stable, and capable of making fast passages. In my opinion, she is a wee bit tender, and I've been told that Kurt Hansen of Whitby Boat Works recommends reducing sail after 18 degrees of heel.

With her high freeboard, shallow keel, and moderate ballast-displacement ratio of 36 percent, the boat does not have an exceedingly high range of stability for that ultimate wave that the offshore sailor hopes he will never meet, so I for one would not want to take her around the Horn or passage in the "Roaring Forties" or "Furious Fifties." However, she is a fine boat for ordinary, well-planned blue water cruises, and a number of these craft have made outstanding transoceanic passages and weathered some heavy gales with few problems.

I'll have to admit that the freeboard is slightly too much for my taste, but it is high for some good reasons. Even though it may prevent the hull from having the lowest possible center of gravity, the freeboard supplies a reserve of stability until the rail becomes submerged. Some experienced sailors also think that high sides are essential for boats such as the Whitby 42 that have center cockpits, because they are so vulnerable to spray when sailing upwind. In an article written for *Yachting* (May 1973), naval architect Frank MacLear decried, with such strong words as "lubberly ignorance," the recent trend toward midship cockpits. MacLear contends that "with experience, owners are going to tire of midship cockpits and their inherent wetness." However, he admits, "the brilliant yachtsman of today

realizes that if he places himself extremely high, the water is less likely to fight gravity and reach him." Of course, Ted Brewer recognizes the problem of spray blowing aft, and that is one reason for the Whitby's high freeboard and also ample flare in the bow sections.

Many of the pros and cons of the center-cockpit/divided-cabin arrangement were discussed in the chapter about the round-stern ketch *Amee*. It seems to me that the Whitby 42 is a better size for this arrangement, because there is room in the after cabin for a large enclosed head, and the larger hull together with high freeboard allows a below-deck passageway between the after and main cabins. The latter feature obviously makes it unnecessary to go on deck in foul weather in order to go from one cabin to the other.

On a boat of this size, the owner's stateroom is normally in the after cabin, but there are certain drawbacks to that location, such as some wetness below from rain or spray when the companionway is at the forward end of the cabin trunk. One might think that the after cabin would be the most comfortable location with respect to the boat's motion, but this is not necessarily true. Although the axis about which a boat turns when pitching is normally well abaft amidships, it is often forward of the after cabin. I was interested to hear that this fact was learned, aboard one center-cockpit boat, from the owner's cat. Many domestic animals seem to have a computer-like efficiency in finding the most comfortable place to sleep. It didn't take this cat very long to move out of the after cabin to a location near the pitching axis. Nevertheless, the after cabin has considerably less motion than the usual forward stateroom.

My wife, Sally, and I had the pleasure of cruising in the West Indies aboard Harry and Nancy Primrose's Whitby 42, *Queen Mab*. Despite a breakdown of the engine, it was a most enjoyable and comfortable cruise. The Primroses, who were at that time homeward bound after completing a circle of the Atlantic, feel that their boat is ideal for cruising with two couples, although Harry told me that he thinks

Revelation *"strutting her stuff" on a spinnaker reach. Her owner, William Fordiani, wrote about this picture as follows: "I am sending along a photo showing a Whitby 42 as it probably has never been seen before: reaching with a ¾ oz. radial head spinnaker, 4 oz. bigboy staysail, main, and mizzen spinnaker racing to Ensenada."*

the boat is a little large for easy doublehanded cruising. I agree, because she has fairly large sails, requires sizable ground tackle, and has considerable windage. Nevertheless, she is easily managed by a crew of four, and they can live aboard in complete privacy and luxurious comfort.

A study of the accommodation plans shows such posh features as a spacious galley with double sinks and refrigeration, two large heads with showers, heating stove, swivel chairs, a folding bar, and almost every convenience except, as a charter yacht broker once told me, "hot and cold running laundromats." In addition, she has a large chart table, workbench, abundant lockers, and a roomy engine compartment that can accommodate a sizable generator and allows good accessibility to the diesel engine (a four-cylinder Perkins 4-107 or 4-236). One Whitby I have been aboard has a transom berth rather than two chairs on the starboard side of the saloon, and this is the arrangement I prefer. You can always sit on the berth, and it may be needed for sleeping in rough weather when there is too much motion in the forward stateroom.

Construction is fiberglass laminate of alternate woven roving and mat with balsa core in the deck and upper hull. This kind of construction provides shell stiffness and insulation without excessive weight, but the outer skin must be thick enough to withstand rough treatment, and it is important that the balsa core be well sealed off from water at every hole through the hull. Ballast is at the forward end of the keel only. Ordinarily, on this type of boat, I would prefer that the ballast be more spread out along the keel length for strength and protection when grounding, but the Whitby's ballast allows a lot of space for tankage in the keel, and the tank's baffle plates form built-in floor timbers to add strength. She can carry 300 gallons of water and enough fuel for a cruising range of from 1,200 to 1,500 miles under power.

Some of the boats I'm familiar with have had a minor problem in regard to support of the mizzenmast. It is interesting that on the construction plans Ted Brewer specified support from the keel to the underside of the cabin sole in way of the bulkhead that carries the load of the deck-stepped mizzenmast, but on *Queen Mab*, at least, there was not really adequate support under the bulkhead. This support is often a problem on center-cockpit boats because the propeller shaft runs directly under the mast (whether it is stepped on or through the deck). The Gibson Island (Maryland) Yacht Yard solved the problem very well on *Queen Mab* with horizontal channel supports and two vertical pipes that straddled the propeller shaft. A further problem was that the balsa core in the cabintop on which the mizzen rested was being crushed, and it was necessary to cut out the core under the mast and fill the void with solid material. Incidentally, the builder uses the Alberg 30 mainmast for the mizzen on the Whitby 42. Ted Brewer told me that he doesn't think the section is heavy enough if the boat is to carry a large radar antenna on her mizzen.

Even if it is on the light side, the Alberg 30 spar supplies a lot of sail area aft, especially when a mizzen staysail or mizzen spinnaker is set (see accompanying photo). Cracked off the wind with everything flying, the boat combines the virtues of a live-aboard cruiser with those of a fast racer. As William Fordiani put it, "Somebody once said that life should be a reach and I agree except it should be reaching on a Whitby 42."

27/ A Tancook Whaler Yacht
A Tasteful Blend of Old and New

Length overall: 25 feet 6½ inches
Length on waterline: 20 feet
Beam: 6 feet 4 inches
Draft: 2 feet 10 inches
Sail area: 301 square feet
Displacement: 3,663 pounds
Designer: Peter D. Van Dine
Year designed: 1972-73

It could not be said that the little Tancook whaler schooner described in this chapter oozes character from every seam only because the boat has no seams, at least not in her hull. It is made of fiberglass, but you'd have to examine the boat closely to find this out. With her white oak rudder, fir thwarts, white cedar decks, tongue-and-groove bulkhead and cockpit lockers, white cedar cabin sides and cockpit coamings (normally finished bright), white oak bowsprit and toe rails, varnished spruce spars, and even her custom-made wood shell blocks, she looks every inch a traditional wooden boat. This is one of the most beautiful little boats I have ever seen, and incidentally, she sails like a witch.

The general Tancook whaler type that originated in the mid 1800s at Tancook Island, Nova Scotia, was probably influenced by the double-ended boats used on whaling vessels. Perhaps the Tancooker's "roots," to use a current term, may go back as far as the Viking ships that visited Nova Scotia, long before Columbus "discovered" America. At least this idea has been suggested. The genuine working Tancooker, of

course, was developed for fishing, but it has a number of features that make it suitable (with certain modifications) for yachting, namely: good looks, speed, docility at anchor, and the ability to hold a steady course with the helm unattended. Desirable modifications would be a bit more freeboard amidships and more initial stability, since there is seldom if ever a need to haul fish, traps, or nets over the side of a sailing yacht. Of course, a cruising version would need a fairly large cabin, and I, for one, would want a small self-draining cockpit well.

The particular boat featured in this chapter has all of these qualities. Although the model illustrated here has an open cockpit with a small cabin, there is also an enlarged cabin version with a cockpit well. This boat was designed and is being built by Peter Van Dine of Annapolis, Maryland. Peter is an artist and craftsman who might be called a practical traditionalist. He has been able to combine traditional design with contemporary materials to produce craft that are both handsome and practical. In addition to the Tancook whalers, he is currently producing

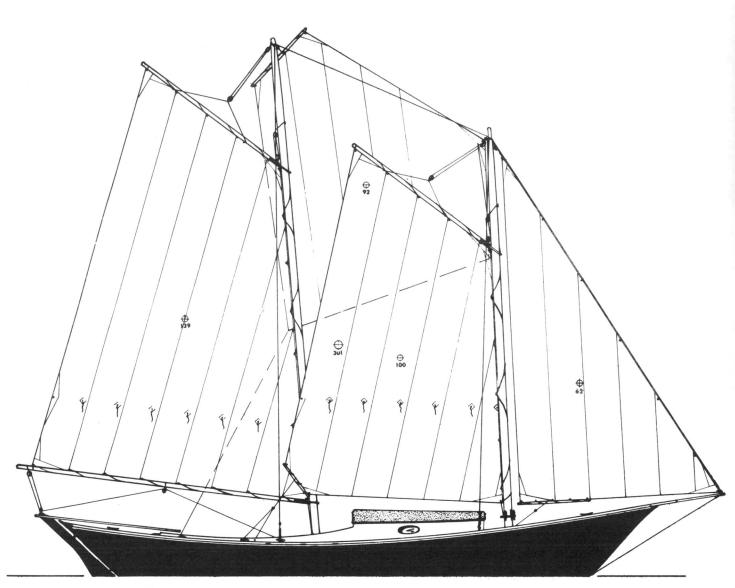

With its vertically cut sails, gaffs, clubs, and varnished wooden blocks, the schooner rig on this Tancook whaler is nostalgic as well as picturesque. Yet the rig is surprisingly sophisticated and versatile.

small Crotch Island pinkies and Banks-type schooners. The whalers are offered in two different sizes: 25 feet 6 inches LOA or 35 feet 4 inches LOA.

The plans shown here are for the daysailing/weekender version of the 25-foot Tancooker. Her hull is narrow and fine-ended, suggesting the ability to knife through choppy seas. Actually, her designer says she is at her worst in a chop, but only because she is small and light. She carries a lot of sail, so if the helmsman can bear off a bit with cracked sheets to keep the sails

"rap full," she has little trouble driving through a sloppy seaway. Her beautiful, almost champagne-glass sections, along with considerable keel ballast (44 percent of the hull weight), give her power to carry the sail, especially since its center of effort is quite low. The gradual curves at the turn of the bilge and the garboards minimize wetted surface, while the easy waterlines and buttocks help assure that the boat will slip through the water in fresh winds without making much of a fuss. A possible weakness with some fine-stern double-enders is lack of

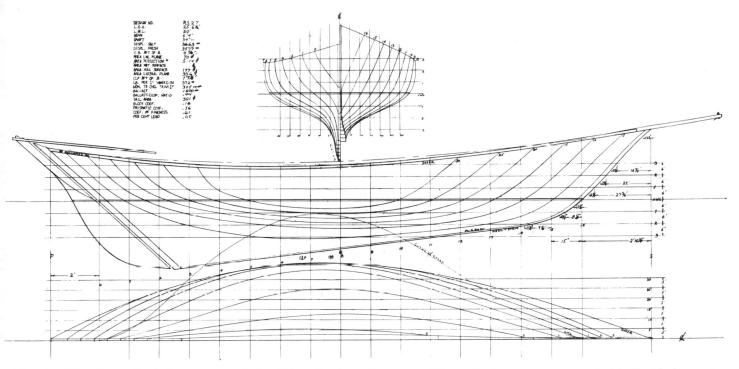

The Van Dine Tancook whaler seems to rival a Viking longboat for grace of form. She has a very symmetrical hull with fine ends, almost champagne glass sections, and considerable drag.

buoyancy aft, but this boat has quite a lot of reserve buoyancy with her sharply raking stern post and considerable flare in the after sections.

Not so long ago, when the Van Dine Tancooker was reviewed in a boating magazine, a young naval architect friend criticized the review, because it did not warn the reader of the possibility that the boat could sink from a severe knockdown. Such an accident could happen to the open-cockpit model, but it would take a tremendous blast to lay the boat down to the point where she would fill and sink. Before reaching that point, her sails would spill their wind; and if the crew released the sheets, she would most probably right without shipping much water. Of course, there is always the possibility that the boat could be rolled down by a large sea, so I would never recommend that the open-cockpit model be taken far offshore. However, the decked-over model with its self-draining cockpit should be perfectly safe for modest offshore passages. This model has an off-center companionway, but there is a high

bridge deck and an even higher companionway sill that would prevent water from going below during any ordinary knockdown.

A friend of mine, Ian Smith, owned the first of the Van Dine Tancookers for several years, and he raves about the boat's performance. According to Ian and also Peter, she outsails many of the standard racing-cruisers of her size. For example, it is said that she can beat the fast Cal 25s in most conditions except when hard on the wind. Of course, gaff schooners normally are not as closewinded as jib-headed sloops, but even so, this Tancooker is no slouch to windward. She can actually sail square, I understand, with one tack 90 degrees to the other. The boat has considerable drag (depth of keel aft), which is typical of the original type, and she has a centerboard to increase lateral resistance. Peter says that she makes so little leeway that the board is really needed only for a light air beat. The board is shaped and positioned so that it will not change the boat's balance very much whether it is up or down. As

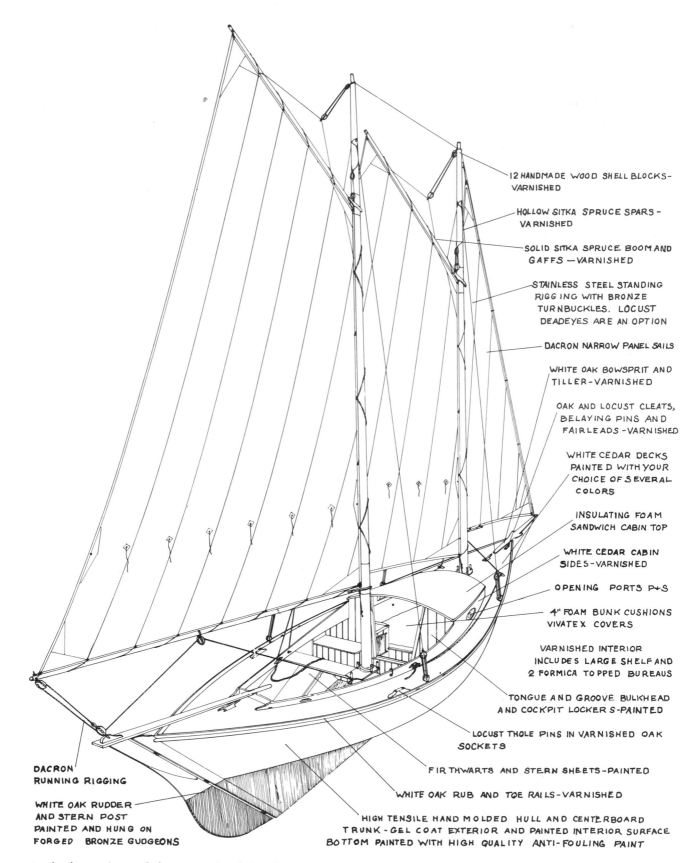

12 HANDMADE WOOD SHELL BLOCKS-VARNISHED

HOLLOW SITKA SPRUCE SPARS-VARNISHED

SOLID SITKA SPRUCE BOOM AND GAFFS-VARNISHED

STAINLESS STEEL STANDING RIGGING WITH BRONZE TURNBUCKLES. LOCUST DEADEYES ARE AN OPTION

DACRON NARROW PANEL SAILS

WHITE OAK BOWSPRIT AND TILLER-VARNISHED

OAK AND LOCUST CLEATS, BELAYING PINS AND FAIRLEADS-VARNISHED

WHITE CEDAR DECKS PAINTED WITH YOUR CHOICE OF SEVERAL COLORS

INSULATING FOAM SANDWICH CABIN TOP

WHITE CEDAR CABIN SIDES-VARNISHED

OPENING PORTS P+S

4" FOAM BUNK CUSHIONS VIVATEX COVERS

VARNISHED INTERIOR INCLUDES LARGE SHELF AND 2 FORMICA TOPPED BUREAUS

TONGUE AND GROOVE BULKHEAD AND COCKPIT LOCKERS-PAINTED

LOCUST THOLE PINS IN VARNISHED OAK SOCKETS

FIR THWARTS AND STERN SHEETS-PAINTED

WHITE OAK RUB AND TOE RAILS-VARNISHED

HIGH TENSILE HAND MOLDED HULL AND CENTERBOARD TRUNK-GEL COAT EXTERIOR AND PAINTED INTERIOR SURFACE BOTTOM PAINTED WITH HIGH QUALITY ANTI-FOULING PAINT

DACRON RUNNING RIGGING

WHITE OAK RUDDER AND STERN POST PAINTED AND HUNG ON FORGED BRONZE GUDGEONS

Deck plan and rig of the Tancook whaler shown in perspective. Notice such traditional touches as the pin rails with belaying pins, the tongue-and-groove bulkheads, and optional deadeyes.

206

The Tancook whaler Ca Va *with former owner Ian Smith at the helm. Notice her speed in such calm weather. No, the engine is not on. As a matter of fact, this boat had no engine.*

said before, the Tancooker excels at self-steering, and with the sails properly adjusted, it is seldom necessary to touch the helm when the wind is forward of the beam. Undoubtedly the boat can be made to steer herself with the wind abaft the beam by attaching the jib sheet (with an opposing piece of shock cord) to the tiller or by some other sheet-to-helm arrangement.

It is rather unusual to have a boat of this size rigged as a gaff schooner, but of course the rig lends character, especially with such optional features as deadeyes and lanyards and belaying pins. Also, there are some practical advantages of the rig. The center of effort is low, and the boat will balance well under main and jib or

207

28/ The Valiant 40

For the Ravages of the Sea

Length overall: 39 feet 10¾ inches
Length on waterline: 34 feet
Beam: 12 feet 4 inches
Draft: 6 feet
Sail area: 840 square feet
Displacement: 22,500 pounds
Designer: Robert H. Perry
Year designed: 1973-74

Surprisingly, the Valiant 40 has been a somewhat controversial boat. I say surprisingly because this handsome double-ended cutter, designed by Robert Perry, looks like an ideal seagoing cruiser capable of making fast passages, and that is more or less the claim made by the boat's developer and marketer, the Valiant Yacht Corporation. She also appears to be a rugged boat capable of withstanding the sea's ravages, and her builder, Uniflite Inc., is so confident about her fiberglass construction that the hull is warranted free from failure "for the lifetime of the boat's original owner." Furthermore, Valiant 40s have completed a number of extremely tough ocean passages without being seriously scathed.

The main controversy seems to be identified with an article that appeared in *The Telltale Compass*, a yachtsman's newsletter and consumer's report with a fine record for accuracy. The article was quite critical about certain aspects of the Valiant 40's design and construction. Then there was the rather disturbing report that one Valiant capsized on two occa-

sions. On top of this, a well-known yachtsman told a friend that his Valiant was the worst pounding sailboat he had ever owned.

I had wanted very much to include the Valiant in this book, but after hearing those adverse reports, I was not so sure. It seemed that the best way for me to form a fair opinion about the boat was to examine her myself and to take a sail on her in a spanking good breeze. At the kind invitation of Francis Stokes, the well-known singlehander, I took a 30-mile ocean sail on his Valiant 40, *Mooneshine* (often spelled incorrectly with one "e"), and we put her through her paces on all points of sailing in winds that varied from eight to 20 knots. In addition, of course, I examined the boat and bombarded Francis with questions about her. Fran is a most likable, easy-going fellow who was not at all defensive about his boat and was anxious to let me draw my own conclusions. He seems to like his boat a lot, and before the day was through, I came to the conclusion that she is an unusual combination of sea boat and smart

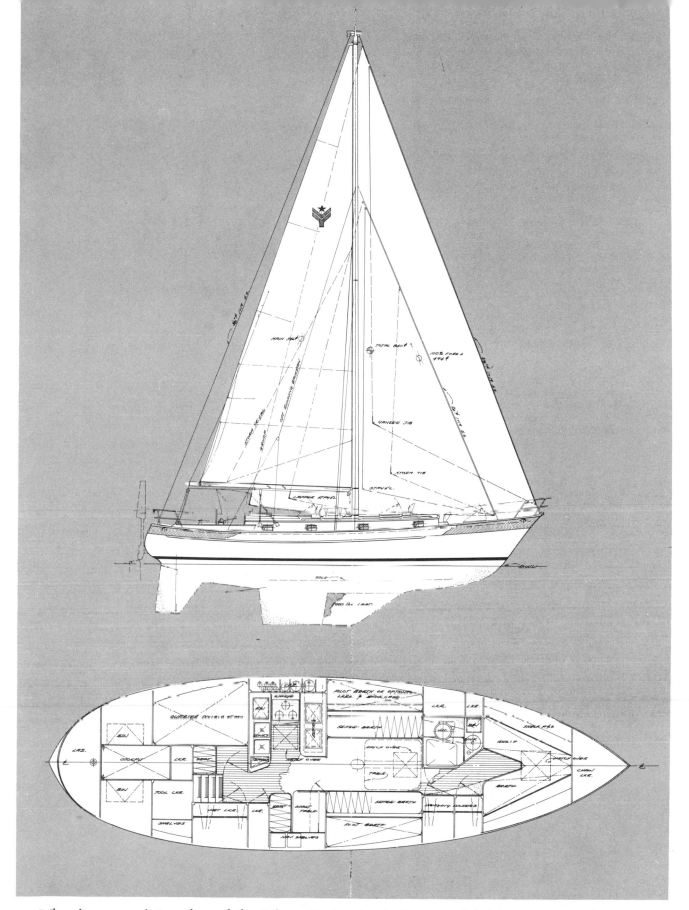

Sail and accommodation plans of the Valiant 40. Running backstays are labeled optional, but they would certainly be advisable at least for offshore work. Note the unusual after cabin and huge wet locker near the companionway.

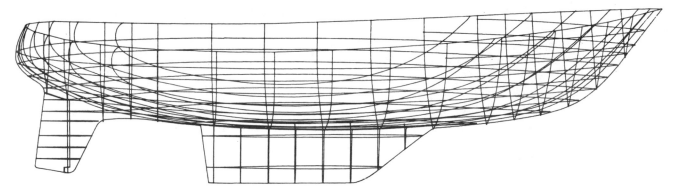

An unusual transparent perspective drawing which shows both sides of the Valiant 40's moderately shallow rounded hull.

sailer with overwhelmingly more good points than bad.

The unfavorable article that appeared in *The Telltale Compass* (Vol. VIII, No. 2) was largely based on a report by Peter Evans, an Englishman who competed in the 1976 OSTAR (*Observer Singlehanded Transatlantic Race*), in which *Mooneshine* and another Valiant 40, *Windquest*, also sailed. Evans had "completed" his own boat, which was said to be so heavily constructed that at least one race contestant called her an "icebreaker," and when Mr. Evans examined *Windquest* following the race, he felt that the Valiants seemed to be relatively lightly built. Based on a reply to *The Telltale Compass* by the producers of the Valiant 40, and some

further investigation, it seems that some of the criticisms made by Peter Evans are partially valid, but most are not. For instance, it is not true the hull and deck separated, nor that a structural bulkhead came loose, nor that the deck was flexing seriously, as implied by Mr. Evans. It is true, however, that a water tank on *Mooneshine* shifted several inches during a gale, although it did not "charge about" as reported. The Valiant hulls do flex to some extent (like many other boats) during the heaviest weather, and the chainplates are on the light side by some standards.

My greatest concern about the boat had to do with the report of severe pounding, the hull flexing, and especially the capsizes. *Windquest*

This bottom-view perspective reveals the shape of the waterlines with their considerable fullness aft.

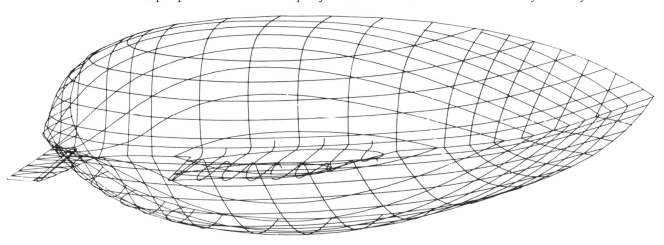

was the capsize victim, and it is my understanding that she was rolled over on two different occasions, once in the Pacific during her 500-mile OSTAR qualifying cruise and once in the Atlantic during the OSTAR itself. On each occasion *Windquest* reportedly rolled over to nearly 180 degrees and then promptly righted without breaking her mast. On one occasion she was lying ahull during a gale, and the other rollover occurred when she was running off in heavy weather. These incidents might suggest a deficiency in the Valiant 40's stability, but I really think it is far more likely that *Windquest* had the unusual misfortune of twice being caught by "rogue waves" that could have capsized any boat.

The Valiant has a ballast-displacement ratio of 34.6 percent, which is not high by today's standards for racing boats, but the ratio is considered ample for cruisers (after all, the famous *Finisterre*'s ratio was only 28 percent), and the ballast is lead, which keeps its center of gravity low. Furthermore, the boat has good form stability, and I would judge from her moderate freeboard, adequate draft, and inexcessive rig weight that the boat has a reasonably low center of gravity for a desirable stability range. During my sail on board *Mooneshine* we carried the full main with staysail and a large yankee jib in a 20-knot apparent wind, and the lee rail was well clear of the water. She certainly could not be considered a tender boat. Just recently, a centerboard version of the Valiant 40 has been introduced, but *Mooneshine* and *Windquest* are keelboats, as shown in the accompanying plans.

Interestingly enough, it was reported that *Windquest* carried an extra 1,000 pounds of ballast, yet she was the boat troubled with capsizings. The more lightly ballasted *Mooneshine* was not too far away when *Windquest* experienced her rollover during the OSTAR, but Stokes said he had no stability problems. *Mooneshine* successfully weathered other gales offshore, including heavy March winds in 1976 during her OSTAR qualifying cruise, and she was not very far from the trimaran *Gulf Stream-*

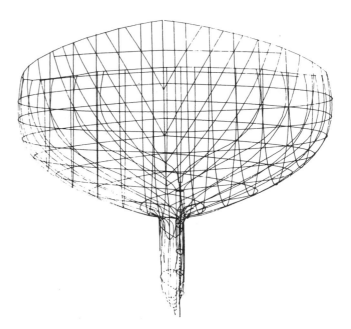

An end-on perspective shows the sections to advantage. Notice that they are well flared forward and rounded amidships, while there is quite a bit of tumblehome aft.

er when the multihull turned turtle in bad sea conditions when both boats were enroute across the Atlantic for the start of the OSTAR. Also, I understand that other Valiants have experienced heavy weather with little difficulty.

As for the hull flexing, Francis Stokes admitted that he had noticed some in the heaviest weather, but there hadn't been enough movement to give him any concern. Most fiberglass boats flex to some extent unless perhaps they are a cored construction (Airex foam or balsa sandwiched between fiberglass, for instance) or are fitted with numerous longitudinal stringers. As a matter of fact, the Valiants do have a few longitudinal stringer-type reinforcements, and this is somewhat unusual for a stock American boat. I think the really important point is that flexing is not extensive and that there are no hardspots near the flexing that could lead to fatiguing of the fiberglass. During my sail with Francis Stokes when we were beating into a moderately choppy sea in a 20-knot wind, I went below to look for any hull movement but could find none. Granted, it was not really rough, but we did cross the wakes of a few displacement fishing vessels, and I still could not detect any panting or oil-canning in the bow or elsewhere, nor was there ever any pounding. Stokes said that *Mooneshine* pounded to some extent when driven hard to windward in a really bad seaway, but he felt that most boats in the same conditions would be pounding as badly or worse.

The Valiant 40 is a delight to sail. She gives you the feeling of great power, yet her displacement is light enough for good buoyancy and responsiveness. Francis said that *Mooneshine* always seems to ride over the bad seas rather than plow into them. The Valiant Corporation claims that she can sail to within 30 degrees of the apparent wind, and this is exactly what she did—30 degrees at six knots of boat speed in 18 to 20 knots of apparent wind, according to *Mooneshine*'s instrumentation, which I had little doubt was quite accurate. Strapped in and hard on the wind, the boat was stiff and quite well balanced, although I would have preferred a bit less weather helm. Francis said he thought that some of this could have been relieved by rigging a Cunningham downhaul, because the mainsail's luff was quite slack, while the leech was too tight. Undoubtedly the sail's draft could have been pulled forward, and the traveler might have been shifted farther to leeward, which would have been helpful; nevertheless, even with the sails not perfectly trimmed, *Mooneshine* could be controlled very well by her Aries self-steering vane gear.

When coming about, *Mooneshine* seemed a bit slow in stays compared with a modern racer, which is not surprising, but Francis kept the staysail sheeted flat until filling away on the new tack; and with the sail held aback, the boat fell off quickly after passing through the eye of the wind. As a matter of fact, the backed staysail was most helpful in guiding the yankee jib through the slot between stays.

The longish fin keel on the Valiant, which undoubtedly contributes to her moderate sluggishness in stays, also helps give her an unusual ability to hold a steady course. Sailing downwind with the jib boomed out, *Mooneshine* tracked so well that even when we disconnected the Aries vane, the boat sailed herself, despite the fact that there were some quartering swells.

There is no doubt that the boat is fast. Under the capable management of Francis Stokes, *Mooneshine* was third in her competitive class in the 1976 singlehanders transatlantic race, and she won both the singlehanders race from Newport to Bermuda and the doublehanders race from Bermuda to Newport in 1977. It has been said that *Mooneshine* has the fastest time from the U.S. mainland to Bermuda of any boat under 40 feet except for Carleton Mitchell's *Finisterre*, and that boat was fully crewed. Stokes, of course, sailed alone, and furthermore, he hove to for several hours prior to finishing the race so that he would not have to approach Bermuda's dangerous outlying reefs in the dark. Another fast passage was made by the Valiant 40 *Foreign Affair* when she sailed from San Francisco to the Marquesas in the South Pacific in 23 days. It was reported that she averaged over 180 miles per day in the southeast trade winds!

Aside from her fine sailing ability, the Valiant is a handsome boat with lots of character, and she has many important seagoing qualities. Some of her safety features are a small cockpit well, a bridge deck, a low cabin trunk with small ports, a high toe rail similar to bulwarks, wide side and forward decks, many hand rails, and high coamings. Her underbody is the modern, low-wetted-area type, not always admired for offshore work, but the configuration is not extreme. And the hull form is well rounded, which not only minimizes wetted surface but provides a degree of seakindliness and strength of form (remember that an egg's shape is not solely for the comfort of the hen). Above the water, the hull is somewhat reminiscent of a traditional double-ender. The Valiant 40 is said to have a canoe stern, but I would call it a Baltic-type stern, which is fuller and more rounded. The true canoe stern sometimes lacks buoyancy, but the Valiant seems to have ample buoyancy aft with her rounded buttocks and full stern sections, as can be seen in the perspective drawings. The bow sections are sharply V'd, but

A bow view of a Valiant 40. Notice the wide spreaders, which reduce compression on the mast, and the small ports, which are not apt to be smashed during a knockdown. The prominent rubrail gives good protection to the topsides when alongside a pier. (Roy Montgomery)

there is a lot of flare for reserve buoyancy and to keep the decks dry.

One would expect a boat like the Valiant 40 to be sluggish in light airs, but her displacement is moderate and she carries plenty of sail with a good sail area to wetted surface ratio of 2.28. The cutter rig divides the sail area very well for easy handling by a small crew; however, the large staysail with its stay so far forward makes it difficult to tack a large genoa jib. I think there should be some arrangement for detaching the lower end of the staysail stay and bringing it aft when the genoa is carried in light airs. There is no need to detach the stay when tacking with the yankee jib. Close trimming of the headsails is not possible because of extra-wide spreaders and outboard shrouds; nevertheless, as said before, the boat will sail at 30 degrees to the apparent wind, and this is closewinded for an offshore cruiser. Furthermore, the large angle the shrouds make with the mast reduces compression on the mast, and the wide spreaders help prevent the main halyard from fouling on the spreader tips when sail is being hoisted on a reach. Francis Stokes said that the boat balances well under staysail alone in heavy weather, but the mast pumps to some extent, and he feels that in those conditions she needs running backstays attached to the mast near the staysail stay's point of attachment. The standing rigging is adequately heavy, but the chainplates seem relatively light to me. Even so, the fact that *Windquest* survived two rollovers without losing her mast give one a lot of confidence in the strength of the rig.

All the running rigging is led aft to the cockpit, which is helpful for shorthanded sailing, but I would prefer that the jib and staysail halyards be secured at the mast in order that lowering can be controlled more easily by one person when he is forward handing those sails. Incidentally, Francis had heavy steel D-rings at the clews of his headsails, but I would rather have conventional grommets to eliminate the possibility of injury from a flailing clew.

The arrangement below is somewhat unusual in that there is a private stateroom on the port side of the boat aft with a large double bunk and a seat (but no head). Just forward of the after stateroom is an excellent U-shaped galley with plenty of counter space, large ice box, and double sinks. On the opposite side is a splendid navigator's niche and abaft that, the largest oilskin locker I've ever seen on a boat under 40 feet. A large engine room affording good accessibility to the Perkins 4-107 engine is under the cockpit. The accommodations forward of the galley are quite conventional, with a main saloon having a pilot berth and lower transom berth on each side, a large head with shower forward of the saloon, and a two-berth cabin still farther forward.

Unfortunately, the after stateroom arrangement requires that the companionway hatch be off-center, a feature that possibly could make the cabin vulnerable to flooding in the event of a severe knockdown on the port tack. There are also off-center cabintop hatches over the stateroom and galley, but these would normally be kept entirely closed in heavy weather. A companionway storm slide will be needed more often on the Valiant 40 than on a similar boat with the more conventional on-center companionway.

My impression of the Valiant's fiberglass construction is that it is strong, although I am not a surveyor and my examination was not really thorough. The hull laminate is said to be 21 layers, laid up by hand with alternate 24-ounce roving and 1.5-ounce mat and with a 50 percent ratio of glass to resin. Incidentally, the resin is a fire-retardant type known as Dion FR Polyester. The builder, Uniflite of Bellingham, Washington, has a good reputation and for many years has been supplying the Navy with rugged fiberglass boats. Although most of these Navy craft are powerboats, Uniflite has also built the U.S. Naval Academy 44-foot Luders yawls, which must be among the toughest of fiberglass sailboats.

There has been some controversy regarding fire-retardant resins, partly because some builders claim that the retarding ingredients adulterate the polyester resin. However, the Naval Academy yawls, which are made of fire-

The Valiant 40 Mooneshine, *owned and frequently sailed singlehandedly by the remarkable Francis Stokes. (Brian Harrison)*

retardant resin, do not seem to show any lack of strength, and they have been well tested. One of these tests was a horrendous collision that occurred between two Navy yawls last summer when a yacht displaying a topless female crew passed close aboard (who could blame the midshipmen?). Although the yawls had been sailing at top speed, little damage was done. A witness told me that the crash would have all but destroyed a lightly built boat.

I did notice a few minor oversights in the wood trim on *Mooneshine.* Some molding near a bunk was omitted, and teak strips were absent from two Lexan hatch covers. The plywood used below is exterior rather than marine grade, which may be all right structurally, but I would prefer marine ply. Also, there were some galvanic corrosion problems due to combining aluminum and stainless steel in way of the mast step and porthole dogs (I understand these faults have been corrected in recent boats). But basically the boat seems unusually sound and strong.

In general, I think the Valiant 40 is a highly successful boat, and I, for one, would not hesitate to take her anywhere. I might have her thoroughly surveyed before embarking on a transoceanic voyage, but that would be a good idea with any boat. She's far from cheap, but there is some truth in the old saw, "You get what you pay for." The Valiant impresses me as being able to withstand the ravages of the sea, and that includes the latest hazard, helmsman's lapse as a result of topless distractions.

29/ The Cabot 36

Sturdy but Smart

Length overall: 35 feet 7 inches
Length on waterline: 29 feet 8 inches
Beam: 11 feet 8 inches
Draft: 4 feet 9 inches
Sail area: 632 square feet
Displacement: 15,000 pounds
Designers: Edward S. Brewer, Robert E. Wallstrom
Year designed: 1974

When I visited with naval architect Edward S. (Ted) Brewer last year at his office-home, in Brooklin, Maine, he showed me a large, thin piece of Airex PVC foam sandwiched between laminations of fiberglass. Then he invited me to take a swing at the fiberglass with an ax or heavy sledge. Judging from some nicks on the convex surface, I suspected that some visitors before me had accepted Ted's invitation, but I declined to take a whack. Although such an action might have helped alleviate some of my more deeply rooted frustrations, it was apparent that I would get nowhere in trying to inflict serious damage. Of course, the fiberglass sandwich was well curved to resist oil canning, but Ted's point was well made, that this kind of construction makes a very strong hull.

This construction is used to build the hull of the Cabot 36. The sandwiched Airex affords light weight, good insulation, and great stiffness, with little risk of core deterioration. The boat's deck, however, has a balsa core, because Airex can begin to soften in temperatures exceeding 140 degrees. A deck can easily exceed this temperature in the tropics, especially if it is a dark color.

The design work for the Cabot 36 was a collaboration of Ted Brewer with Robert E. Wallstrom, who is not only a designer but also one of the top marine surveyors. Ted wrote me that he "did the prelims and lines and Bob handled the rest." With two such capable architects, I tend to have a lot of confidence in the design and specifications for the Cabot. Furthermore, both designers feel that the builder, Cabotcraft Industries, Ltd., of Cape Breton, Nova Scotia, has done a very conscientious job with the construction. In fact, Ted told me he thought the boats were almost half again as strongly built as specified. Unfortunately, I have recently been told that Cabotcraft has gone out of business and the 36s are no longer being built, although the tooling has been sold to an Ontario firm that might again produce these fine boats.

Plans of the Cabot 36 show a wholesome, moderate, but fairly beamy hull with below-average draft for a keel boat. The draft is a good

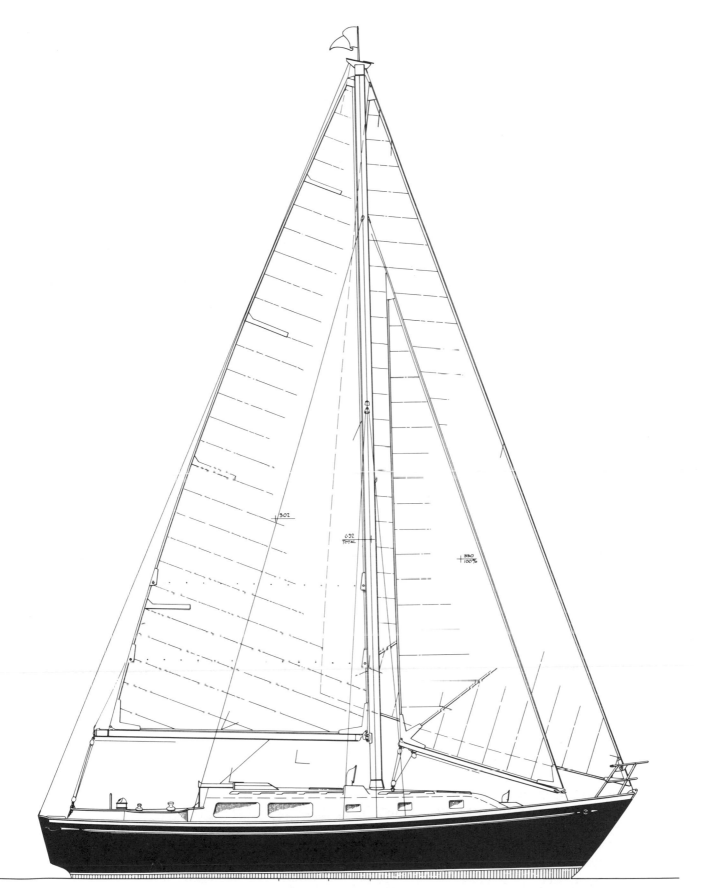

The Cabot 36's rig is a handy one for shorthanded sailing, especially when the jib is fitted with roller furling. The yankee's leech line should be adjusted before hoisting, as it cannot be reached from the deck.

219

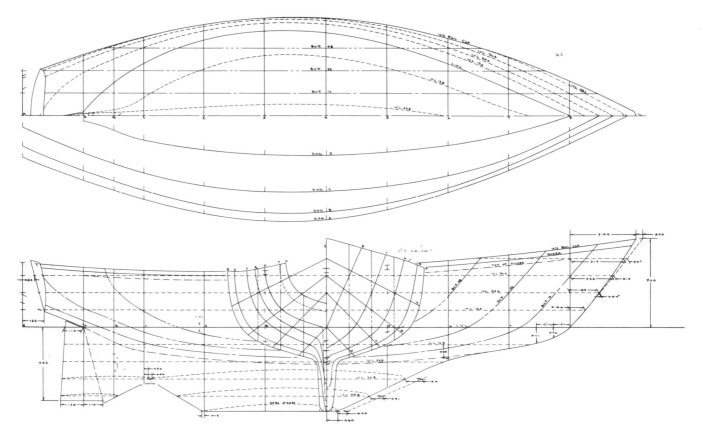

Lines of the Cabot 36 show a seakindly hull with plenty of reserve stability. Note the keel cutaway aft, which is helpful to maneuverability.

compromise between a shallow keel for gunkhole cruising and a deep keel for reserve stability and windward ability. Ted Brewer has developed a rather distinctive keel profile for many of his cruising boats. The keel is quite long and the rudder is attached to its trailing edge, but there is a cutaway area just forward of the rudder. This allows the rudder to be located far aft for the most effective steering without undue sacrifice to wetted surface, and the aft cutaway allows maneuverability and quickness in stays seldom found on a long keel boat. It is interesting that the lines show a hint of separate streamlining for the keel abaft and forward of the cutaway, almost as though the after part of the keel is considered a completely separate skeg. The keel shape also allows easy hauling on a marine railway, and its raked leading edge gives assurance that it cannot be fouled or badly damaged by contact with deep-floating flotsam.

The submerged waterline (12B) shows a slightly hollow entrance, but the "particulars" on the lines plan show an "overall" (considering hull and keel together) prismatic coefficient of .553, which means that a fair amount of fullness has been carried into the boat's ends. This fullness in the bow takes the form of a moderate forefoot just under the waterline ending. The forefoot is not so sharp or deep as to cause rooting when running before following seas, but it is sufficiently deep to help keep the bow from blowing off when beating into head seas. A boat such as this, with the high freeboard forward, might tend to "lose her head" when pitching if she had a very shallow forefoot and cutaway keel forward.

Ted Brewer was one of the early proponents of the bustle soon after it was developed in 1966 for the *America*'s Cup 12-meter boats. This fullness or protuberance beneath the aft end of

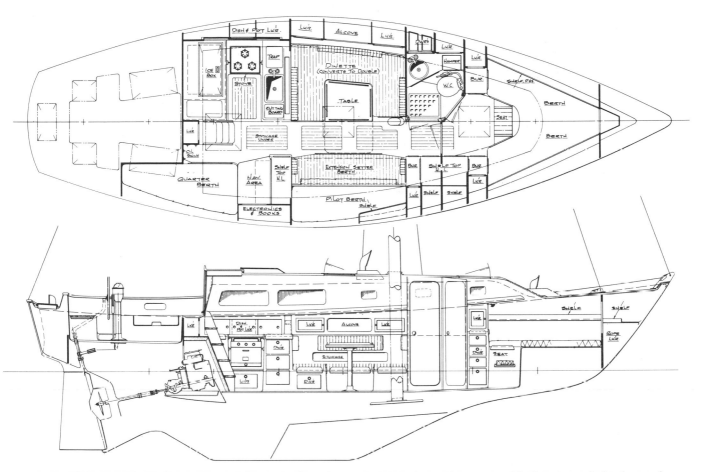

For a 36-foot boat, the Cabot has almost unbelievable accommodations. This is possible because of the boat's long waterline and great beam.

the load waterline can reduce the quarter wave and lessen turbulence as the water flow leaves the hull. The bustle is said to delay flow separation (detachment of the flow from the hull) and produce the effect of a longer sailing length by delaying the coincidence of bow and stern waves when the boat is near hull speed (about 1.3 times the square root of the LWL). The Cabot 36 has a moderate bustle fairing into the keel's after end above the aft cutaway. This is shown in the after sections, waterline 12B, diagonal D, and the dash-dot buttock line. On a recent sail aboard a Cabot, I was impressed with her low quarter wave and smooth wake in moderate winds.

The Cabot 36 has a bold sheer that gives her a seagoing look, but for purely aesthetic reasons, I might prefer that the sheerline aft be a wee bit lower. This would reduce the size of the transom and perhaps give the boat a slightly more sleek appearance. Nevertheless, the high stern together with the hull's ample buoyancy aft helps ensure that the boat will not be pooped by a following sea.

Neither the builder nor the designers claim that the Cabot 36 is a racer. She is intended solely for cruising, and there was no need to sacrifice any desirable feature for the sake of obtaining a good handicap rating. It is possible that the boat could do well under the PHRF (Performance Handicap Racing Fleet), but competitive or not, she is quite a smart sailer. During my aforementioned sail aboard a Cabot 36, the cutter-rigged *Mimi VI,* owned by Steve Batchelor of Melbourne, Florida, I found the boat to be responsive, well balanced, maneuverable, and surprisingly fast for her type. We sailed in light to moderate but occasionally puffy winds on Florida's Indian River. Under yankee jib, forestaysail, and full main, the boat seemed stiff, easy to steer, and directionally stable. She also sailed to windward well, although we had no instruments or nearby boats by which to measure accurately her upwind performance. Steve says she has a slight lee helm in light airs, and the sail plan shows that the center of effort (CE), at the middle of the mast, may have a slightly greater than normal lead over the center of lateral plane (CLP), which is directly under the forward end of the companionway scabbard. Nevertheless, *Mimi* seemed exceedingly well balanced with just the slightest weather helm during my sail on her when the wind was moderate.

The cutter rig seems a very sensible one for cruising this boat shorthanded. The ample spread between the CE and the CLP allows her to balance quite well under staysail and main. When it breezes up, it is not necessary to change jibs; one simply lowers or rolls up the yankee. Steve uses jib roller furling, his particular system being a Hyde Stream Stay above the roller drum. In a real blow, it is not very difficult to jiffy-reef the main, and then the staysail and main will be nicely matched, and the CE should be close to its designed position. The yankee supplies a lot of power in lighter winds, and its high cut allows good visibility and prevents excessive twist when reaching; however, Steve told me that he would prefer a lower clew so that he could reach the leech line. Coming about is no problem, because the yankee slides through the slot between headstay and forestay quite easily, and of course the staysail is self-tending with its sheet on a traveler. *Mimi* does not have running backstays, but they are shown on the sail plan. I think they are important to counteract the staysail's pull and to hold the mast steady in a seaway. These stays are all but essential in very heavy weather if the boat will be sailing under staysail alone.

One of the outstanding virtues of the Cabot 36 is her below-deck arrangement. There is a good chart table and a magnificent U-shaped galley with a three-burner stove, deep sink, a seven-cubic-foot ice box, and lots of counter space. The main cabin is roomy, bright, well ventilated, and comfortable, with a U-shaped or optional L-shaped dinette to port and a berth-seat to starboard. The large enclosed head with sink and shower has double doors, one leading to the forward cabin, to provide maximum privacy. Lockers, shelves, and bureaus abound, although I would prefer that the hanging lockers be a bit larger from top to bottom. Also, I would prefer a grab post in the main cabin and hand rails on each side of the boat. *Mimi* has an overhead hand rail above the dinette, but Steve told me this was a mistake. It should have been put in a corresponding location on the boat's opposite side. Originally, there was a problem with access to the Volvo diesel engine. It could not be serviced easily on the port side nor cranked in the event of starting motor failure. But now a large galley cabinet has been mounted on hinges to allow a gaping access.

There is not much doubt that the Cabot is a good sea boat. She was competently designed and built as an "offshore cruising auxiliary." Before taking her on a long ocean passage, however, there are a few modifications that should be made, in my opinion. The windows are fairly large, and the "glass" is quite flexible, so it might be a wise plan to carry storm shutters. Some electrical wiring runs through the bilge, and I noticed that even on our easy sail, the wires were damp. Even if the insulation is first class, it is not the best practice to run the wires under the cabin sole, so I would reroute them at a higher location.

The cockpit has a splendid bridge deck, but the volume of the T-shaped well is fairly large, and coamings are high all around the cockpit. A heavy sea breaking aboard could conceivably weigh down the stern, and water could run below before flowing over the coamings. Ocean racing inspectors often insist that clearing ports be cut through the coamings when they are too high. It would be helpful if this could be done to a Cabot 36 before she set forth on a tough offshore passage. Another feature I'd like to see, although it has nothing to do with safety, is a dodger coaming to keep water from sweeping

A Cabot 36 reaching off at near hull speed under roller-furling jib, main, and staysail. The staysail probably would set a little better if its traveler slide were pushed to leeward.

Right: The bow of the Cabot 36 Mimi VI *silhouetted against the sunlit water. The perforated rail is handy for attaching nets or fittings. (S.D. Batchelor)*

Below: The author, at the helm of Mimi VI, *does not seem to be concentrating on his sailing. Note the handy gallows frame with furled bimini top attached.*

under the forward edge of the dodger when driving into head seas with the spray flying aft.

Aside from the need for those modifications and a few minor alterations (such as replacing the flimsy mainsheet traveler stops), there is little else that should deter a seaman from taking a Cabot 36 anywhere in the world. Some of these boats have already been well tested. For example, I understand that Dr. Raymond Kennedy has circumnavigated Newfoundland in his Cabot, and the story goes that he encountered a hurricane with 75-knot winds and 30-foot seas. Apparently his boat behaved well running off before it under bare pole (with engine idling). Dr. Kennedy is a veterinarian from Nova Scotia, and I hear that he occasionally visits patients in Newfoundland by his boat. How frequently he does this, I cannot say; but if I were a sick animal that had to wait for the doctor to come by sailboat, I would be happy to know he was coming by a safe, speedy, and reliable Cabot 36.

30/ The Ranger 28

Versatility in the New Breed

> Length overall: 28 feet
> Length on waterline: 21 feet 8 inches
> Beam: 9 feet 7 inches
> Draft: 4 feet 6 inches
> Sail area: 376 square feet (tall rig)
> Displacement: 5,108 pounds
> Designer: Gary W. Mull
> Year designed: 1973

A ditty about our first naval architect tells us that "old man Noah thought he knew a thing or two." As a matter of fact, Noah not only thought so, but he did know a thing or two. And so did many early yacht designers. They knew more about what produces good performance than many contemporary sailors seem to realize. The most modern racing-cruising boats are often considered breakthrough designs, but an old-timer like Nat Herreshoff, for example, knew as much about the basics of what makes a boat go fast as Doug Peterson, Ron Holland, or any other contemporary designer. I suppose that statement makes me seem like an old fogy, but there is no denying that the famous designers of the past knew about the factors that produce boat speed. The basic "fast factors," of course, have to do with sail area, stability, displacement, wetted surface, and sailing length. Although there have been recent refinements in such areas as bustles, high-lift keels, and upwind efficiency from high-aspect-ratio rigs, the main reason why the new breed of racing-cruiser is so fast is that it has a highly favorable combination of fast factors at a low charge in handicap rating. In other words, the new-breed boat is not a breakthrough; it is simply a long, light, stable boat with minimal wetted surface and a big, tall rig that rates exceedingly well under the International Offshore Rule.

The Ranger 28 is one of these new-breed boats, but she is better than most, in my opinion, because she is so unusually versatile. She is not only fast, but also relatively easy to handle, and she is a comfortable boat with amazing cruising accommodations for a 28-foot racer. Gary Mull designed her in 1973 to be competitive under IOR and under the MORC and Off Soundings rules as well. Since her first appearance, she has had an impressive string of triumphs, including a "Boat of the Year" title in the highly competitive New Orleans area.

Recently, I had the pleasure of sailing on the highly touted 30-foot C & C Mega against the Ranger 28 in a match race. I was most impressed with the Ranger's performance, especially going to windward in a moderate to fresh breeze with choppy seas. She actually beat us to the wind-

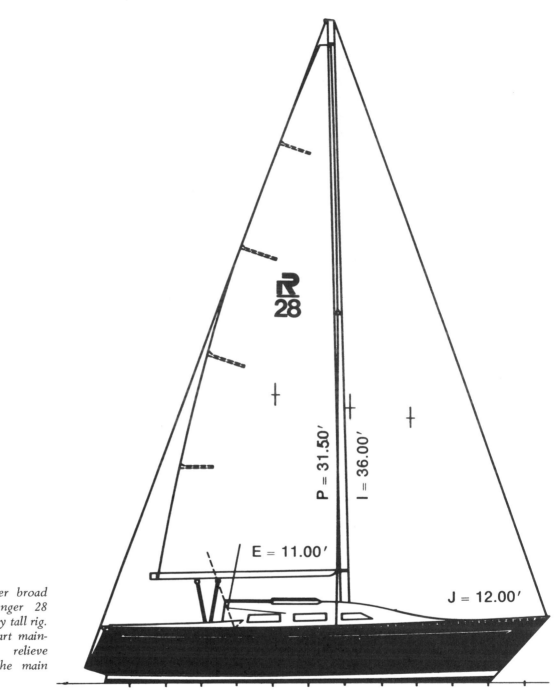

Because of her broad beam the Ranger 28 can carry a very tall rig. The spread-apart mainsheet blocks relieve pressure on the main boom.

ward mark, even though she had a much lower rating.

There is little wonder that the Ranger 28 is fast, with her long waterline, minimal wetted surface, and a mast that's 37½ feet high. Such a tall rig, of course, gives her speed in light airs, but she is not overburdened in fresh winds because of her 9-foot 8-inch beam (considerable for a 28-footer) and high ballast-to-displacement

ratio. The short keel is not too different from the so-called Peterson type, popularized by the One Ton cup boat *Ganbare,* except that the Mull-designed keel has more rake. This feature helps somewhat with directional stability, and of course, it helps prevent snagging flotsam, such as seaweed, or lobster pot lines. One would not expect the keel's aspect ratio to be extremely high, because the boat draws only 4½ feet of

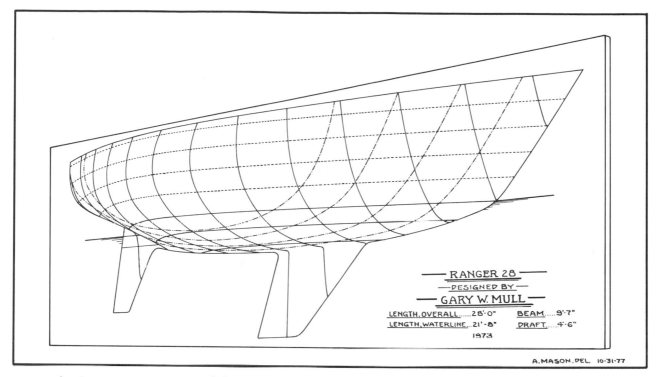

RANGER 28
DESIGNED BY
GARY W. MULL
LENGTH, OVERALL......28'-0"   BEAM.....9'-7"
LENGTH, WATERLINE....21'-8"   DRAFT....4'-6"
1973

A. MASON. DEL. 10-31-77

Even this bow-view perspective of the Ranger 28 gives a hint of the bustle aft. Note the wide sections with tumblehome amidships.

The Ranger 28's wide beam gives a surprising amount of room below, although the slightly pinched-in bow detracts from footroom in the bunk forward.

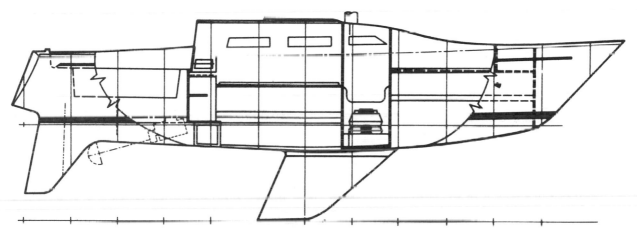

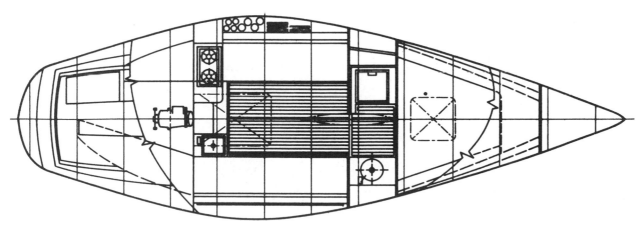

water, but the hull is quite shallow and this permits an efficient long-span, high-lift fin to be carried up relatively close to the waterline. The keel seems slightly farther forward than the norm for this type of boat, and you might think it would produce a bow-down trim, since the boat has a fine bow and a stern that is fairly full; however, the Ranger carries a sizable engine that is located quite far aft. Actually, on such a small boat it is good to have a very slight bow-down trim when there is no one aboard, so that the addition of crew weight in the cockpit will put the boat on her lines.

Looking at the keel's profile, it is hard to believe that there is sufficient area to prevent leeway, but the boat's lateral plane is augmented by an ample skeg and rudder. This configuration also helps with tracking and steering control. There is a moderate bustle or fullness at the base of the skeg and slightly farther forward with the hull lines fairing into the skeg. In theory, this extends the boat's sailing length and smooths the quarter wave, and it also directs the water flow against the rudder in such a way as to delay stalling. Certainly, this rudder should not stall as easily as a spade type with no skeg.

The Ranger 28 has a definite wedge-shaped hull with her fine entry, full stern, and her maximum beam well abaft amidships. Many a modern boat of this type, which also has a deep, sharp forefoot (a feature that has been encouraged under the IOR), may tend to root or bury its bow when running before following seas in a fresh wind. The Ranger 28, however, does not have a deep forefoot. Hers is only deep enough to extend the sailing length forward and carry some buoyancy into the bow to help balance the buoyancy aft.

Although she has the new look with wide beam, considerable tumblehome, reverse transom, and a blister-type cabin trunk, I think a traditionalist should find the Ranger 28 a lot better-looking than many modern boats of her size. The stern is not so extremely chopped, and there is a slight counter to balance a not-unpleasant bow overhang. The cabin trunk is low and the blister effect is not so pronounced

that the crew might have to step on slippery windows (as on some modern boats). The stern is neither pinched nor extremely wide. I would prefer somewhat less tumblehome, as it gives the boat a slightly pregnant look. (Is there such a thing as being slightly pregnant?) However, the bulgy topsides do help keep the rail out of water in a fresh wind. By and large, there is a certain harmony to the various parts of the hull, and an advertising caption tells the truth when it says, "the Ranger 28 looks fast even when she's lying at her dock."

Most modern competitive racing-cruisers of this size have minimal accommodations, and many are "skinned out," as yachting reporter Red Marston once described a boat, "with the craft of an Alaskan trapper." Not so the Ranger 28. She has bunks for five, a complete galley, and an enclosed head that includes a wash basin/vanity and hanging locker. Because of the boat's broad beam, there is a surprising amount of space in the main cabin. An adequate dining table is hinged against the main bulkhead so that it can be folded up out of the way when it is not in use. There is a quarter berth on the starboard side that is a bit cramped and awkward to get in and out of, but it makes a good sea berth and can be used for sail stowage when not needed for sleeping. Up forward is a double V-berth, but I understand that the newer boats have a small cutout area that allows one to step into the forward cabin. A filler piece is then needed to make the berth a double.

The galley stretches across the after end of the main cabin. It has a deep stainless steel sink to starboard with an optional two-burner stove to port. There is a 40-pound-capacity ice box that originally was to be located under the companionway, according to early literature, but it is now on the boat's port side. This location necessitates a short settee berth on the port side, but extra length is gained with a foot well, a sort of cubbyhole cut through the main bulkhead. The well extends into the head, but it is not obtrusive, because it is hidden under the vanity. Foot wells may detract somewhat from sleeping comfort, but at least they make good

The Ranger 28 showing her speed under tri-radial spinnaker. The mast appears to be bowing forward quite a bit, which indicates the need of a baby stay to help straighten the mast. The vertical wrinkles in the main might be relieved not only by straightening the mast, but also by slacking the sail's luff.

stowage compartments for folded-up bedding. There are quite a few lockers and drawers on the Ranger 28, but I must say that I don't like her locker door latches, which are the friction type, because they have been known to fail in heavy weather.

Headroom below is 5 feet 10 inches, and I'm glad the designer resisted the temptation to give full headroom to tall people, because this surely would have hurt the boat's appearance. Actually, most people of average height can stand up and walk about quite comfortably, and if one should bump his head, there is a soft liner that will cushion the blow. This liner is a foam-backed Herculon material, and not only is it attractive, but it also is supposed to take care of the condensation problem that is so common on fiberglass boats in cold weather. I'm not prepared to say how well the liner will hold up over a period of time. There are zippered panels at various locations in the material so that one can reach the underside of the deck to install bolted fittings or to tighten existing nuts.

Unlike many boats with shallow bilges and bolted-on fin keels, the Ranger 28 has a bilge-water sump, which I think is highly desirable. The cast lead fin is mounted on a short keel stub that is part of the hull, and this provides a catchment for any water in the bilge. Unfortunately, the sump is not very deep, so the bilge needs regular checking. A permanent bilge pump is mounted in a cockpit seat locker, but I would prefer a through-the-deck type so that the locker lid would not have to be opened in heavy weather to operate the pump.

Above deck, the boat has many desirable features, including a comfortable cockpit with a small well and narrow bridge deck, which keeps water out of the cabin if a sea should happen to break aboard. There are wide side decks, and the foredeck is nearly flush to facilitate crew work forward. There is a very small after deck so that ventilators for the Universal Atomic gasoline engine need not be mounted on the side decks, where they are vulnerable to taking in water when the boat heels. The tiller extends to the forward end of the cockpit within easy reach of the mainsheet, which slides on a traveler across the bridge deck. With halyards leading back to the cockpit, the boat should be quite suitable for singlehanding.

The shrouds are set inboard for flat sheeting of a genoa. There is only one set of lower shrouds, so I would by all means install a baby stay to hold the mast steady in a seaway. There are certain rig options, and it is possible to have a slightly shorter mast (the original rig) for cruising or racing in heavy-air regions. For sailing in exposed waters, I would prefer a slightly heavier headstay and stemhead fitting.

Although her construction is on the light side, the Ranger seems reasonably well put together. There are bolts, for example, rather than pop rivets or screws holding the deck to the hull. The builder, Ranger Yachts, a division of Jensen Marine, produces a lot of boat for the money. The 28 is not my choice for extended offshore cruising, but she's a good boat for daysailing, weekending, racing, cruising on soundings, and even some coastal passages. As the advertising literature says, "the Ranger 28 is not the boat for everybody," but she should certainly satisfy a great many sailors because of her great versatility in this modern age of limited-purpose boats.

The Ranger 28 seems a fitting design with which to conclude this book, since it is one of the best of the newest type of fast cruiser. And so we have presented some outstanding designs that date from 1928 through 1974. As every sailor knows, there are good and bad boats, but in my opinion, there are few boats that are really horrible. Sure, there are some home-created monstrosities, some ugly ducklings, and more than a few stock boats that could be much better built. But in a general way, I tend to agree with the old salt who opined that "there is no such a thing as bad rum, it's just that some brands are better than others." This same philosophy could be applied to boats, and I feel that some of the better if not the best boats have been presented here. At least I think it is safe to say that there are absolutely no bad ones on these pages.

Index